SYAMA PRASAD MOOKERJEE

HIS VISION OF EDUCATION

SYAMA PRASAD MOOKERJEE

HIS VISION OF EDUCATION

EDITORS
ANIRBAN GANGULY | AVADHESH KUMAR SINGH

wisdom tree

In association with

Dr. Syama Prasad Mookerjee
Research Foundation

First published 2017

Photographs courtesy SPMRF

ISBN 978-81-8328-496-7

Published by
Wisdom Tree
4779/23, Ansari Road
Darya Ganj, New Delhi-110 002
Ph.: 011-23247966/67/68
wisdomtreebooks@gmail.com

Printed in India

सत्यमेव जयते

प्रधान मंत्री

Prime Minister

MESSAGE

Dr. Syama Prasad Mookerjee occupies a place of eminence in India's history. His contribution in the domains of education and politics in the 20th century has been remarkable. Besides being a front-ranking statesman he was an outstanding educationist and education administrator.

His deep reflections and vision of education was rooted in India's civilisational ethos and along with that was modern as well as futuristic. It is indeed interesting to note that his educational formulations, made decades ago, in the form of convocation addresses, lectures and speeches remain strikingly relevant even today.

Broadly speaking, Dr. Mookerjee advocated the need for spreading education right up to the grassroots, emphasised the importance of technical and skill education for the empowerment and for the upliftment of the masses, focused on women and adult education, supported the strengthening of Indian languages and spoke of the need to restate India's cultural and civilisational vision through education.

Dr. Syama Prasad Mookerjee Research Foundation in New Delhi has made a commendable effort to compile these valuable speeches for wider dissemination and more importantly for posterity. I congratulate the editors, Dr. Anirban Ganguly and Professor Avadhesh K Singh for this initiative and hope that the book generates a wide and dispassionate discussion on the fundamentals of Indian education as envisaged by Dr. Syama Prasad Mookerjee.

(Narendra Modi)

New Delhi
21 June, 2017

CONTENTS

On Advancement of Education

For Education

PREFACE

Every human being is unique and has multiple selves or layers with infinite possibilities. Exceptional are those who leave indelible imprints on history with their vision, voice and accomplishments. Syama Prasad Mookerjee was one such personality who played a pivotal role in Indian history in the first half of the twentieth century and continues to exercise influence. After more than half a century of his demise, the full measure of his contribution demands consideration and study, as the existing discourse tends to focus more on his active political engagements in the last one and half decades of his life, and other critical facets of his persona as a thinker—educational, cultural and political—have remained ignored.

Historical beings often get reduced to images as seen throughout human history. For instance, the symbols of Mohandas Karamchand Gandhi are the knee-length dhoti (loincloth), round-rimmed glasses and a lathi (staff). In addition to these, he is also closely associated with concepts like ahimsa (non-killing, not non-violence, as many would like us to believe) or satyagraha. Gandhi was more than the sum of these parts put together. Like Gandhi, Mookerjee has also been a victim of perceptions, mainly political, as his contribution in the public sphere has been reduced to being known as the founder of Bharatiya Jana Sangh or as a crusader for Kashmir. Consequently, his contribution to domains beyond politics remains unacknowledged. His political affiliations did not help Mookerjee, the educationist either, as after Indian independence, the political dispensation—averse to his ideology—was at best indifferent to him and at worst critical or contemptuous of his achievements. His own party in its new avatar, preoccupied in establishing an alternate political narrative, was too engrossed, and rightly so, in his political views to fathom his contribution as an educational thinker and administrator. A serious and vigorous consideration of his educational views and vision still eludes us and is not a part of the discussions in the mainstream education system in India even today.

Mookerjee was an academician at heart who deftly donned the mantle of a politician too. His discontent with the then power structures and pressures persuaded him to join active politics, which he perceived to be a potent means of changing the nation in general and its education system in particular.

When talking about the few instances of isolated interests in his views, a slim volume entitled *Educational Speeches by Dr Syama Prasad Mookerjee,* edited with a brief Foreword by Dr Sarvepalli Radhakrishnan, needs to be mentioned. To give Dr Radhakrishnan due credit, it must be stated here that he at least took note of Mookerjee's views, as he was aware of the interest Mookerjee had taken in the rise of scholars like him. However, the volume has a few inadequacies. Firstly, it is not a complete written work in itself as it contains only some of Mookerjee's discourses, and leaves out many that might not have been available to the editor then. Secondly, it contains a few factually-wrong statements, as the book claims that 'Dr Syama Prasad Mookerjee's principal achievements in the fields of education were during the years of his vice chancellorship of the University of Calcutta between 1934 and 1938'. The statement undermines Mookerjee's contribution to Indian education against the facts because his concerns began in early 1930s and continued till his death. It would be erroneous to limit his contribution to the period of his position as the vice chancellor. It also does gross injustice to his concerns and views expressed in a vigorous and sustained manner from different fora, including his speeches in the 1940 and 1951 debates in the then state assembly and the Indian Parliament.

Dr Mookerjee was a strong believer in Indian cultural values like service, sacrifice and care for all, among others, and advocated the primacy of social harmony, for he saw internal conflicts as the main cause of India's plummeting fortunes. On umpteen occasions in his discourses, he stressed the need for harmony, and saw education as the main instrument of enforcing it in the country. Discrimination on no ground—region, religion, gender, caste or creed—was tolerable to him. He invoked all segments of the society, particularly students and teachers to play their roles, as his educational discourses reveal to us. It is now imperative for us to study Mookerjee's discourses, as they exist, and in relation to the discourses of other thinkers. Why was Mookerjee, like other leaders of his time, speaking to the student community about these issues? The reason was that he saw hope in the youth, as his own generation in some way failed them, at least in practice. The moot point here is that Mookerjee needs to be read from the viewpoint of the cultural history of the Indian subcontinent.

Belatedly though, the present volume endeavours to put together Mookerjee's educational discourses culled from almost all known sources in the form of his convocation addresses at different universities, various academic bodies and associations, and interventions in debates in the meetings of the university statutory authorities, the state assembly and the Parliament, among others. They need to be revisited because his educational views were the essence of his concern for national and human values.

The volume is a tribute to Mookerjee, the educational thinker who was committed to high ideals of Indian education and culture, and strove to implement his vision in his different capacities. It is expected that the volume will help in furthering our understanding of Mookerjee, the educational thinker, and inspire the scholars to study his vision from different viewpoints.

Our most profound gratitude to Shri Narendra Modi, Hon'ble Prime Minister of India for his deeply inspiring message for the book and for his dynamic and moving assessment of Dr Syama Prasad Mookerjee.

Before concluding this prefatory note, let us mention that the task of preparing this volume would not have been possible without the support and cooperation of various institutions and individuals. The editors are indebted to Nehru Memorial Museum & Library, New Delhi, Dr Syama

Prasad Mookerjee Research Foundation (SPMRF), New Delhi, University of Calcutta, University of Delhi, Saha Institute of Nuclear Physics, Kolkata, Visva-Bharati, Santiniketan (West Bengal), Parliament Library, New Delhi, Sri Aurobindo Ashram Trust, Puducherry and Sri Aurobindo Ashram Archives, Puducherry and their office bearers for allowing permission to access their resources pertaining to the life and work of Dr Syama Prasad Mookerjee.

Various individuals took interest in the volume and provided unstinted support and help in preparing the volume at various stages. We would like to express our profound gratitude to Shri Amit Shah, National President, Bharatiya Janata Party (BJP), and trustees and office-bearers of SPMRF, viz Shri Ram Lal, General Secretary (Organisation) BJP; Shri Arun Singh, Secretary, SPMRF and General Secretary BJP; and Shri Shyam Jaju, National Vice President BJP. Shri Shakti Sinha, Director, Nehru Memorial Museum & Library; Dr Narendra Shukla, Head Human Resource Development, Nehru Memorial Museum & Library and Head of the Manuscript Section, Nehru Memorial Museum & Library; Shri Amit Kumar, Executive Assistant, SPMRF; Shri NS Bisht SPMRF; Shri Devesh Khandelwal, Research Scholar; Shri Tarun Vijay, former Member of Parliament; Shri Matriprasad, Secretary; Sri Aurobindo Ashram Trust and Shri Amarjeet Singh, Officer on Special Duty to the Governor of Bihar deserve special mention.

Our acknowledgements are due to many unnamed people who contributed in as many innumerable ways as they themselves in preparation of this volume. Last but not the least, we put on record our gratitude to Shri Shobit Arya, Wisdom Tree, New Delhi for undertaking publication of this book with his commitment for qualitative production.

INTRODUCTION

Syama Prasad Mookerjee's Vision of Education

Syama Prasad Mookerjee was among the leading intellectual academicians and educationists of his time. His engagement with education was not coincidental. He came from a family of educationists. His father, Asutosh Mookerjee, was vice chancellor of the University of Calcutta, and had earned the sobriquet 'lion of Bengal'. Incidentally, like his father, Mookerjee also served as the youngest vice chancellor of the university from 1934 to 1938. It was perhaps the largest university in Asia if not in the world at that time with problems of great magnitude and complexity. The son continued the unfinished agenda of his father and strove to modify the university in accordance with the ethos of the region, nation and human values. His efforts should by no means be regarded as accidental or isolated instances of university programmes. They form components of a well-considered plan of future reorganisation of education in India.

Mookerjee advocated reforming the Indian education system in the light of rich Indian intellectual and cultural traditions. He did not take recourse to the easy task of just critiquing the colonial education system, but as a critical insider, he provided reasons for doing so in larger Indian historical perspective and prepared a blueprint and implemented it too in his capacity as the vice chancellor.

The higher education scenario before the tenure of Syama Prasad Mookerjee as the vice chancellor of the University of Calcutta deserves a brief scrutiny to contextualise his contribution to education. The report of the Education Commission of 1882 after the establishment of universities in three presidencies reported a relatively quick growth of higher education in the next decades. The phenomenon led to the appointment of the University Education Commission of 1902 to 'enquire into the condition and prospects in British India and to recommend such a measure as may tend to elevate the standard of the university teaching and to promote the advancement of learning'. It was followed by the University Act of 1904 that focussed on the main recommendations of the 1902 Commission and reconstitution of the governing bodies of Indian universities. The Government Resolution on Education Policy in 1903 spelt out the policy in regard to higher education. Accordingly, universities were established at Dacca, Aligarh, Banaras, Rangoon, Patna and Nagpur, though the World War I delayed the establishment of universities in Banaras and Patna that came into existence in 1916 and 1917, respectively. The new universities desired the establishment of the inter-universities board to coordinate the work of universities after a conference of vice chancellors in 1924 and the report of the Central Advisory Board on Educational Development in 1943.

During this period, Sir Asutosh Mookerjee (1864-1924), father of Dr Syama Prasad Mookerjee, revolutionised Indian higher education by changing the character of the Indian universities from mere college-affiliated academic bodies to postgraduate departments of teaching and research. Asutosh Mookerjee, who was vice chancellor of the University of Calcutta from 1906-1914 and from 1921-23, launched many academic graduate programmes of teaching and research like applied psychology, Indian history and culture along with Islamic culture, anthropology, industrial chemistry and comparative literature with the study of Sanskrit, Pali, Hindi and Bangla in the university. His revolutionary step persuaded the then government to appoint a commission for comprehensively examining the problems of the University of Calcutta. The secondary education and its problems were also included in its terms of reference (TOR). The report, submitted in 1919, did not produce the desirable impact due to many reasons, primarily financial, yet new universities were established in Mysore, Hyderabad, Aligarh, Delhi (1922), Nagpur (1923), Andhra University (1926), Agra (1927), Rajputana or Rajasthan (1947), Sagar (1947), Poona (1948), Kashmir (1948) and Baroda (1949).

In this period, Bengal was leading the 'national' education movement. Thinkers like Sri Aurobindo, Acharya Satish Chandra Mukherjee, Bipin Chandra Pal, Subodh Chandra Mullick with Gurudev Rabindranath Tagore were products of the colonial education system but they critiqued the system from outside for its un-Indian character that led to the subjugation of spirit and culture that was brought out by KC Bhattacharya in his seminal essay 'Swaraj in Ideas'. Gurudev Tagore, on the one hand, proposed the notion of '*vishwa manav*' (universal man), and went on to chart out his ideal education in the form of Visva-Bharati. It is worth noting here that Syama Prasad Mookerjee had fought in the Parliament for autonomy and sanctity of Gurudev's vision when the Visva-Bharati Bill was discussed in 1951.

While many Indian thinkers brought out the deficiencies of the colonial education from outside, Mookerjee did so from within the system during his tenure as vice chancellor of the University of Calcutta between 1934 and 1938 and tried to reform the system by bringing about changes in perceptions regarding mother tongue as the medium of instruction, India's intellectual and cultural heritage, science and technology education, woman education, adult education, employment and research among others. He contributed to the rich legacy of his father in different fields of higher education and invited Gurudev Tagore to deliver the convocation address in Bangla which was unprecedented in the history of the university. When he introduced Bangla as a subject and medium for the highest examination, that is, PhD in the university, he paid his tribute to his father whose epitaph reads thus: 'His noblest achievement, surest of them all/a place for his mother tongue—in stepmother's hall.'

Syama Prasad Mookerjee's concerns with education continued subsequently, as may be seen in his discourses at different forums until his untimely death. Mookerjee's formative years were shaped, on the one hand, by the two world wars that humanity witnessed as the darkest, cruellest and meanest chapters in history, and, on the other, by India's struggle for independence against the colonisers. Most part of his life passed in this turbulent period marked by the highest and lowest points in the history of colonisation and its consequences. Before World War I, the colonial expansion was at the highest with 85 per cent surface of the earth colonised. However, it was at its nadir in the years after the World War II, as the empire that was solid melted away gradually. In case of India, apart from its indirect participation in the War, the period was paralleled by India's freedom movement along with attendant narratives of exploitation and brutal suppression like the Jallianwala Bagh massacre and the famines. When India attained its freedom ultimately, its celebration was attended by the dispossession, displacement and massacres due to the vivisection of the subcontinent. It pained all alike, as Faiz Ahmed Faiz voiced it, '*Yah dag dag ujala, yah shab-guzida subah*' (This is speckled light, and this dawn is wrapped in darkness).

Equally pertinent it is to note that Mookerjee was from Calcutta (Bengal) that was still the intellectual and cultural centre of India, though the political capital of India had been shifted from Calcutta to Delhi. Bengal was both a beneficiary and victim of the process of colonisation. It was natural that the resilient Bengali psyche observed and resisted colonisation in the form of intellectual argumentation, peaceful and even violent protests. No surprise that the suppressed yet belligerent Bengal, on the one hand, produced the most outstanding intellectual and spiritual leaders, politicians and revolutionaries, and on the other, produced the best of babus who were co-opted by the colonisers for their utilitarian value. Swami Vivekananda left this mortal world a year after Mookerjee's birth, though the impact of his ideas then was limited in comparison to the resurgence of interest in him later. Gurudev Tagore had earned literary accolades from people all over the world. The word swaraj was in the air in the political sense of the term. It was KC Bhattacharya who lent it a new dimension with his 'Swaraj in Ideas' that he first delivered as a talk in October 1931 in Chandernagore under Sir Asutosh Memorial Lecture Series. The impact of the ideas of Sri Aurobindo, the true inheritor of Swami Vivekananda's intellectual and spiritual legacy, was being felt with his transition from the political to the spiritual sphere. Mookerjee, who later went to address his ashram's proposed university one year after Sri Aurobindo's demise, imbibed all these ideas and lent his voice to them.

The colonial forces had systematically replaced the Indian judicial, revenue/economic, socio-cultural, intellectual and administrative systems with their colonial counterparts. Education suffered the most, to take recourse to Gandhi's words, they killed the beautiful tree called 'Indian education'. However, it should be counted among the greatest ironies of colonial history that the colonial education system produced a generation including Shyamji Krishna Verma, Swami Vivekananda, Sri Aurobindo, BG Tilak, Veer Savarkar, Mahatma Gandhi, Bhagat Singh, Subhas Chandra Bose, BR Ambedkar, S Radhakrishnan among the rich array of freedom fighters and thought leaders, that resisted, subverted and fought against the colonial ways of exploitation of Indian resources—natural, human, economic and intellectual—till India threw away the yoke of thraldom. Mookerjee resisted the negative influence of the colonial system from inside with the intent of improving it. Though he was a product of the colonial system, and for a while a part of it with the highest positions that he held in higher education, yet he was the one who wanted to reorient the Indian education system holistically. In the process, he decolonised one of the principal pillars of colonial enterprise in India. His discourses reveal that he never missed any opportunity to assert his identity, his rich cultural and intellectual heritage and the way the then system had failed to respond to the needs of the Indian youth. His discourses reveal that he spared no opportunity to vehemently criticise unfair policies and actions of the then rulers, but not without justification. His discourses also reveal that even in independent democratic India, no vice chancellor would demonstrate the courage and sharpness of tongue in his criticism of the rulers, as he did then.

Mookerjee's concerns for education were integral to his yearning for India's independence. For him, freedom was indispensable for education, which was the means of social advancement leading to the attainment of its pristine glory and freeing India from the colonial yoke. That is the reason why his educational vision is inseparable from his national vision, and his concerns were attended by a historical sense through which he saw the present India.

Mookerjee understood Indian education in relation to Indian history. During colonial rule in India, and even today, the question that was often asked was: Why did India lose its glory and independence, if it was so great culturally and powerful because of its people? He too posed the question and answered it. In his address at Patna University, he said, 'Would it be true to say that the catholicity and universal sympathy that contributed so much to the everlasting freshness of India's civilisation, concealed in them the germs of her political downfall? Did they engender that other-worldliness that spelt ruin to the prospect of India's freedom?' He tried to see the answer in Indian history, and found these propositions preposterous, 'India's culture has not been responsible for India's bondage.' Validating it with evidence, he stated,

> Did not India produce Chandragupta and Samudragupta, Pratap Singh, Shivaji and Ranjit Singh, in spite of the pacific teachings of our ancestors? Did not the nameless but illustrious heroes, the Indian Argonauts, who explored the mysteries of the unchartered seas and spread Indian culture to the furthest east, prove that Hindu pacifism did not eliminate enterprise and love of adventure? Indian sages and philosophers never suggested that cowards and weaklings would ever be the torchbearers of India's great heritage.

Mookerjee was of the firm opinion that Indian culture is primarily inclusive to which different cultures and religions contributed. In this attribute lay its strength. According to him, Hindus and Muslims had directed their energies in the past to the task of India's unification. They cooperated to establish an edifice of Indian culture marked by 'liberalism, toleration and a broad-mindedness that did away with the artificial barriers raised by racial and religious prejudices. The structure stood till the recrudescence of intolerance and arrogance levelled it to the ground, to the eternal misfortune of our country'.

In another convocation address, Mookerjee further elaborated it and considered the issue of Indian unity and its attributes. He said that if 'Indian unity is a desideratum; its essential prerequisite is a broad toleration in every sphere of life'. On its basis, he charted the spirit of the new India that 'must be born of struggle and arduous labour and sacrifice, of noble scorn of ease and luxury, of thirst for knowledge and its widest application to the alleviation of human misery and suffering, of a broad-based toleration and justice affecting the rights of the vast multitude of the Indian people, of a burning and unalterable faith in the political integrity of the country, of loyalty to truth and faith in God'. Here it needs to be borne in the mind that he was not in favour of artificial unity. Also, he opined, 'Unity need not imply uniformity in every respect. In a country like India, with its huge extent, teeming population and diverse culture, a dull uniformity is not to be encouraged.'

Mookerjee never forgot to remind his audience that the Indian ideal is 'harmony and not discord, freedom and not slavery, not warring factions, castes and communities, each distrustful of the other, a united India—marching resolutely towards the goal of self-realisation'. His India included all, as he remarked, 'May we not regard ourselves as her sons and daughters—Hindus, Muslims, Buddhists and Christians—all loyal to our flag, but all equally determined to find for our great country an honourable place in the Commonwealth of Nations, to restore it to its position of glory and freedom.'

The question of India's colonisation bothered Mookerjee who sought reasons for it. There were many answers already around him. Karl Marx had his explanations to this question. He limited the canvas of considerations from the Mughal period onwards. According to him, the Mughal rule was weakened by their subedars whose decline was made a reality by the Marathas. The Afghan invasion enfeebled Marathas. It was natural, that the society such as this in the course of time was taken by colonisers. Mahatma Gandhi in his *Hind Swaraj* examined this phenomenon and said that British did not take India. We, that is, Indians gave India to them. As a proud Indian, Mookerjee could not digest India's fall, and so he studied the issue in his own way and found that it was mainly because people were at the critical hour divided and disorganised. The internal strife ceased only for a time when great kings like Asoka and Akbar ruled over India who united the subcontinent by the bond of a common aspiration and a passionate longing for the eternal code of righteous conduct, charity and understanding.

> A strong and united India fearing none and loving all, brought the message of peace and goodwill to a distracted world. But as soon as the sceptre dropped from their hands, when their grip over the country was loosened through weak and short-sighted successors, when narrow selfishness and mutual jealousy and distrust overpowered our souls, when local feuds and religious strife raised their ugly heads giving rise to social exclusiveness and moral decadence, unity was lost; freedom, man's priceless treasure, disappeared; the country broke into fragments and relapsed into a state of conflict

> and struggle. While the national and political unity of India was successfully achieved by great individuals, the masses did not at all times feel an abiding interest in its preservation. Thus, although all culture has survived the storm and stress of time, we find ourselves in the strange and tragic position of the representatives and exponents of an ancient civilisation, yet alive but in bondage.

Rather than blaming others, he examined problems within, and shared the lessons from history. According to him, the English came to India as traders and exploiting India's weakness due to lack of unity, became masters of an empire. However, he gave credit to the British where it was due to them—for the progress of India—but as a self-respecting Indian that did not prevent him from criticising them for disturbing the vitals of Indian life in the form of 'a general decay of the creative Indian arts...the decline and disappearance of the indigenous industries of India...cottage industries...deplorable neglect of the health and welfare of the villages of India'. He traced India's poverty and distress to 'a systematic pursuit of an economic and industrial policy which has not been prompted and administered in the sole interest of India and her inhabitants but for serving colonial interest'.

Mookerjee went on to add that the illiteracy of more than 90 per cent of the people at his time was among the worst problems of Indian life. Also, he found another vital weakness among Indians that 'they have not been adequately trained to defend their own hearth and home'. For him an autonomous India was 'unthinkable without a national army and a national navy controlled and manned by Indians themselves'. His canvas of concerns was not limited to progress but the heavy price that India paid due to its colonisation. Without losing sight of core aspects of the Indian eco-socio-cultural realities, he realised that no reform was possible until and unless India becomes free. Freedom was his pre-condition for India's rise from fall. So he remarked, '... no reforms of a radical character in any field of activity will ever be possible, nor can India rise to her full stature spiritually and economically, until and unless she takes her rank among the free nations of the world. No material gain, no earthly possession can ever compensate for the loss of man's liberty'. Also, in absence of freedom, the country will not be a society of enlightened citizens which was according to him 'the ultimate goal of enlightened man'.

Every individual should be free to 'think, worship, speak and act as he would, subject to the similar rights of others, free under the protection of the equal justice to pursue his lawful business as he chooses, free from the absence of restraint and in the presence of opportunity'. To him, liberty was not a single and simple conception. It had four elements—national, political, personal, economic.

> The man who is fully free is one who lives in a country which is independent; in a State which is democratic: in a society where the laws are equal and restrictions at a minimum; in an economic system in which national interests are protected and the citizens have the scope of a secure livelihood, an assured comfort and full opportunity to rise by merit.' But the freedom, so truly and courageously longed for by him, was not India's lot in the colonial period. He stated in no ambiguous terms, 'Until this condition is reached, India will never achieve true greatness or happiness, based on the glorious features of her past civilisation.

Mookerjee's trajectory of educational thinking, revealed as it is in his discourses, sees education in regional, national and international terms. Since he was a nationalist, he thought of India, free from the colonial clutches. But his concept of nation (*rashtra*) was based on the foundation of region (*kshetra*), that is, Bengal in his case. In Indian thinking, *kshetra* is a core cognitive category. It cohabits space with other contiguous *kshetra*s. Its contact with other contiguous *kshetra*s leads to creation of clusters of *kshetra*s, followed by the formation of *chakravartin kshetra* with the cohabitation of different *kshetra*s, as discussed by the ninth century Sanskrit poetician Rajashekhar in his *Kavyamimansa*. Mookerjee's vision rests on this paradigm which is applicable to his world view and educational vision. A strong nationalist that he was, his nationalism was not a parasitic concept. The nation was a geo-cultural entity and an emotional and cultural construct with long shared and lived experiences. In his framework, Bengal was the foundation of his vision, India was the trunk of the tree, and entire humanity its sky. That is why in the early part of his thinking about education, Bengal is the focal concern. If Bengal of his ideals was to become a leader, its education system needed revamping. He wanted to create 'a new Bengal that is destined to lead and not be led'. This Bengal of his vision did not know discrimination on the grounds of religion, caste and creed. His ideal was a generation of young intellectual warriors whom he termed as 'able-bodied intellectual youths, Hindus, Muslims and Christians, trained and brought up according to the highest ideals of service, capable of responding to the call of the nation and ready to unfurl the flag of truth and sincerity, of progress, unity and freedom'.

In other words, Mookerjee's love, concern and commitment for Bengal did not come in conflict with the nation. Rather they were at the disposal of the nation. Hence, *kshetra* and *rashtra* did not clash for him. His *rashtra* was a composite whole of different *kshetra*s or regions. His concept of *rashtra* was in consonance with Sri Aurobindo's, but differed from Gurudev Tagore's notion of nation that was informed by the west and by the ravages of various wars fought in Europe. It made Tagore denounce 'nation' in his lectures in Europe. Mookerjee's nation was based on the Vedic concept of *rashtra* and analogous to Mahatma Gandhi's concept, as he saw *rashtra* as an entity to maintain unity within and resist colonisation and exploitation by alien rulers. Mookerjee, too, did not see any adversarial relationship between '*kshetra*' (Bengal) and '*rashtra*' (India). Also, he did not gloss over the world beyond the nation, and seemed to have agreed with Gandhi whose happy nationalism led to happy internationalism. Mookerjee wanted an able nation built on cultural ideals to ensure a stable world for humanity. All nations, thus in existence, would lead to the creation of a positive world order.

In accordance, Mookerjee's vision of education rested on the scaffolding of *kshetra* (region), *rashtra* (nation) and *vishwa* (world). He sought systemic reforms in Bengal's education at the level of region, nation in terms of federal policy of education but without oversighting or glossing over universal ideals. This is discernible in his discourses delivered in the second half of 1940s. Since he addressed academic assemblies in different parts of the country, he saw to it that the *kshetra* was respected. Be it Calcutta, Patna or Mumbai, he invariably referred reverentially to cultural and intellectual traditions of the region and sought changes in the education system accordingly. Thereafter, he envisioned requisite changes for reforming the education system in India. For this purpose, he knew in no uncertain terms that for a strong India, strong Bengal, like other *kshetra*s in India, was needed. He stated that to play her part in the remaking of India, Bengal must produce through her educational institutions 'a race of men and women, strong in body and mind, true, resolute and self-reliant, burning with hefty patriotism and idealism, not carried away by emotions but capable of exercising critical and reasonable judgment, trained both to be leaders and soldiers, amenable to discipline—discipline imposed by the combined will of themselves—devoted to duty, determined to work not as a class or community but in a spirit of corporate service, and ever willing to place their services in all capacities, humble and great, for the good of society and for the advancement of the highest interest of the nation'. This makes it clear that *rashtra* and *kshetra* do exist together without any threat.

Holistic Revamping of Education in India

For revamping education, Mookerjee conceived of education holistically in terms of elementary, matriculation and higher education. Though he worked in the higher education sector primarily, he never considered it in isolation from other segments of education. He sought a sound policy of national education, which will ensure a steady advance from the lowest stage to the highest. He wanted to see primary education as 'developing widely and laying the foundations of literacy, of right conduct, of healthy activity and of a breadth of outlook which will render possible the growth of a national consciousness'. With primary education as the foundation, he wanted to see 'secondary education spreading far and wide, satisfying the requirements of a sound and liberal education and leading its recipients to diverse fields of intellectual, useful and productive activity'. At the third stage, he wanted to see university education as a natural continuation of such a varied type of secondary education, providing for higher and advanced work, not only in the liberal and professional studies but also in science and technology, in commerce and agriculture'. He wished a young learner growing up not as 'a mechanised recorder of information and theories, not as a dry specialist, but as one whose latent power is well roused, whose critical judgement is strengthened and whose capacity for wide thinking and application of knowledge to problems of life is developed to the fullest extent'. Also, he felt a strong need for a liberal and useful education, on which will be raised the superstructure of such departments of study as will produce men and women trained in diverse branches of knowledge, theoretical and practical, which will make them fit persons in the service of the nation. In unequivocal terms, he spoke about ideals of a university that can ill-afford to gloss over the needs of the land on which it stands. He wished that each university should adequately reflect the peculiar needs of the country and should produce men who would possess both knowledge and culture. He put his formula about education succinctly thus: 'To put it differently, we can say that true education should include the local idea, the national idea and the international idea.' One discerns in it an echo of Sri Aurobindo's words who wrote in his 'Preface on National Education' (1920-21):

> It follows that this alone will be a true and living education which helps to bring out to full advantage, makes ready for the full purpose and scope of human life all that is in the individual man and which at the same time helps him to enter into his right relation with the life, mind and soul of the people to which he belongs and with that great total life, mind and soul of humanity of which he himself is a unit and his people or nation a living, a separate yet inseparable member.

Entrenched that he was in his ancient Indian intellectual cultural traditions, Mookerjee saw education as the means of eradicating the evils plaguing Indian society. Education was an instrument of sustaining cultural values, and of preserving, creating, disseminating and applying knowledge. Ancient Indian education based on the *gurukul* system considered the teacher a pedestal higher than parents and even God. As a well-structured system, it took care of the holistic development of disciples. The colonial education system was utilitarian and aimed at producing a generation that was useful to the colonisers, disregarding the native educational culture and heritage. That is why it earned censure of all thinking souls in that period.

Among his illustrious contemporaries, Mookerjee was the most qualified to speak about education. He could see through the colonial project of educating Indians in the mirror of Indian educational tradition. He knew that the day the history of education in British India will be traced by an impartial historian, the record will be hardly creditable to the ruling class. India, according to him, suffered not for want of zeal and devotion for education on the part of Indians but 'on account of the colossal blunder made by our rulers while formulating their educational policy a little over a century ago'. He knew that the policy was influenced by the advancement of the interests of the ruling class. Hence, with its roots cut-off from the ground, education was doomed to failure, fostering an artificial growth, producing a race of imitators. He was aware of colonial records that disclosed a lamentable lack of knowledge of India's civilisational past by the rulers. The colonial education systems portrayed a remarkable 'over-emphasis on the so-called virtues of western culture and an unconcealed contempt for everything Indian'. He did not deplore the fact that the gates of western knowledge were thrown open to Indians, but that knowledge was imported at the sacrifice of India's cultural heritage. Consequently, a proper synthesis between the two systems did not take place and led to neglect and destruction, of the Indian base. He knew that the reason for sustenance of western education in India was largely due to the glamour of State service. Despite this, 'the national consciousness of educated Indians could not be suppressed and far from being blind supporters of an alien rule, they themselves became the torchbearers of revolt'. Since the education of the masses was neglected, the educational system failed to serve real needs of India. Mookerjee suggested a thorough overhauling of the entire system. In Gurukul Kangri University, he boldly stated that 'the problem of education can never be fully solved in a manner acceptable to self-respecting Indians until and unless it is left in the hands of a government representing the national will and freed from foreign domination. We move indeed in a vicious circle. Without education properly outlined and directed, we cannot easily attain our freedom. Without freedom and full control over our own destinies, we cannot reshape our educational policy entirely according to our will and requirements'.

As Mookerjee saw *kshetra*, *rashtra* and *vishwa* in relation to each other, he saw primary, secondary or matriculation and university education not in three segments but as parts of the whole. 'The future of university education depends vitally on the secondary education and to my mind a reference to these regulations is not only justified but also necessary. Most of the unsatisfactory features of undergraduate and postgraduate education have their origin in a defective system of secondary education. He referred to it in his address to the conference of representatives of teachers in the university and its colleges. He furthered it:

> Education wisely planned and rightly executed will ultimately be the principal factor on which the future peace, progress and happiness of the Indian people will rest. Primary, Secondary and University education—all stages demand a balanced attention from the State and the public. Expansion and not curtailment must be our motto, preservation of equality must be our constant aim.

Also, he saw segments of education—primary, secondary and university—in a non-hierarchical manner and proposed that 'each should receive the unstinted support of the State and the public'.

Similarly, Mookerjee considered the issues of higher education in terms of their past, present and future. He could perceive the disconnect between the present and ancient university systems. He found that universities of modern India had very little in common with ancient or medieval centres of learning. 'It is well known how the British authorities planned the establishment of universities in India about one hundred years ago mainly for their own administrative purposes. Consequently, the masses were neglected, villages became stagnant and poverty reigned supreme in India. Elementary education suffered and so did Indian languages.' He lamented the neglect of 'that great storehouse of Indian knowledge and wisdom—the mother of most of our languages, Sanskrit. The aims and purposes of education were inconsistent with national aspiration. Respect for the noblest features of our great culture and civilisation dwindled away due to ignorance and disbelief'.

For him, education was not a static phenomenon. So he opined that its syllabi must change with 'the passage of time and with the altered conditions of the community it seeks to serve and elevate'. He also wanted it to be 'closely related to the life of the people' lest it becomes 'stagnant and soulless and instead of uplifting society tends to retard progress of the country'. Free India of his dreams was an able country capable of catering to the needs of all stages of education as parts of one comprehensive national system—from primary to university levels. He saw education in India holistically: genders—men and women; areas—rural and urban; religions—Hindus, Muslims and Christians; all segments from primary to higher education; and all constitutive elements of human personality—physical, mental, intellectual, rational, aesthetic, relational, moral and spiritual—as equal participants. He argued that,

> There need not be any conflict amongst primary, secondary and university stages, nor amongst literary, scientific, technical, vocational and agricultural courses of study. A national system of education must conceive of a balanced structure where due and proper emphasis will be laid on every section so as to maintain its harmony, its strength and solidarity. Today after freedom the universities must be conscious of much wider conception of their duties and responsibilities than before.

Without getting limited to the domain of education, he went on to add that there was an urgent need for 'adequate' leadership in the professions, in commerce and industry, in politics and administration.

As early as 1937, he had stated in his address to Bombay University that 'the time has now come for initiating a new policy of education, suited to our needs and aspirations and consistent with the best traditions of our past'. He was aware of questions being then raised against the university system, so he wanted to guard against its critics and zealots both.

> As home of progressive thought and culture, the university could be the mouthpiece of national hopes and aspirations, a medium for conserving and advancing the bounds of knowledge, and for preserving and raising the intellectual life and thought of a nation, breathing an atmosphere of freedom and truth, drawing together men and women of all castes and creeds, inspired by a zeal for devoted and unselfish service.

Mookerjee, with the heritage of Takshshila, Vallabhipur, Vikramshila and Nalanda in his mind, held universities in high esteem. He saw universities as institutions 'whose paramount task is to produce not only leaders of thought and action but also workers dedicated to the service of the nation'. For this to happen, he believed that there is need to 'set our house in order' for younger generation of 'Hindus, Muslims and Christians alike—to combine and resolutely stand for the permanent well-being of our province and to rescue her from the deadly stagnation which now seems to envelop her'. He termed his generation 'as trustees of our national honour', and called upon them to invest in the university for the future, 'It is for us to realise the supreme need of abandoning paths of hatred, violence and destruction. It is for us to concentrate on constructive plans of reform and expansion in different fields of activity for the promotion of national prosperity.'

Dr Mookerjee had roles fixed for all stakeholders for rebuilding of a new India. For this, Indian universities 'must not regard themselves as exclusive institutions which exist apart from the currents of the country's life'. They need to 'train their alumni in a worthy manner, saturate them with the lessons of Indian history and civilisations, instil into them unity and reason, strength and dauntlessness, inspire them with skill and knowledge and teach them to apply themselves devotedly and unselfishly to the service of their fellowmen'. He added,

> If the university is to be true to its salt, if it is to fulfil its mission in awakening a true national spirit and the consciousness of the people, it must contribute in every possible way to the building up of the youth of the country and train them in all spheres of useful and constructive activity. The teachers should consider it their sacred duty to be the interpreters of India's heritage, the seekers of truth and knowledge, and prove to the world that Indian scholars are second to none in their efforts to serve the cause of the humanities and the sciences in relation to the unfettered progress of India and of human civilisation itself.

He could never see higher education with its links severed from Indian heritage, pursuit of knowledge in all domains like humanities and sciences and entire humanity.

Reorienting Education in India

Education to Mookerjee was the instrument for attaining independence. He had imbibed the principle that true education liberates but this liberation (*mukti*) was not an abstract category but an ontological category that meant freedom from causes of sufferings and bondages—economic, social, political and spiritual. For him, immediate liberation was freedom from colonial rule in which education had a principal role to play. 'It is through education that the ultimate battle of Indian freedom will be won.' After Independence, he saw that the gigantic task of reconstruction—cultural, social, economic and political—can be achieved through 'the coordinated efforts of bands of trained and disciplined Indians'. His ideal of educated and trained Indian was one who was 'armed with the knowledge of India's past glory and greatness, her strength and weakness, it is they who can place before their country a programme of work, which while loyal to the fundamental traditions of Indian civilisation will be adapted to the changing conditions of the modern world'.

With his critical acumen, Mookerjee could perceive then that the colonial system of education was incapable of realising these objectives. Hence, it demanded reorganisation immediately. For any 'scheme of reorganisation of education, truly national in character' he spelt out eight primary conditions thus:

> First and foremost, a system of education, consistent with the genius of the people of India and suited to modern life and conditions, cannot be fully achieved unless and until India enjoys a political status which will give her the liberty to decide for herself what constitutes her national needs and how best they can be satisfied. Call it dominion status, responsible self-government or *swaraj*, I am not concerned with the nomenclature; I am concerned with the supreme fact that the constitution must give us real and not shadowy rights and powers and enable India to be the mistress of her own destiny. Secondly, there must be less of degrading poverty and less of disease and pestilence, now nationwide in extent, which are sapping our vitality and energy and shutting out the inrush of joy, light and beauty into this land of proud and ancient civilisation. Thirdly, the State must spend far more adequately and generously on education, in all its grades, than what it has done in the past. All schemes for reconstruction will remain unrealised until this paramount condition is wholeheartedly fulfilled. Fourthly, there must be an elaborate system of elementary and secondary education which will form an enduring foundation on which the great structure of university education will be built, shining like a crown of purposeful achievement drawing inspiration and strength from the abundance of materials which the lower stages will bring to its doors. Fifthly, education at every stage should be as cheap as possible while its quality will be maintained at a high level.... Sixthly, while expressing our deepest gratitude to our past benefactors, let us emphasise that the universities must inspire private benefactions on a much wider scale than they have hitherto done. ...But this disparity is nowhere more staggering than in this unfortunate land of ours. If our wealthy men who have amassed

> fortunes, whether through personal efforts or through the accident of birth or otherwise make up their minds to allot a portion of what they possess for the uplift of their brethren, for the wide diffusion of knowledge and culture, for the alleviation of suffering, they will be uprooting feelings of hostility and antagonism and will inspire the affection and confidence of the masses whose prosperity and improvement they will thus have helped to stabilise. Seventhly, there must be a close and honourable connection between education and trade, industry and commerce, so that men trained in different branches of practical skill and knowledge will have a natural scope for their talents. ...Lastly, the universities must be given the amplest freedom to work out their salvation. We must free education from the undercurrents of political and communal strife. Let each university have a constitution judiciously planned on academic considerations and truly representative in character. Let the men chosen for their administration be of the right type inspired solely by the idea of training youths who will be an asset to the cause of Indian progress.

Education, according to him, demanded to be seen in the light of these eight principles or *asthata siddhanta* which are equally true even today. While seeking revamping of the Indian education system, he favoured multidimensional education as against 'education of one type' for that is not equally good for all people. But for this was needed immediate reorientation of the present system. Stressing this, he mentioned three requisites for reforming education in his address to the University of Calcutta dated 2 March 1935 in the form of '(i) sufficient funds, (ii) expansion of education and not its curtailment in any shape or form, and (iii) the control of education vested in a body of men endowed with full autonomy and chosen primarily on academic considerations'. While stressing the vital need of reforms, he sounded a caveat that 'it would be nothing short of a national disaster if the prestige and the authority of the university are sought to be curtailed or its influence minimised'. He respected the university as an institution and advocated preservation of institutional autonomy and sanctity.

Ideals of Education

To Mookerjee, educational institutions were not as 'factories for the production of clerks and subordinate officers'. Their task was 'to supply the country with the leadership and skill in different branches of activity—economic, commercial, and industrial; municipal, provincial and national—such men and women were to be animated with the ideals of service, imagination, courage, catholicity of outlook and resilience of nature'. He saw them as 'the living organs of national reconstruction'. It was the task of the university to discover the best means of blending together both the spiritual and the material aspects of life. It must equip its alumni irrespective of caste, creed or sex, with individual fitness, not for its own sake, not merely for adorning varied occupations and professions, but in order to teach them how to merge their individuality in the common cause of advancing the progress and prosperity of their Motherland and upholding the highest traditions of human civilisation. That constitutes the perennial ideal of a university rooted in Indian soil and expresses one of the greatest needs of the hour.

In the university education, he favoured promotion of all disciplines of knowledge—philosophy, literature, archaeology and architecture, fine arts including music and painting, the Indian languages, classical and modern, history and polity—in such a way that 'the correct interpretation of the manifestations of the genius of India in the realm of thought and culture will be faithfully and courageously given'. But they were not to be 'a mere catalogue of past achievements'. In the process, he outlined the attributes and functions of a modern scholar,

> The modern Indian scholar must have the training and the vision to connect our ancient history and civilisation with our present needs and conditions and to suggest rules of conduct and formulate an outlook on life which the Indian society of today can worthily accept. Economics and banking, particularly the position of this country in relation to foreign trade and competition, and the conditions of a prosperous and an economically free India must be investigated. Politics and constitutional law and theory must be critically examined, especially the fundamental aspects of the government and constitutions of countries which are attempting to rehabilitate themselves on the ruins of their former existence. Education and psychology will form the subjects of active investigation. A department of educational research will devote itself to the study of local problems as also of great experiments,

> made in countries far and near, particularly in Russia and Japan. Important languages of the east and the west will be studied and the achievements of other civilised nations brought home to our rising generations. Indeed, while the Indian universities will maintain the great characteristics of India's past culture and civilisation, omitting all that is pernicious and anti-progressive, it must not summarily reject what the west may give us. If western ideas can be assimilated into our system without detriment to its national character, we shall welcome them. If such acceptance denationalises us, we shall reject them without hesitation.

It is necessary to mention here that he dwelt at length on the place to be given to religious education in the system. Religion, according to him, played a dual role in the evolution of mankind, and has done 'enormous good to humanity', but had been utilised as a convenient excuse for senseless oppression of mankind. He criticised the policy of secularisation of Indian education 'according to a policy of religious neutrality' pursued by a foreign government which has had in some respects 'devastating effects on the Indian mind'. Mookerjee recognised religion as a reality in India and hoped that religious education would lead to greater understanding of other religions. But he knew the problems in the practicability of religious education as a subject for study in schools and colleges, and open to youths belonging to various religious faiths. 'The danger lies in the fact that this instruction is likely to be imparted by men who will lay greater emphasis on the practices of religion than on its principles and thereby sow the seeds of exclusiveness and fanaticism, ruinous for the growth of Indian nationhood.' Keeping these issues in view, he wanted religion to be left mainly to the home of the learners. However, he urged for 'a regular and well-balanced study of the great truths and the beauties underlying the different religious faiths, presented in a manner which will not seek to proclaim the superiority of one to the other, nor emphasise minute differences among one another. The text which will require most careful preparation, will record the ultimate triumph of truth and righteousness, lay stress on the essential unity of all religions and aim at the foundation of a common sympathy, a just and equitable understanding and a sense of universal brotherhood'.

Role of Teachers and Youth in National Life

Mookerjee considered teachers as the foundation of the education system so the selection of the right type of teachers was vital for the success of an educational scheme. Teachers equipped with character and learning will regard their task as a 'sacred mission—men who will inspire the respect and affection of their students and will act as their guides, philosophers and friends'. However, seeing universities as 'the mouthpieces of that liberty of thought and expression to be upheld by a true democracy', he stressed on a student-centric education. It demanded cordial relationship on the campus. He had before him the ideal of the traditional relationship of deep understanding, cordiality and reverence between the teachers and the disciples in ancient days. 'No university can exist unless it can evoke a spirit of affection and loyalty in the minds of the students,' he averred. But he was clear that mere 'extraneous rules and regulations of discipline' cannot bring about an atmosphere of goodwill and cordiality.

Mookerjee criticised the British system of education for its evil influence on Indian cultural and social life. But he did not ignore its contribution. He was not a blind detractor of the western education system, as he stated: 'Western education has helped to rouse our political consciousness, has to a large extent unified the scattered elements spread throughout this vast country, and has had remarkable effects on our national awakening'. No one can forget the inestimable value of these contributions. He further stated it in his address to Bombay University that students produced by the system stood out as illustrious workers in diverse fields of Indian life including the struggle for the attainment of *swaraj*. He mentioned many names who were alumni of Bombay University.

'If Shivaji coined the expression *swaraj* 300 years ago, Bal Gangadhar Tilak brought it back to the minds of the sleeping millions of modern India and roused their energies to constructive work which has had far-reaching effects on the destinies of our country...Of those living, the name of Mahatma Gandhi naturally comes uppermost in our minds as one whose greatness and goodness have given India a new position in the eyes of the world.' It may be construed from his arguments that they could achieve their goals because they never disowned their allegiance to the spirit of our 'beloved Motherland', and accordingly called upon the youth of the university, 'whenever the occasion needs it, do not hesitate to proclaim yourselves as Indians first and anything else next'.

Like Swami Vivekananda, Mookerjee underscored the importance of the role of youth in India's future. He had understood the simple but cardinal truth that the future of Bengal—nay, of India—lay in 'the younger generation of her men and women that she will be only what they shall make her to be'. For the task of national reconstruction, he pinned his hopes on a race of Indian youths, 'proud of their culture and traditions, armed with western skill and knowledge, fearless and straightforward, determined to work and stand united under a common banner of progress and service'. He wanted the youth to be 'saturated with the highest ideals of Indian life and culture', but they should 'imbibe the best elements of western science and knowledge'. Moreover, he did not want them to 'grow up as an aggressive nationalist utterly forgetful of their ultimate loyalty to the spirit of humanity at large. Neither do I minimise the value of his attachment to his community and province'. The community, province, nation and humanity at large constituted the contours of his vision of life, world view and education. He knew that nationalism that ignores community and region is parasitic in the manner internationalism is if it glosses over nation.

Dealing with the responsibilities of university teachers, he referred to the problem of unrest in the student community also. He did not propose that students with immature minds, or with no training, should be allowed to dictate policies to teachers and administrators. 'But students sufficiently grown up, students who have become adults and students who have obtained a sufficient amount of higher education, should be permitted to deliver their considered opinion on important political, social, economic and educational problems confronting the country, without becoming partisans in active politics.' Against the old ideals of teacher and the student relationship as that of father and his son, he noted that in modern days, the atmosphere in educational institutions does not always lead to the formation of 'a healthy social life between the teacher and the student'. With his association with the student community, he unhesitatingly asserted that authorities should miss no opportunities of discussing with students all those problems that agitate their minds, for it would create 'an atmosphere of mutual trust and confidence' but he did not encourage them 'to make the educational institutions the forum for expressing their disapproval of questions of public policy'. Though he did not favour students 'remaining aloof from the burning questions of the day', he did not, however want them to be engrossed in party politics, for he believed that they should maintain their independence of outlook and zealously cultivate that spirit of critical thinking, that free power of reasoning, which should be their main asset as they enter upon public life on the completion of their educational career. He added that nothing, however, should prevent them from an active study and discussion of important political questions of the day, and even, should they so desire, sympathising with particular schools of thought which they individually or collectively might choose to support.

Moreover, Mookerjee wanted universities to be 'a healthy training ground for future citizenship', for which occasional outbursts of youthful feelings should not worry educational administrators if they do not interfere with routine academic work, or create deadlocks on issues, small and insignificant'. Else 'they become a disease which, if unchecked, will destroy the very foundation of that strong disciplined character'. He wanted education to be free from party politics, and would have been pained to see the present scale of politicisation of some campuses in the country that have become non-sites of intellectual disputations. He underscored it when he remarked, 'We want to see such a wide and beneficent policy of education, receiving unstinted aid from the State and from the public, and freed from the baneful influence of party politics and communal wrangles.'

As an upholder of students' rights, he had reacted against a notification issued by a provincial government that had laid down severe penalties for the maintenance of discipline among students including debarring of students from government service. He opined that threats of punitive action would defeat the very object which the authors of the order themselves allege to have in view. He added, 'Any attempted transformation of the free and sacred temple of learning into a branch of the Intelligence Department is a sure method of destroying the soul of India's manhood.' The enforced discipline, such as the above, must make room for discipline from within, because, to him, the mass student mind was 'sound and pure'.

Last but not the least, for him, learning was valuable but learning itself was 'not always of the greatest value.... But it is not the man alone that the university is to make. Let us teach our students and let us ourselves demonstrate that no man lives to himself, that no task can be more patriotic than that of binding the whole community together by common association and aspirations'. For him, 'the great object of every university' was 'production of the individual man' whose influence shall live forever in the weal of humanity.

Girls' Education

While defining the role of youth in building a new India, girls' education formed an integral part of Mookerjee's vision. Aware that he was about the intricate problem of education of girls, he understood his responsibility as a university authority and as an enlightened member of the society. In a period when women's education was picking up, he not only supported the cause but also facilitated it by providing amenities for the purpose. He wanted women's education to 'enable them to take their rightful place in family and social life'. While welcoming the steady increase in the number of girls joining education and appearing at the examination, he noted that the phenomenon brought to the forefront 'the special claims of women's education and the role they may play in the service of the people'. Though he was sad at the fact that many girls did not study beyond the matriculation stage, it was heartening that quite a large number of them joined higher education. For this, he considered ways of 'making proper arrangements for their study and recreation' in the form of providing infrastructural facilities including hostels for girls among others.

Adult Education

Mookerjee envisaged inclusive education in India. For this purpose, he expressed his view that the doors of the university should not be limited to its walls. Rather they should be 'thrown open wider still, so that it might elevate the nation and rouse the self-respect of the people of this land'. He favoured expansion of education for ensuring education for all in all age groups, in all places with no discrimination. Though the participation of youth was increasing in higher education, a huge number of adults could not get education at the right age and remained beyond the reach of education. For illiterate adults, adult education was an option that he proposed to be introduced for. For this, he argued that education cannot be limited to youth only. It should include all those adults who were deprived of education in their youth for reasons beyond their control. 'The influence of the university in this democratic age cannot safely be limited to the period of youth but must include systematic and organised effort for the education of adults. In the present state of our national existence, I cannot but emphasise the reality and the greatness of this need,' he averred thus.

Physical Education

Mookerjee was a dedicated subscriber to Indian philosophy and culture so he considered spirituality to be the principal pursuit of human life. But wrong it would be to limit it to spirituality alone, as it left enough space for material pursuits, provided they were attended by righteous conduct. The human body was considered to be the means of spirituality and pursuing *purushartha chatushtaya*, that is, four obligations of human life. '*Shariramadhyam khalu dharmasadhanam*' (Human body is the principal means of pursuing dharma), stated Indian tradition. If it be so, can education ignore physical health? Certainly not! He recognised the importance of physical education for youth of India because education is of no worth if youths in general are 'physically weak or unfit, unable to stand the stress and strain of modern life'. Also, he disliked mere tokenism exercised in this regard in the form of health check-ups. 'What is education worth if we cannot turn them into men physically strong and well equipped as they should be intellectually sane and robust? We have not remained satisfied with a mere examination of their health?' He was unambiguous in his assertion that the main objective should be to give to the Indian youth an education which will be a true preparation for life. It 'cannot be achieved by fostering intellectual activities alone'. For this, it is necessary 'to raise the physical standard and efficiency of the rising generation and must aim at creating a sound mind in a sound body'. But he did not stop at merely mentioning it. He wanted that 'physical education must be made compulsory in schools and colleges'. Subscribing to it, he implemented physical education in the University of Calcutta and enhanced facilities for the purpose. Also, he stressed on the supreme question of supply of cheap but nourishing diet to students without which physical culture is meaningless, if not harmful.

In his consideration of physical education, he went a step further and recommended that military education be made part of the education system. He emphasised that military training should be made compulsory in education so that Indian youth can defend itself and the nation as and when the need arose. But his justification for it was that its objects will not be to proclaim the doctrine of might is right but to 'instil into the minds of our students a sense of discipline, alertness and organisation, so essential for building up character. It will also serve to show that, given adequate scope, Indian youths may worthily form the foundation of a national force, capable of defending our hearth and home; this will deepen a sense of self-respect and self-confidence in the minds of our people and remove an unjust stigma of our capacity and character'. He believed that 'the policy of keeping Indians unarmed and unprepared for national defence has not only put this country in a highly perilous state but has practically emasculated the manhood of India'. For this, he called upon Indian universities to 'demand with one voice provision for compulsory military training fully related to mechanised warfare'. Unfortunately, his voice remained unheeded, and the country had to remain content with NCC in the post-Independence period.

Moral and Spiritual Education

Along with physical education, he never lost sight of the moral aspect of education. As he remarked in his address to the University of Calcutta in 1935, 'Its great and important task will be to promote not only the physical well-being of our boys and girls, to assist the needy and the deserving, but also to develop in them a sound moral character; to create men and women who in the home, in the village and in the city, in their influence on government and local administration and on national policies, will act righteously, fearlessly and for the attainment of the general welfare. If education in India were to remain divorced from the moral and spiritual consideration, Indian education would be neither value-based nor Indian in its character.'

Vocational Education and Employment

Education in general, and university education system in particular, has been perennially faced with the question of employability of educated youth.

The Indian higher education has in the last few decades also been under stress for producing unemployable graduates. Mookerjee was pragmatic enough to realise that mere ideals would not serve the purpose. Those who would pass out from their educational institutions would need financial support to run their lives in the form of employment or vocational occupations. He stated it clearly that economic depression 'chills the soul of man', and anticipated the gravity of the issue many decades ago and considered employment as an integral part of education. According to him, the time has long passed by when it was possible to quote 'cheap platitude that a great centre of learning should not apply itself to the solution of the "bread problem" and that its motto should be "education for education's sake"'. He, however, did not suggest that a university should directly make itself responsible on any large scale for finding employment for its alumni because no university can practically resolve the problem of unemployment. He believed in the middle way, that is, the university should take care of education first and attend to life and the issue of livelihood as well. Without shirking from his responsibility, he admitted in this respect that much remains to be done by universities. For this, the State, according to him, needed to play its role as well. 'But the main task is for the State to see that they may be absorbed in employments and occupations made available to every son and daughter of India according to his or her ability.' He put it in unambiguous terms, 'What contribution can our educated youth make to serve society or to revive the glorious aspects of our culture and civilisation in accordance with the needs of the modern age if we cannot provide for them a decent standard of life?' He was realistic enough to realise that education would not be able to sustain itself without providing vocational engagements to educated people. However, he sounded a caveat in his address at Banaras Hindu University thus: 'It is not feasible for the university to find employment for all its alumni, although the university should do all it can to establish close contact with those men and institutions that control the fields of commerce, business and industry. These must know and understand one another and work in harmony for the larger welfare of the community. It is indeed one of the primary duties of the State, more than that of anybody else, to solve the problem of unemployment.' To facilitate the process, he had suggested close interaction between educational institutions and corporate houses in the 1940s which in its modern avatar is industry-institution interaction established in Indian universities now with varying degree of success in realising their objectives.

Notwithstanding his commitment for employment for students, he did not see universities as 'factories for producing clerks'. He had already rejected the colonial project of producing a class of clerks for its utilitarian purposes. In consonance with his concerns, he found that the great problem of the hour was not only to provide the right kind of training but also to save the educational system from being a soulless machine. For employment of the youth, he suggested that there must also be close relationship between the university and businesspersons in whose hands lies the control of established trades and industries, for that alone will prevent us from making our teaching too theoretical. In this manner, he anticipated the present-day stress on Industry-Institution Interaction Cell (ICC) in the higher educational institutions.

Mother Tongue: Vernacular as Medium of Instruction

Mookerjee was among the first in India who realised the importance of mother tongue in education as a medium of instruction. While detailing the scheme of subjects to be taught, he undertook the issue of medium of instruction and observed that,

> In the first place, our mother tongue is to be recognised as the medium of instruction and examination in all subjects other than English. In the second place, the present list of subjects has been revised in important directions so as to render the entire course more up-to-date, useful and practical. History and geography are to be made compulsory and elementary science is for the present, included in the list of optional subjects with the proviso that it will be made compulsory after five years. In the third place, certain new subjects, such as domestic science and music, which are especially suitable for girls, have been added to the list. They are of course in addition to the subjects which are open to all. The educational needs of boys and girls are not exactly the same and the university must provide for the special requirements of the latter. In the fourth place, there is provision for imparting instruction in a number of 'practical' subjects which may to a certain extent be expected to meet the demands of vocational education. I am under no illusion that the

> introduction of these subjects will immediately solve the burning problem of unemployment among educated youths.

It showed his concern with the subjects to be included in the syllabi to be taught but the issue of medium of instruction was principal.

In his address to the Patna University, he said that for more than a century, education imparted through the medium of English has produced 'a class of men who are unconsciously so denationalised that any proposal for the recognition of the Indian languages as the vehicle of instruction up to the university stage is either ridiculed as impossible or branded as reactionary'. He pleaded for vernacular language 'out of a firm conviction that the fullest development of the mind of a learner is possible only by this natural approach and also that by this process alone can there be a great revival of the glory and richness of the Indian languages'. He not only advocated but implemented the policy of making Bangla as the medium of instruction and examination. For Bangla as the medium of instruction, textbooks were needed in the language. He thought seriously about it, as is evident from his following note: 'I have been discussing for some time past with various persons in and outside the university the desirability of bringing out a series of books in Bengali dealing with different branches of knowledge.' Accordingly, in his tenure as the vice chancellor, Mookerjee invited renowned writers for bringing out a series of books in Bengali dealing with various subjects, in arts, science, politics, history, sociology, economics and religion, 'written in a manner which will make useful knowledge accessible to all'. He went a step ahead and allowed research scholars to write their dissertation in Bangla. His tenure saw the award for the first time of the degree of doctor of philosophy to a successful candidate who wrote his thesis in Bengali.

Mookerjee wanted to enrich India's national languages for which it was essential to make them the vehicle of instruction and spread knowledge far and wide in diverse branches through them. He charted out his plan: 'Acceptance of our national languages as the media of instruction and examination up to the highest standard is a fundamental condition which has yet to be fulfilled. ...Each province has its own major language and this should be accepted in its own educational sphere. If there is another language which has a substantial number of adherents, this may also receive recognition under suitable conditions, although the multiplicity of languages within the same provincial zone may lead to obvious complications.'

Mookerjee favoured the use of Indian languages as the medium of instruction but was not a blind detractor of English as a language per se. While pleading for the due recognition of our own languages, he recognised that English should remain a compulsory second language and that it should be taught to all, mainly for the purpose of a correct expression of ideas and assimilation of knowledge to be gathered from books written in that great language. Despite his insistence for the mother tongue, he was not against other Indian and foreign languages. He pleaded for provision for the study of important eastern and western languages. 'We cannot at the same time forget that our economic and political progress and cultural advance are closely bound up with western science and literature through medium of western languages, especially English. Reconciliation between these two points of view is possible and must be found for the sake of our future national growth.' Rather than fostering a hostile attitude towards English blindly, he adopted a pragmatic attitude toward it. In his address to Gurukul Kangri University that prides in its use of Sanskrit, he reiterated that a working knowledge of English is adequate for ordinary purpose, excepting a 'limited number of scholars who may study English language and literature as part of their academic training. Similarly, a working knowledge of Hindi is indispensable for direct contact among peoples of different provinces. The study of different subjects like history, economics and social science has to be dealt with in relation to Indian environments'. For science, he wanted that the 'nomenclature should remain as in other parts of the world for keeping in touch with world progress, and retaining contact with others'.

Elaborating his scheme regarding the use of language, he proposed that up to the secondary stage 'the medium of instruction should be the mother tongue of the students or where it is not feasible, due to the paucity of numbers, the regional language should be the medium, with full facilities given to them to study their mother tongue. In many states, the regional languages will be rich enough to be the medium of instruction at collegiate and university stages also.

With such an encouragement of the Indian languages, we will be endowed with creative force, and enrich the heritage of Indian literature.' He considered Hindi as a link language in the country. He said that it will act as 'a powerful unifying force'. Moreover, with its acceptance as the official language of India, it should be learnt by all without any hesitation.

Equally interesting it might be for us to note regarding the use of English, he responded to the so-called purists who insisted on the use of 'correct' English, that is, that to some was the Queen's or King's English. 'I do not think that we want the average student who passes the matriculation examination to be a scholar in English; it will be sufficient if he is able to clearly express his thoughts in simple English. To tell you frankly, we need not be ashamed or be filled with horror, as some of us often are, if our boys cannot speak or write English as correctly and properly as an Englishman would do, for, after all, it is a foreign language—and one may ask legitimately, how many Englishmen, bachelors and masters of great universities in the west, who have spent their lives in Bengal can speak or write Bengali as well as even the average matriculate students can read or write English.' His linguistic pragmaticism harboured no prejudice against the English language, for what mattered to him was the attitude towards it. He had no servile attitude towards it as the coloniser's language. He was wise to realise that its exclusion altogether would render Indian education imperfect. He stated: 'India needs to utilise her two-centuries-old acquaintance with the English language to her best national advantage increasing our capacity to compete with the rest of the world in spheres of higher education and international contacts.' He urged for the systematic study of important Indian languages at each university centre. When no systematic study of comparative study of languages and literatures was in vogue in India, he proposed it. 'A comparative study of Indian languages will be greatly facilitated, if under State patronage a scheme is formulated for bringing out well-known publications from different Indian languages in their original texts but printed in Devanagari script. I would urge also the revival of the study of Sanskrit and granting of special facilities for this purpose.' In his scheme, Sanskrit was the foundation, native languages with necessary space for foreign languages constituted the edifice. The pertinence of his linguistic views, based as it was on realities and requirements of the land, may be witnessed from major documents that deliberated on the issue of language in the post-Independent India. They are a prefiguration of the views that were later reflected by the Radhakrishnan Report and the Kothari Commission.

Examination System

Along with considering systematic aspects of education like recruitment of competent teachers and their training, teacher-student relationship, syllabus, pedagogy, research and employment opportunities, assessment and evaluation did not escape Mookerjee's attention. He wanted reforms in the education system, and was against the Indian education system's obsession with examinations that had adversely affected the march of progress. Rightly so, because acquisition of knowledge was the central body of education and examination the tail. However, so much importance came to be attached to the tail that the tail began to wag the body. Failure in examination would become a stigma on the students' psyche. The increasing percentage of failures in the examinations of many universities bothered him. He called for a thorough revision of the system of examination and for exploring the conditions under which it would be possible to dispense with the rigours of the examination system by securing a more satisfactory recognition of the work done during a student's career in educational institutions. He had stated in this regard:

> The rigidity of our university examinations can be removed only if we can provide for a more extensive tutorial system and make the final results dependent not on one examination but the performance of students during the entire session. He saw the major drawback in the fact that Indian students had to then learn and appear in examination in the medium of a foreign language.

Thus, he not only sought revision of the system but also focussed on its minutest aspect in the form of proposing the medium of language to be used in the examinations because the language of examination, if it happens to be other than the mother tongue, not only puts extra burden on the examinees' mind but also privileges it to languages, particularly the native languages for whom Mookerjee had fought relentlessly.

Research

Research held a central place in Mookerjee's scheme of education. For him, a university was 'not worth its name which does not provide for both teaching and research of the highest order in diverse branches of knowledge'. Only through it, according to him, 'India would be able to produce her own band of discoverers and conquerors of new realms of thought who will help to raise the intellectual level of the country and call forth the spontaneous homage and respect of nations far and wide.' He considered research as one of the primary and essential duties of university teachers, and so he remarked: 'We are bound to search after fresh principles if we desire to lay firm foundations for a progressive practical life. In our relations with the student community also we must search after such fresh principles.' Outlining conditions for research, he told the members of the Royal Asiatic Society that research does not mean 'a mere excavation of the past; its main task lies in building for the future'. Also it should be 'conducted in an atmosphere of truth and freedom, unhampered by worries and anxieties in all domains of knowledge like arts and science both and that must be closely related to Indian conditions and constantly aim at their betterment'.

He felt that a lot needed to be done in the field of research but to his dismay he found the garner of research, meaningful in Indian context, almost empty. He posed an upfront question regarding the relevance of research being conducted:

> What serious study, I ask, has been made of the urges, habits, outlook and modes of life of millions of men and women, of diverse castes and tribes, living under varied conditions, in plains and hills, in towns and villages, speaking a multitude of languages, but all cheerfully owning themselves as the sons and daughters of mother India, and swayed by common spiritual impulses? ...No country has ever spent too much on research either in the domain of arts or science. It matters little if we do not get a quick return, for we can never render a commercial account of research and investigation. Let our universities provide for basic training according to approved standards and maintain fellowships and scholarships on a well-planned basis. Let research for truth and knowledge be carried on in a spirit of harmony and cooperation, under the guidance of enlightened Indian teachers selected for their merit and efficiency.

Also, he insisted on research in the field of pedagogy to provide ideas for changes in teaching and learning processes. Thus, he was concerned with guiding principles of research in the Indian context so that it may impact the lives of Indians and contribute to critical knowledge at the world level.

Laying stress on the need for developing the scientific study and research activities of our universities, Dr Mookerjee, with his experience, stated that it may not be possible for every university to specialise in every department of science due to want of resources and manpower. He suggested a way out that 'the basic sciences must be a common factor and specialisation may be shared region-wise'. In a way, he suggested special research centres in different regions in the country in order to avoid duplication or wastage of efforts.

He raised the issue of validity of western methodology too. 'In our study of the past, we have received from the west an unassailable method, but it must be admitted that this method alone cannot unfold the past in its true perspective. Those who are born in the tradition, who have inherited the culture of the land through ages and have a sense of respect for that heritage, are in a better position to apply the method with the greatest amount of success.' In a way, he suggested a complementary role for the western and indigenous Indian methodology. Moreover, he warned against the mechanical nature of studying the past. He averred on the occasion: 'The study of the past does not mean the dissection of a carcass. The past is not a dead past. It has brought the present into being and those who live in that present are best qualified to discover the subtle links between the past and the present which constitute the very life of a civilisation.'

As an aside to the discussion, it needs to be added here that Mookerjee, who had a high opinion of research conducted by the Asiatic Society, appreciated the efforts of Indologists and Orientalists. It did not prevent him from exposing the vested interests of the colonial projects. He punctured the self-proposed myth of colonisers as the protectors of Indian heritage. He referred to the reports that during the time of Lord William Bentinck, the Taj Mahal was on the point of being destroyed for the value of its marbles. It was he who sold by auction the marble bath in Shah Jehan's palace at Agra. Also after 1857, a solemn proposal was made by the then government to raze to the ground the Jama Masjid at Delhi that he termed as one of the noblest ceremonial mosques in the world and as late as 1868, the gateways of the Great Stupa at Sanchi in the Bhopal state were on the point of being destroyed and one of them, the eastern one, was about to be presented to Napoleon III, the emperor of the French. He went on to add other examples like *Adhāi-din Ki Jhomprā*, and marbles from Brahmanical and Buddhist shrines of great antiquity.

Indology, for him, was 'more than a mere study of India's past language and literature'. It was 'a message born out of healthy mass-culture, a message of the people of India to the world'. People of India were catholic in their assimilation of other cultures. There was a thousand-fold diversity no doubt, but this diversity was never compartmental; it blended into a unity in the ultimate purpose—the welfare of mankind irrespective of one's birth, wealth, creed or religion. Education was given the highest place. 'The learned are respected everywhere, the king only in his own land.' The average standard of education was high enough to produce scholars, and the kings were ever ready to support them, to fund their material needs so as to ensure them abundant leisure for following study and research. His understanding of India, its culture and heritage, and body of knowledge being created, was uninformed by stereotypical colonial phrases and criteria.

Regulating Higher Education

True education is space for free interaction of ideas, unhindered by unreasonable regulation. Regulation kills soaring imagination and ideas. With his faith in Gurudev Tagore's vision articulated among others in the poem 'Where the Mind is Without Fear' that he often used to cite, Mookerjee, in principle, was against regimentation of education because he believed that 'regimentation of rules and adoption of a rigid pattern in the sphere of education virtually give it a death blow. They strike at the root of its life and lead to deadly stagnation'. He wanted reformation of Indian education for Indian national construction with very limited role for regulation. However, the educational administrator in him knew well that for a large country like India, it was not possible to maintain the system without some sort of regulation for maintaining standards. So he deliberated on the role of a regulatory body for higher education also.

For higher education, he considered the establishment of Universities Grants Committee (UGC) for serving the central and state universities as an urgent necessity. He wished the committee to be so composed as to 'command the confidence of universities as well as the public with adequate funds at its disposal for distribution amongst the universities in accordance with a planned and systematic development on a national basis'. However, this committee was not to encroach upon the autonomy of universities. He pointed at the danger in the general tendency to believe that grants and control necessarily go together. 'The need for maintaining the autonomy of the universities and not making them subservient to the State on the plea that they receive State grants must be emphasised by all well-wishers of the country.' Also, he did not want the UGC to become 'a super-university by itself, developing extremely complex machinery, deadening the soul of all universities in India and making them rigid and stagnant.' He prophetically added: 'If such an authority is to enjoy executive powers, it will lead to a regimentation of university education which even totalitarian countries or autocratic regimes dared not experiment in.'

Without underestimating the importance of maintaining adequate standards of university instruction and examinations and the urgency of avoiding wastage and unnecessary duplication, he suggested multi-tier pattern—to be undertaken, 'first by each university acting in a rational manner, balancing regional requirements with national progress; secondly, by the inter-university board which, though having advisory powers, must be helped to develop healthy conventions and whose well-considered recommendations cannot be easily flouted by any university; thirdly, by well-informed deliberations in state legislatures and Parliament at the time of voting of demands on grants, and lastly, by the Universities Grants Committee…' His inclusive and federal model of self-regulatory internal and external mechanism is relevant even today, and would remain so in future as well.

He was of the view that good education needs good financial support. Therefore, he sought generous funding for education. 'Education is one sphere of activity on which the State can never be accused of overspending. If our planning is sound and administration correct, the more we spend, the more solid will be the results leading to national prosperity and solidarity.' This profound statement should have earned perusal and implementation by the governments at least in the post-Independence India for ensuring and sustaining globally competitive education. The fact known to all of us, however, is that the subsequent Indian governments did not pay heed to his advice and the result is that Indian education could not prosper the way it was desired. If speculative indulgence is not unwarranted, one would be tempted to ask a question: What would have been India's educational scenario, if Syama Prasad Mookerjee was the Education Minister of India?

Science and Industry

Mookerjee knew that the future of civilisation depends on widening and deepening of the scientific habit of the mind. So he considered it the urgent duty to think out and promulgate practical methods. For this, he advocated cultivation and development of scientific temper that would include 'that questioning, impartial, problem-solving attitude of mind, which must obtain if truth and sanity are to rule the world'. He saw that India was faced with international conflicts of gigantic proportions, so he believed that scientific and industrial development of a country like India is indispensable not only for its prosperity but also for its very existence. However, he favoured judicious use of science. 'Science, like fire, is capable alike of good and of evil and like fire it needs to be used with discretion and care. The good that science has done is obvious and immense. If used exclusively for the good of mankind, it is capable of promoting peace and happiness in this world and of conferring benefits beyond imagination,' as he observed in the joint session of the British Association for the Advancement of Science and Indian Science Congress on 3 January 1938. For this purpose, he did not see any problem with the spirit of science but with the moral and social failure of the people who handle it. 'Science in a comprehensive sense provides us with the material appliances of life. It is the spirit of man who uses them that requires to be educated.' He suggested that 'the view of science should be supplemented by the vision of beauty and truth'. It is a truth or reality that has been understood by subsequent caretakers of Indian education.

Along with sciences, Mookerjee emphasised on subjects related to the present Indian problems or to the basic conception of Indian culture and civilisation like Indian history, Indian thought and philosophy, Indian art, architecture, music, and Indian sociology. He was sure the fruits of the study and investigation of Indian scholars would 'produce new light which will help us in remodelling the structure of our society and the pattern of our lives in a worthy manner'. Science and technology take care of provision but without poetry or humanities they are visionless. He knew that science in wrong hands may prove to be disastrous. So he was for science but not without poetry. He stated: 'Poets are often said to be the guides of mankind in the realm of thought, for they give shape and form to men's ideas. The same is no less true of men of science, with this difference that, while poets may draw inspiration from the limitless fountain of imagination, science, though not without its romance, cannot deviate from accuracy and truth.' He favoured balance between science and liberal arts and humanities for which he wanted provision for a sound liberal education, so as to find the correct synthesis between cultural education and vocational and technical training. He advocated for providing 'the amplest facilities and privileges to our teachers so that they may be endowed with learning, character, and freedom'. Apart from teachers, he wanted 'unification of educational purposes to draw out the best qualities that lie hidden in our youths and to train them, intellectually, physically and morally, for devoted service in all spheres of national activity—in villages, in towns and in cities'. He stated it in his addresses to the Royal Asiatic Society of Bengal in 1944 and 1945, and sought proper evaluation of India's cultural heritage but without becoming a jingoist so that it does not become over aggressive, for he knew 'what harm an aggressive nationalism can do to humanity'.

Education, Harmony and Humanity

Mookerjee knew that the inherent power of assimilation has been the strength of the Indian mind. So he stressed on it time and again. 'The aim of our culture has been the complete realisation of life. Nature, man and God make for life's entire knowledge; and service and love are the materials which go to the making of man complete.' According to him, true education consisted 'more in spirit it conveys than in the instruction it imparts'. The challenge was to strengthen those invisible bonds of understanding which unite man to man, irrespective of caste, creed and community, or whether we have betrayed this ideal and imposed artificial restrictions on natural sympathies and brotherhood. From this view, he was sad to note that 'many of our educated men are today often the victims of narrow provincial and communal feelings'. Without casting a reflection on any province or community, he wanted every teacher to pause and think when he finds that uneducated men are often free from these trammels and we, who claim to be educated, are trying to inoculate them with this severe poison. He believed that so long as the present environment of distrust and suspicion continued, it would be impossible to attain its cherished goal of a united and regenerated India. In his address to the All India Educational Conference in Nagpur (1935), he stated his lofty vision thus: 'Communalism, cliquism, cabalism are but cultural nullities—from them come only freakish growths and perverted performances. May we be endowed with strength and courage to regard ourselves, however humble and unworthy, as soldiers in the war of liberation of humanity, marching proudly for the promised land of the swaraj of the intellect, the mental emancipation of man!'

Alternative Models of Education

Mookerjee had witnessed the colonial system of education from closest quarters and served it in highest capacities. Seeing it in the perspective of Indian tradition of education, he could see its adverse impact on the Indian system and culture. He had seen the British model inside out. He had the ideal model of *gurukul* system and Takshshila and Nalanda universities before him, and also experiments that were made in different parts of India. Since he was convinced that in a vast country like India, uniformity of higher education is neither desirable nor feasible, so he thought of models like Banaras Hindu University (BHU), Varanasi, Gurukul Kangri Vishwavidyalaya, Haridwar, Visva-Bharati, Shantiniketan and the proposed Sri Aurobindo University, Pondicherry. He was not against the western education system per se, as he was aware that many thinkers, social reformers, educationists, freedom fighters and revolutionaries were products of it. His problem with it was that, barring a few instances as mentioned above, it produced a de-Indianised educated class that was not only indifferent but also contemptuous of everything Indian without accessing it in unprejudiced manner. He articulated its adverse consequences. 'Nothing is more ruinous to the cause of our country's progress than to create a separate class of so-called educated Indians, entirely out of touch in outlook and mode of living with the vast millions of their less fortunate fellow countrymen to whose service they must dedicate their lives.' So instead of turning westwards, he proposed rebuilding Indian society fundamentally on an indigenous model. He said: 'In a country such as ours with people following different religions and faiths, we must so adjust our movements as to permit full scope for intellectual and cultural development to all essential units, each remaining loyal to its creed, helpful to and trustful of each other, and all owing allegiance to the imperishable spirit of Indian unity.'

This persuaded Mookerjee to look for alternatives, and he did find a few institutions. Swami Shraddhananda's Gurukul Vishwavidyalaya, Gurudev Tagore's Visva-Bharati, Mahamana Malaviya's Banaras Hindu University and the proposed university in Sri Aurobindo's name in Pondicherry. It is not incongruous to mention it here that Dr Mookerjee was the chairman of Sri Aurobindo Memorial Convention constituted to deliberate on the formation of a university in the sage's name. The proposal ultimately evolved into Sri Aurobindo International Centre of Education. Dr Mookerjee presided over the convention held in April 1951 in Pondicherry (now Puducherry) at the special invitation of the Mother. Also, he singled out Gurukul Vishwavidyalaya for its foundations on the *gurukul* system in which the relation between teacher and student used to be such as between father and son. In his convocation address to the university, he stated,

> Your basic concept of *gurukul*—the home of the teacher—is a gift of the ancient Indian mind and has seldom penetrated into the artificial atmosphere of residential schools, copied from the western pattern in many parts of India. An Indian *gurukul* cannot separate education from the mainspring of Indian dharma, interpreted in its broadest sense. The heritage that belongs to an Indian youth must be clearly and boldly held before his mind's eye. The eternal value of the teachings of the ancient seers must be explained to him—not for lowering his vision or choking his spirit of inquisitiveness, but for making him judge for himself their fundamental values. Civilisation in our society meant progressive socialisation of our lives by developing all

> the finer feelings which helped us to realise our own selves in others and others in our own selves. This is why our social life had been dominated more by moral consciousness than political. If today we suffer from divisions and disruptions, the fault lies with those interpreters who for historical reasons clung to forms and practices and narrowed the base of the original structure of our society striking at the root of service and equality so manifest in the teachings of our ancient seers.

He appreciated that the *gurukul* had demonstrated that education in this country can be organised by 'a correct synthesis between the fundamental aspects of Indian civilisation and the true requirement of a scientific age'.

Mookerjee looked around and found another model in Tagore's Visva-Bharati. He saw it as a new hope for India's education. He admired Tagore and subscribed to his notion of mind without fear, free knowledge, unfragmented and unwalled world, truth, perfection, uncluttered reason, mind ever widening into thought and action, and ever awakening country in the heaven of freedom. In his address to Visva-Bharati University in 1950, Mookerjee referred to the farsighted wisdom, vision and patriotism of Tagore in founding for the first time in modern India a seat of learning that could be truly called international.

Mookerjee found in Tagore's vision a new alternative that could serve as the model for Indian education. Education, according to Tagore's plan, must be a matter of joy and not a burden, both for the teacher and the pupil; it could only prosper in the right atmosphere which he helped in creating. He also believed in combining the best Indian traditions with the wholesome gifts of the west.

Tagore, Mookerjee said, was dissatisfied with the system of education prevailing in India under the British rule. He realised that a mere tinkering with the problem would not achieve the results he wished for. He started by establishing a school amidst natural rural surroundings, the main object of which was not any regimented imparting of instruction on the western pattern, but the full and harmonious development of the scholar's body, mind and character, based on a radically revised curricula and methods of teaching. He laid emphasis on the use of one's mother tongue at every stage. The subjects taught were comprehensive, dealing with arts and letters, science and agriculture. Thus, year after year boys and girls who went out to the world after receiving their training at Santiniketan bore upon them the impress of the poet's idealism and practical realism.

India's uniqueness, according to him, lay in the fact that it had been the confluence of diverse thoughts and movements. Indian universities should contribute to this culture. But Mookerjee found that it was not happening. Tagore's vision took care of it, as in his (Tagore's) university at Santiniketan special emphasis was laid for the study and research of various aspects of eastern culture and civilisation. Tagore's dream was the creation of a seat of learning in India where scholars, irrespective of race, creed or colour, would assemble from all parts of the world and actuated by a truly scientific spirit not only resurrect old wisdom now forgotten, but also create new knowledge. He entertained an abiding faith in a spirit of harmony in human culture. Since Tagore believed in '*vishwa manav*', he claimed that the ultimate peace of the world could be discovered not through ugly competitions between one nation and another, not through political and economic strife, not through domination and exploitation, but by emphasising upon points of common contact and purpose, representing the mighty efforts of generations of seers and savants of each nation towards the fulfilment of human destiny and the advancement of human civilisation.

Tagore had laid out the concept of '*vishwa sahitya*' in his address in 1907 that he considered equivalent to comparative literature. Mookerjee was beholden to it in practice and advocated it in practice, as he stated,

> Art, architecture, philosophy, languages, literature, religion—all could be and should be studied from a comparative standpoint so as to discover that great unity in diversity which might ultimately form the basis of a lasting international understanding at once peaceful and harmonious. It is but natural that if a university in India has to keep so high a purpose in view in the sphere of international relations, it must be able to lay a firm foundation in respect of studies connected with Indian culture and civilisation.

Visva-Bharati, however, represents a type of its own. Mookerjee was for diverse models of universities in India. He saw no reason why India should not maintain different types of universities located in various sites, each fulfilling its purpose and serving the cause of progress. While coordination of the activities of Indian universities is desirable, avoiding unnecessary duplications, yet, there should be no attempt to mould all on a similar pattern or to ignore the claims of special institutions.

However, he wanted to guard Visva-Bharati University 'against the possibility of being yet another university turning into 'a mere machine or a lifeless administrative body, overloaded with laws and bye-laws, forgetting or minimising the free and invigorating conditions of its existence'. He cautioned the successive administrators of Visva-Bharati, 'Let not all energy and attention be devoted to the making of a golden cage, the bird inside it dying for want of free air and light.' His deep involvement with Tagore's educational vision and its realisation in Visva-Bharati are to a good measure evident in the proceedings of the parliamentary debate on the Visva-Bharati Bill in which, among other parliamentarians, he vigorously sought to preserve the autonomy, funding and preservation of its uniqueness.

Further, Mookerjee had diagnosed the cause of India's suffering and degeneration that according to him lay in spiritual decay and an erosion of this component in the educational sphere. His idea of a university for spiritual education found expression in Sri Aurobindo's University Centre in Pondicherry. He found that India was suffering not so much from the poverty of the means of material existence but from the bankruptcy of her spiritual resources. He remarked in this regard: 'High purpose is reserved exclusively as an adornment of pontifical pronouncements from high offices. The scene is virtually littered with the debris of the spiritual achievements of a people that was once great.' He found that India had failed to achieve in spiritual and cultural aspects of national life even a few years after Independence. Sadly, he saw no serious efforts being made in this direction. He realised that India had lost track of her real culture. He searched for a university that will 'symbolise the world's urge for a new spiritual rebirth; it will stand out as an oasis amidst the barren tracts that breed jealousies, suspicions and petty conflicts'. This he found being taken care by the vision of Sri Aurobindo and the work undertaken accordingly to realise it. He found a new hope and alternative in Sri Aurobindo, the crusader for India's political freedom and the searcher for the freedom of the spirit. He found the two Aurobindos, the political fighter and the yogi, merged in one, 'a true Indian'. Commenting on Sri Aurobindo's vision, he said: 'The culture of a people may be roughly described as the expression of a consciousness of life which formulates itself in three aspects. "There is a side of thought, ideal, upward will and the soul's aspiration; a side of creative self-expression and appreciative aesthesis, intelligence and imagination; and a side of practical and outward formulation." Philosophy and religion belong to the first of these three aspects of culture; art, poetry and literature to the second; and society and politics to the third. In India, however, the master idea that has governed the life, culture and social ideals of her people has been the seeking of man for his true spiritual self and the use of life.' He found that Indians had lost track of this noble idea. 'A base hedonistic view of life seems to inform all our activities today, even where they belong to the realm of the first two aspects of culture.' It had resulted in settling with compromise or appeasement that in modern terminology is called diplomacy. 'Consequently, those spiritual moorings seemed to be utterly broken, and the spirit of man lost, given to the devil.'

Mookerjee saw another model in BHU that was based on a synthesis of traditional Indian knowledge and modern systems, and he spoke at length in his convocation address to the university.

Two other discourses of Mookerjee help us in peeping into his realist mind as an educational thinker. His address to the first All India University Teachers' Convention, Allahabad, in 1947 is significant, as it was delivered just within six months of Independence. One can discern change in his tone, tenor and sense of responsibility because with India's independence, one of his conditions was fulfilled. So he focussed on three topics of the convention: (i) The place of university in society and national life, (ii) Teaching and research in the universities, and (iii) Problems of finance and administration. He noted with dismay that the modern Indian universities derived their origin from foreign inspiration and ideals, so they were not in sync with Indian cultural and educational ideals. 'Indian universities, in spite of their best efforts have not been properly related to our national life and needs.' Hence, the university would need two things above all others—freedom and finance—to perform their functions adequately. He spoke of freedom first and remarked:

> We all know of the frightful results of lack of freedom, creative thought is stunted and it speedily leads to doctrinism and degeneration. Let us not forget what happened in the fascist countries as soon as political control was installed on the universities. The latter lost their autonomy and became a handmaid of the political party in power. Education—creative education was replaced by dogmatic indoctrination. We have seen the spectacle of a whole nation being indoctrinated and led by the political party to action, with apparent initial success but also ultimate chaos.

Mookerjee knew it well that knowledge prospers through circulation of ideas. Subscribing to the Rigvedic hymn *'Ano bhadrah kratavo yantu vishwatah'* (Let the noble thoughts of the world come to me), he warned against ghettoisation of education. For avoiding this, he proposed exchange of teachers and students in Indian educational institutions. He stated:

> I would plead for exchange of university teachers on a planned basis along with programmes for visits of teams of university students from one centre to another. While our universities must be so equipped and administered as to make it unnecessary for Indian students to go abroad for studying ordinary subjects, our scheme for foreign scholarships and fellowships should be more liberal than at present.

Since attainment of independence, he emphasised on the role that the universities in India are destined to play in new India. By the time he delivered his address to University of Delhi on 13 December 1952, the Radhakrishnan Commission had submitted its report on the need for a planned and thorough reorientation of university administration and teaching. He found the report valuable, but as a realist he said then, 'Unfortunately like other distinguished commissions that had previously reported on Indian universities, this report also is in danger of being pigeon-holed on account of want of financial resources. It is not through changes only in the external pattern of the administrative machinery of universities that we can expect to see the ushering in of a new era of reform and expansion.' His words captured the essence of exercise of various commissions and reports and their predicament along with the reasons why Indian education remains trapped in the quagmire of old problems that rather than being mitigated are getting aggravated due to lack of will and resolution to implement them on the part of the authorities.

Conclusion

The cardinal principle that Mookerjee wanted to be implemented in Indian education was that India's young generation, coming out of our education system should be physically, intellectually and morally ready not merely for the purpose of qualifying for any special calling, but to 'bring up good citizens, useful members of society; men, true and fearless, capable of bearing their part with credit in public and private life. Such university-trained men are needed in rich abundance in India today.' In other words, he envisioned integral education culled from different models, and yet based on the Indian socio-cultural ethos. The preceding discussion proves that Mookerjee, in his vision of education, catered to the main principles of holistic and integral education that, inferred from his discourses, may be enumerated as physical well-being, emotional well-being, intellectual or rational well-being, aesthetic well-being, relational well-being, moral well-being and spiritual well-being.

It was a tribute to Mookerjee's perspicacious thinking about education that he was invited to deliver convocation addresses in all major universities of his time all over the country. He did not let them remain as ceremonial occasions but used them to chart out contours of his educational vision. He made them as sites of collaborative thinking. Here, it is to be borne in mind that most of Mookerjee's educational discourses are in the form of lectures, convocation addresses and participation in debates. Since only their written from is accessible to us, other aspects of the discourse, that is, body-centric (performative aspect of his discourses, that is, use of sound, body, supplementing sign-language and gestures among others) and phonocentric (speech) are absent from the discourses. Hence, it is not possible to see the overall impact of his discourses. Frozen words are always not true indicators of the worth of a talk. But they are the only signifiers. However, his vision emerges from his discourses in a clear manner.

Mookerjee's discourses on education reveal that he was concerned not just with the theoretical aspect of education but as a practitioner. He did not philosophise about education and its lofty ideals as an armchair academician or educational thinker. He saw the importance of the role of education in shaping lives of India's young generation and in nation building, and in creating a new world order with contribution from enlightened Indians. He thought of the state of the then education system holistically from primary to higher education and specialised education. In the process, he considered each and every aspect—building, classrooms, library, teachers, syllabus, pedagogy, medium of instruction, examination, employment and extension activities or social service.

Since most of our present-day educational problems are bequeathed to us by the past, particularly in the last two centuries, there is a need to understand them. Mookerjee was an upright critical insider of the educational system in the colonial period with unflinching commitment to national culture and its interests. It is imperative for us to learn from him ways to make our education rooted locally in the region, committed to national and cultural ethos and international in perspective and concerns. Since it is not possible to better his views, it would be congruous to conclude with his own words:

> Let us unreservedly stand by our conviction that whatever our detractors may say, Indian universities are bound to play a large and noble part in the emergence of a new India which will be the mistress of her own destinies, the proud inheritor of an ancient civilisation, rebuilt and reshaped with the changing requirements of the age. Let us stand united to make our universities centres of culture and independent thought nurseries of honest and open-minded teachers and scholars pursuing and advancing knowledge, from which will go forth manly and useful citizens, brave and self-reliant, patriotic and fair-minded, capable of making sacrifices and judging issues and problems critically and fearlessly. Let the Indian universities mould their activities in full remembrance of the fact that the progress of a nation, if steadily maintained, can alone prevent degeneration, that there must be new life and purpose or there will be weakness and decay. At this crisis in the history of human civilisation, when cherished doctrines of liberty and democracy are often discarded and freedom of thought and opinion suppressed, let Indian universities and their sons and daughters proclaim the noblest ideals of Indian teachings and thought, which may once again secure for her that supremacy in the world of intellect which is truly her birthright. And let the Indian universities prove to the world that India can achieve this simultaneously with a progressive and systematic pursuit of western knowledge itself. Let Indian universities be the worthy participators in a

> constant movement towards a higher and nobler civilisation, a civilisation that will make its conquests without resort to war or oppression and achieve its greatest victories pursuing the path of peace and justice.

In the preceding elongated citation from Mookerjee, the term 'university' may be read as a trope for higher educational institutions in India. Also, it underscores the fact that the subsequent generations have to return to him again and again to learn from his vision.

The Educationist.

As Vice Chancellor.

At All India Science Congress, Calcutta with famous scientists,
Acharya Prafulla Chandra Ray (third from left) and Prof Satyen Bose (fourth from left).

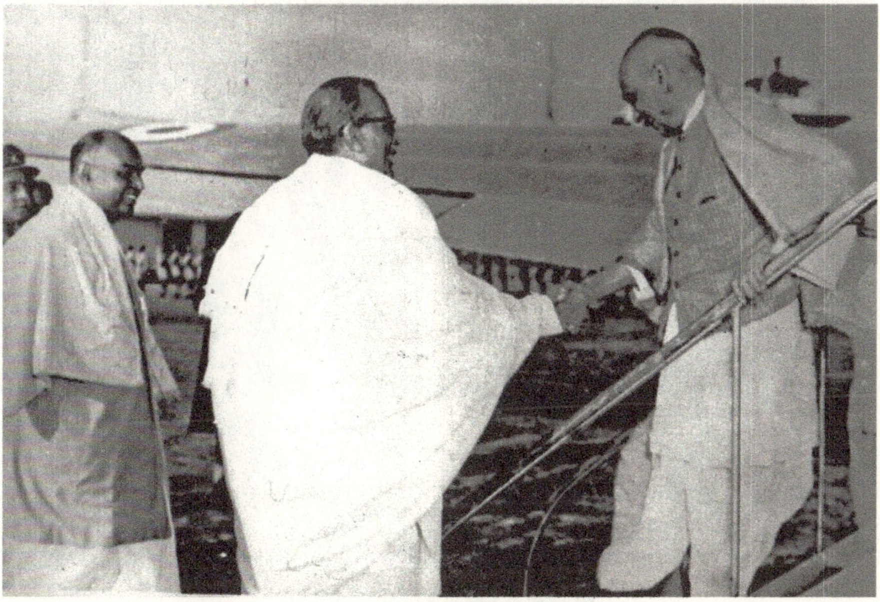

Receiving Sardar Patel along with Dr BC Roy at Kolkata.

In 1950 at Calcutta Shaheed Minar;
Dhwajarohan at RSS Rally.

Unveiling the statue of Sri Aurobindo in Kolkata on 17 August 1950. Founder of Prabartak Sangha and revolutionary Motilal Roy is seen standing behind him.

Sitting right to left: Dr Syama Prasad Mookerjee, Rajkumari Amrit Kaur, Babu Jagjivan Ram, John Mathai, Sardar Vallabhbhai Patel, Dr Rajendra Prasad (President), Pandit Jawaharlal Nehru, Maulana Abul Kalam Azad, Sardar Baldev Singh, Rafi Ahmed Kidwai., BR Ambedkar.

With Dr S Radhakrishnan, carrying the sacred relics of Buddha's chief disciples Mahamogallana and Sariputta.

With Vinayak Damodar 'Veer' Savarkar.

Reorganising Education Holistically

1

EDUCATION IN BENGAL

Problems arising out of the present educational system of our country present such diversity and complexity that I cannot possibly venture to deal with all of them in the course of my address. I accordingly propose to refer only to some of the urgent questions which have recently been before us, and particularly to the almost universal dissatisfaction with our present educational system. Most of the unsatisfactory features of undergraduate and postgraduate education have their origin in a defective system of secondary education. And though this is a conference of representatives of teachers in the university and its affiliated colleges, I shall be forgiven if I first take up the new matriculation regulations which have been recently passed by the Senate. The future of university education depends vitally on the reorganisation of secondary education and to my mind a reference to these regulations is not only justified but also necessary. You would have noticed that they aimed at several reforms of a comprehensive character. In the first place, our mother tongue is to be recognised as the medium of instruction and examination in all subjects other than English—a change which is long overdue and which is justly regarded as of far-reaching significance. In the second place, the present list of subjects has been revised in important directions so as to render the entire course more up-to-date, useful and practical. History and geography are to be made compulsory and elementary science is, for the present, included in the list of optional subjects with the proviso that it will be made compulsory after five years. In the third place, certain new subjects, such as domestic science and music, which are especially suitable for girls, have been added to the list. They are, of course, in addition to the subjects which are open to all. The educational needs of boys and girls are not exactly the same and the university must provide for the special requirements of the latter. In the fourth place, there is a provision for imparting instruction in a number of 'practical' subjects which may to a certain extent be expected to meet the demands of vocational education. I am under no illusion that the introduction of these subjects will immediately solve the burning problem of unemployment among educated youths. But I do feel that the reorganised courses of study, now made varied and practical, will stimulate our students to mental effort and will help to make them more earnest and self-reliant. The regulations are fraught with great possibilities and although there may be a difference of opinion as regards the details here and there, I believe there is general agreement that the scheme is on the whole sound and will prove beneficial. You will remember that these changes were formulated by the university nearly eleven years ago and we are anxious that there should not be any further delay in giving effect to them. They are now before the government and we trust will soon receive sanction and begin to operate in the near future. I hope and trust the university will not remain satisfied with merely recognising the vernacular as the medium for the matriculation examination but will proceed to take the necessary steps with a view to make it the vehicle of instruction and examination for all, including the highest examinations of the university and thus give our national language its rightful place in the scheme of university studies.

The question of girls' education is assuming considerable importance and magnitude. It is not perhaps generally known that the number of girls appearing at the matriculation examination is steadily increasing. In 1920, only 116 girls appeared at the matriculation examination, in 1926, the number was 183 and in 1932, it rose to 670. This is a welcome sign. It is true that many of these girls bring their educational career to an end at the matriculation stage.

Still, quite a large number of them join the university and study in some of our affiliated colleges. The question of making proper arrangements for their study and recreation has, therefore, to be very carefully considered. I have no desire to cast any reflection on the authorities of the only affiliated college for girls maintained out of public funds. The fact, however, remains that a large number of guardians prefer their wards to be educated in non-government institutions. A special responsibility, therefore, rests with the authorities of these colleges. I would ask you to consider the question of future arrangements for imparting instruction to girls in our affiliated colleges, particularly the question of co-education, and also to suggest, if you think it proper, any changes in the courses of study so as to make them suitable in every way for girls.

One of the questions now before the university is with regard to the congestion of students in our Calcutta colleges. It appears that the number of students in mofussil colleges is decreasing rapidly and also that some institutions in Calcutta have on their rolls a disproportionately large number of students. Apart from the fact that too large a roll strength makes it difficult for the college authorities to properly look after the individual needs of students, there is another aspect of the matter which requires our serious consideration. Calcutta has its attractions, and its temptations. It will certainly be better if immature boys who generally matriculate at the age of fifteen or sixteen prosecute their studies at least for the intermediate examination in institutions near their homes and continue to remain as far as possible under the protecting influence of their parents and guardians. This perhaps is one of the reasons why the university has encouraged the establishment of small intermediate colleges outside Calcutta. Unfortunately, however, a majority of mofussil colleges are not in a prosperous condition. I do not think it necessary to discuss the question in detail at this stage but I would ask you seriously to consider if it is possible or desirable to check the congestion of students in Calcutta, and if so, it is our duty to indicate the lines on which the university should proceed in the matter.

While dwelling on this topic, I would also like to refer to the possibility of securing greater contact between the colleges, at least in Calcutta. Much may be gained if we can work out a scheme which would make it possible for students reading in different colleges to attend lectures on selected subjects in particular institutions which enjoy special facilities for teaching them. This may with advantage be done with regard to certain honours subjects. Every college need not necessarily arrange for honours teaching in all subjects. Such inter-collegiate arrangements will not only benefit students but will also lead to a better understanding among the colleges themselves, a better utilisation of existing resources and may ultimately result in economy. We should also consider whether we should not request the university to permit its professors and lecturers to deliver special courses of lectures for the benefit of the students reading in our affiliated colleges. Many college teachers work as part-time lecturers in the postgraduate department. There is no reason why postgraduate teachers also should not cooperate and impart instruction in special subjects to students of affiliated colleges.

I would next refer to another question which has for some time past assumed considerable importance and has evoked some controversy as well. I mean the question of deprovincialisation of government arts colleges and schools. I am glad to find that you have given this subject the special importance which it certainly deserves and propose to hold a separate meeting for its consideration today. I have no desire to anticipate the discussion but you will permit me to place before you certain aspects of this important question. I shall not deal with the deprovincialisation of government schools but shall refer to arts colleges only. There are forty-five arts colleges in Bengal; of these ten are maintained by government and thirty-five are non-government institutions. Roughly speaking, about 3,500 students are on the rolls of these ten government colleges, while more than 17,000 students are reading in the other thirty-five non-government colleges. Government spends more than eleven lakh of rupees annually for the maintenance of these ten colleges and provides grants-in-aid to twenty non-government colleges to the extent of about Rs 2,60,000 only. It is admitted that there is room for radical improvements in our affiliated colleges. It is further acknowledged that improvements on any wide scale are not possible without financial assistance. It is also conceded that the finances of the provinces being what they are, it may not be possible for government to spend more on education than what it is doing at present. Even if some money is available, it is more than probable that it will be required for primary education. It might have been a different matter if government had unlimited funds at their disposal, but things being what they are, what justification can there be for government for spending eleven lakh of rupees for 3,500 students to the comparative neglect of the interests of the great bulk of the Bengali students reading in non-government colleges? The interest taken by government in non-government colleges has been amply proved by their decision to suspend the non-recurring grant of Rs 1,29,000, distributed for many years through the university. I am fully aware that if the policy of deprovincialisation is accepted, the period of transition will be one of considerable difficulty. Existing contracts must be observed. Further, deprovincialisation does not necessarily mean abolition of government colleges, but it involves their being handed over to non-official bodies and their administration in accordance with a system of grants-in-aid. The saving in the first few years may not be considerable but the policy of deprovincialisation must be accepted and a beginning made immediately.

There is one aspect of the matter on which I would lay great stress. We must demand that the money released must be spent on the improvement of collegiate education. To put it plainly, we do not want the introduction of a scheme of deprovincialisation, followed by a reduction of State expenditure and the absorption of the available surplus in the departments of police and jails. If that be the result of our efforts for deprovincialisation, I would much rather leave the government colleges as they are and wait with what patience I may [have] for better days to come.

It is not possible for me in the course of this address to examine in detail the arguments usually urged against deprovincialisation. But I cannot help referring to one objection which is raised whenever this question comes up for discussion. It is stated that generally in non-government colleges discipline suffers and that political and extra-academic considerations usually play a large part in the actual administration of the institutions. I am not desirous of entering into the rather delicate comparison of government colleges with non-government colleges. But I refuse to believe that government colleges have proved ideal places for maintenance of discipline and that non-government colleges have proved the reverse. If discipline be interpreted as meaning that the patriotic feelings and sentiments of the youths of the province have to be trampled underfoot, if discipline means the threat of mass punishment of students for the alleged guilt of a few, or their drastic punishment if boys do not always behave in strict and rigid conformity with the old and musty departmental rules which were framed to meet the requirements of a remote bygone period, if discipline means that boys are to be brought into their classrooms by the show of police force, then I would say that government colleges are superior to non-government colleges. But if discipline implies firmness accompanied by a sympathetic understanding and a tactful handling of difficult and delicate situations, if discipline is to be broad-based on obedience, spontaneously evoked more by personal respect and affection than by mere frigid authority, then I would refuse to place government colleges in a position of superiority. I claim to know the inner workings of many educational institutions both belonging to government and outside their sphere of influence, and I feel no hesitation in saying that, on the whole, the authorities of non-government colleges, although they had to pass through times of abnormal anxiety and excitement, have carried on their difficult task of administration and maintained order and regularity in a manner worthy of commendation.

Equally strongly do I feel that there is no foundation for the charge that the authorities of non-government colleges are likely to be desirous of regulating their policy by political or extra-academic considerations. On the other hand, we may legitimately point towards the tendency on the part of government to introduce openly and flagrantly extra-academic considerations in the matter of making appointments in government institutions. We consider it deplorable that religion or community, and not merit, should be the deciding factor in making appointments to the teaching staff. We feel that the policy of deprovincialisation, if followed with adequate safeguards, will make education free from the cross-currents and undercurrents of political and communal intrigue and place the institutions under the control of autonomous governing bodies whose sole aim would be to promote academic interests.

You will permit me to make a suggestion or two for carrying out some improvements in certain branches of activity of your association. I would invite you to consider for a moment whether the magazine of your association which is making its influence felt in educational circles, cannot extend its sphere of influence and make itself a more powerful organ for the spread of culture throughout the land. The promoters of the magazine have only to exert themselves a little in order to utilise to the fullest extent the vast intellectual resources at the disposal of the association. A powerful press is a very potent influence both for good and evil and the association can most effectively further its interests by extending and strengthening its activities in this direction.

I would further request the members of your association to direct their attention to another field of activity which does not seem to have attracted much notice up to the present. Physical education, games and sport have been relegated to a minor position and though the prevailing agitation for improving the national physique has caught the imagination of the students, it does not seem to have found any corresponding response from our teachers as a body. I would ask the teachers of colleges to guide this growing movement for improving physical education. Apart from its obvious and manifold advantages, it presents to them a unique opportunity for strengthening their hold on the affection and respect of the student community.

Before I bring my address to a close, I would like to say a few words on the general question of remodelling the present system of education. I have no desire to review historically the different stages which the present system has passed. I fully recognise some of the great benefits which it has conferred on the people of this province. Even under this system, we have had many eminent personalities who in various fields of activity have shed undying lustre on their names and have served the best interests of their Motherland. Western education has helped to rouse our political consciousness, has to a large extent unified the scattered elements spread throughout this vast country, and has had remarkable effects on our national awakening. No one can forget the inestimable value of these contributions. Leaving aside these generalisations, when we come to the immediate present, we are faced with a situation which appears to be almost baffling in character. The fact remains that the present system of education has now come to what practically amounts to a stage of collapse. The people of the province have from the beginning displayed a unique eagerness to take advantage of the educational facilities which were open to them and Bengal has witnessed a remarkable growth of secondary and collegiate education. But what do we find to be the present state of affairs? The average student who we are producing are not equipped to fight the battle of life and the question of unemployment amongst the educated middle-class population of Bengal is becoming more and more acute. The time has long passed by when we could console ourselves by quoting the cheap platitude that a great centre of learning should not apply itself to the solution of the 'bread problem' and that its motto should be 'education for education's sake'. I do not mean to suggest that a university can directly make itself responsible on any large scale for finding employment for its alumni. But it has certainly an obligation to impart instruction to the youths of the country on lines which will not only keep alive in them their zeal for knowledge and truth but also make them manly and useful citizens, well-equipped to earn a decent living by means of some honest trade or profession. The present system of education does not generally fulfil these conditions and the time has come when the entire system has to be overhauled and given a predominantly practical turn. I have no sympathy with those who suggest that the remedy lies in simply reducing the number of educational institutions and curtailing the facilities now open to our youths. That is a policy of destruction, a negative policy which can only be worthy of reactionaries who are no genuine friends of our country. To my mind, the remedy lies not only in reorganising the present scheme of studies but also in the establishment of new types of institutions which would provide adequate training in technical, commercial, agricultural and allied subjects immediately after the matriculation stage. This would give the thousands of boys who pass through our hands every year a chance of choosing their careers, instead of being compelled to follow one type of education, which is predominantly literary and is practically the only avenue now open to them.

It is conceivable that many existing institutions may suitably reorganise their activities and provide for necessary instruction in one or more of such vocational subjects. One of the drawbacks of the present system is too much rigidity and standardisation by rules and regulations. I would certainly welcome the possibility of some institutions developing themselves according to their own light and providing for instruction of a specialised character. They cannot obviously do it single-handed; financial assistance must be rendered to them and they must be encouraged to move on generally approved lines in accordance with a well-thought-out scheme. There must also be a closer relationship between the university and practical businessmen in whose hands lies the control of established trades and industries, for that alone will prevent us from making our teaching too theoretical. The university is at present considering a proposal for the establishment of small institutions where agricultural education, both theoretical and practical, will be imparted to a select number of students. We do hope that some acceptable scheme may be formulated and carried into effect in the near future.

The problem of future reorganisation of the educational system is one of vast complexity and magnitude. It will require the united action of the government, the university and colleges and must ultimately depend on public support. I would ask you to give this matter your most careful consideration and, if possible, to make some constructive proposals. In view of the present financial depression, it may not be feasible for us to launch upon too ambitious a scheme but it may be worth our while if we can make even a small beginning.

I do not intend to conclude this address with a note of despondency. However discouraging the present may appear, we must on no account lose our faith in the future. Believe me when I say that your share in bringing our present struggles for solving our immediate problems to a speedy and successful termination will be considerable. But you must proceed on the right lines with that boldness of vision, which should always characterise persons who take upon themselves the sacred task of moulding the character of the rising generation. Though the teachers of this country have not yet been given their rightful place in society and though some of the facilities for work and service to which they are entitled by virtue of their profession and self-sacrifice are even now being denied to them, it will yet have to be acknowledged that they continue to exercise tremendous influence over the destinies of the future citizens of the country. I would appeal to you to examine with the utmost care all problems of educational reconstruction, only some of which have just been outlined by me and to lay down principles which should guide our future activities. I would again appeal to you to realise the vastness of the responsibilities that rest on your shoulders. It is for you to educate public opinion on right lines, to advise the university and government in solving the complex educational problems of the day, such as the adjustment of the needs of primary, secondary and university education; the conflicting claims of literary and vocational education; the coordination of various courses of study; the removal of the evils of the examination system; the building up of corporate life in our colleges; State aid and government control over educational institutions; the reconstitution of university bodies; the maintenance of a proper standard of teaching and examination; and the improvement of the conditions of service of teachers. It is for you to give concrete shape to the measures that may be agreed upon after mature deliberation and to carry them out with steadfast loyalty and devotion to the sacred cause of education. It is also for you to not only inculcate in the minds of youths the passion for knowledge and truth and the spirit of reverence, but also to foster in them that love of their Motherland—that real patriotism which impels one to sacrifice everything for the good of one's country. I look forward to the day when our teachers will be regarded as leaders of society not only in realms of thought but also in fields of action; when the nation will look up to them for initiative and guidance in its different spheres of activity. That day, I fervently hope, is not far distant, and in the meantime it may be expected that no efforts will be lacking on your part to rise to that eminent position to which you may legitimately aspire by virtue of your noble and sacred vocation.

Speech delivered as president of the All-Bengal University and College Teachers Conference at Albert Hall, Calcutta, on 22 February 1933

2

REORGANISATION OF MATRICULATION EDUCATION

One of the most far-reaching questions now before the university is undoubtedly the reorganisation of the matriculation course. To understand exactly how the present situation stands, it will be necessary for me to drop lightly into history for a few moments. In 1921, when the non-cooperation movement was at its height and the University of Calcutta was branded as a House of Slaves, Sir Asutosh Mookerjee, in response to an invitation from Lord Ronaldshay accepted its vice chancellorship. Apart from the sweeping condemnations of all activities of the university, some definite charges were prominently mentioned against the present system of education. One of them concerned secondary education which was declared to have proved abortive, unsuited as it was to present needs and conditions.

One of the first steps taken by the late vice chancellor was to convene in May 1921, a number of conferences to which were invited headmasters of the recognised schools and representatives of managing committees of the institutions. The net decision of these conferences was a declaration to the effect that the present system of secondary education was hopelessly out of date. The conference proposed drastic changes which were duly considered by the different bodies in the university and ultimately embodied in the form of new regulations. These were transmitted to government for sanction in September. Towards the end of October of that year, the government acknowledged receipt of the university letter. In August 1924, that is, after a lapse of about two years, the university was favoured with the views of government on the new regulations. We need not pause to discover the forces which were at work behind the scene and which made it possible for a communication to take nearly twenty-four months to travel from Dalhousie Square to College Square.

Let me here give an indication as to the nature of the changes advocated by the university. The chief reform suggested was with regard to the medium of instruction and examination. Vernacular, the university declared, should be the medium for matriculation, in all subjects other than English. There was an important proviso attached to the section in question which empowered the syndicate to direct the suspension of this rule in respect of special classes of schools.

The second principal change advocated was to the effect that candidates for the examination would have to produce a certificate of training received for a specified period according to prescribed syllabus and under an approved teacher in at least one vocational subject. There were some other changes proposed, such as, geography was made compulsory, study of Indian history was obligatory and option was given to the candidates for the study of elementary science.

The letter from the government to which reference has been made above was placed before the Senate in September last and a committee has been appointed to consider the criticisms made by the government. The pivot of the scheme is undoubtedly the vernacularisation of the present system of secondary education. The government has practically expressed its inability to accept the proposal of the university as it is.

The apprehension that the proposed change will lead to a deterioration of the knowledge of English does not, on a closer examination, appear to be based on solid grounds. What is the present arrangement? To take one illustration, every student in a school now studies Indian history at least twice, once as vernacular in the earlier stage of his career, and again through the medium of English at a later stage. Valuable time is thus undeniably wasted, the student neither learning English nor his vernacular properly, the teaching being conducted in a mixed jargon, half English; half vernacular. It will be admitted that if all subjects other than English are taught and examined through the medium of the vernacular, considerable time will be saved beyond doubt and the knowledge acquired will be real and substantial.

Another objection advanced is based on the supposition that the interests of the Mahomedans will be seriously jeopardised. It seems difficult to realise how this apprehension can reasonably be maintained, for the university does not for a moment say that all students in secondary schools must read Bengali. What the university desires to introduce is that all students must be taught through the medium of vernacular. So far as Mahomedans whose vernacular is Bengali are concerned—and they undeniably constitute the majority—their case should present no difficulty. Those whose vernacular is Urdu are welcome to offer Urdu and it is nowhere suggested that they will be compelled by the university to take up Bengali instead.

It need not be denied that there may be some practical difficulties in the actual working out of the scheme in respect of all the 900 schools under the university. We should, however, consider the proviso empowering the syndicate to deal with particular cases to be sufficient for the purpose.

As a solution, the government, in a spirit of compromise, has asked the university to agree for the present to allow the students the option of writing their answers either in English or vernacular. We hope the university will stand firm and refuse to accept this compromise which, in other words, only helps to put off the evil day. This is a change which every responsible citizen will admit, is long overdue. The university must not forget that the changes formulated by them have as their foundation the considered verdict of the headmaster themselves, persons who being in direct and daily touch with the student community can well be expected to be aware of their needs, capacities and limitations. This is a change, we need not conceal, which is calculated to sow the seeds of national education. It has been remarked and rightly so that the present system of secondary education has been followed by an almost scrupulous disregard of every national feeling and characteristic. A Bengali boy has as much right to be taught through the medium of his vernacular as an English lad, practical difficulties there may be and there will be. They will have to be boldly yet cautiously faced and overcome; they must not, on the other hand, be allowed to overawe us.

3

EDUCATIONAL RECONSTRUCTION

In India, education has recently been receiving close attention at the hands of people belonging to diverse schools of thought, and we are confronted today with a long catalogue of criticisms, suggestions for reform and reconstruction, almost bewildering in character. This situation is capable of logical explanation. Valuable as education is at all times in the history of every civilised nation, to us Indians, it is of paramount importance at the present juncture. Differences there exist as to the means which should be adopted for the realisation of India's political rights, but there is complete unanimity of opinion that no real and permanent advancement is possible unless education of the right type spreads far and wide till it saturates the teeming millions of this vast subcontinent. I believe it is this aspect of our future national growth that has inspired many, though not all, of the recent reports and utterances on education.

One of the criticisms with which we have grown familiar is that education in India has been a complete failure. I have no desire to underestimate the evils inherent in the present system, but I believe there has sometimes been a definite tendency to overstate the case. It would be idle for us to ignore the fact that, but for the education which we and our forefathers have received, we could not have made the progress achieved by us in different fields of thought and activity. There can be no question that western education has brought us into closer contact with the culture and civilisation of progressive countries other than ours. There can be no question that it has laid the foundations of an Indian nationhood; it has helped to awaken our national consciousness, to broaden our intellectual horizon and to kindle in us dreams of a better and a mightier India we all long to see realised. It has taught us self-respect and has inspired us with a sense of equality and fearlessness prompting us to stand up as men, demanding justice and fair play. We need not feel unduly nervous if it has helped to disturb the placid contentment of our people or if it has shaken accepted beliefs and dogmas, for it is only through such unsettlement that the right path of future reconstruction can be discovered.

I am not suggesting for a moment that everything that our educational system has to offer is good, or that all products of western education are animated by the spirit of service, culture and patriotism. The system has undoubtedly its weak points and a change in its outlook and objective is imperative. But let us not minimise, much less forget, the great contributions it has made.

One of its gravest defects is to be traced to historical reasons. The growth of universities in India marked a definite stage in the progress of Indian education. But university education was introduced primarily for the supply of the agency for running the administration of a bureaucratic government. The government stood in need of central organisations which could test the capacity of the students, educated in schools and colleges, on the basis of public examinations, and the universities were brought into existence. They were not meant at the first stage to be seats of culture and learning, nor were they intended to foster higher teaching and research or to train leaders of a democratic community. More than seventy-five years have come and gone; universities have undergone vital changes and do not today exist only for conducting examinations. They have adopted other ideals more appropriate to their true functions and are trying to discharge their obligations with varying degrees of success and efficiency. But a machine-like spirit still persists and continues to deprive these institutions of their full share of life, faith and vigour without which they cannot contribute to national wealth and welfare.

English was deliberately chosen as the medium of instruction and examination to the deplorable neglect of vernacular languages. Indigenous institutions suffered decay and existed merely as shadows of a bygone past. It was apparently thought that a new race of Indians would gradually grow up who would become influenced by the culture and civilisation of their rulers and out of feelings of loyalty and gratitude would be the strongest champions of British interests in India. I need not enter into the details of this aspect of the history of Indian education. That our vernaculars should be developed and given their rightful place in any scheme of national education is now widely recognised. We cannot at the same time forget that our economic and political progress and cultural advance are closely bound up with western science and literature through the medium of western languages, especially English. A conciliation between these two points of view is possible and must be found for the sake of our future national growth.

There is another matter which deserves notice. Primary education was neglected until recently and that, in a manner, which gave rise to widespread resentment. It was thought at one stage that higher education, if extensively given, would itself become an instrument for the spread of primary education among the masses. This hope has not materialised to any satisfactory extent. It is now recognised that the spread of free and compulsory elementary education is one of the pressing needs of the day and, in many provinces, ways and means are being discussed for giving effect to this idea. Lack of funds is usually advanced as the reason for the delay in fulfilling this sacred obligation which rests on government. But we refuse to believe that money cannot be found if there is a will to find it. I voice your united demand when I say that there should be no further delay on the part of government to remove this stigma of middle-class unemployment. It will, however, be a mistake to take an exclusive view of vocational or technical education. We must devise means of shaping our policy in such a way as not to neglect the supreme value of a sound liberal education. There must also be ample provision for scientific education and for the spread of technical knowledge. While emphasis may be laid on one or the other in accordance with the aptitudes and requirements of different classes of students, we must not encourage one aspect to the detriment of any other.

It is important for us to bear in mind that a mere supply of trained youths, qualified in various scientific or technical pursuits, will not solve the question of unemployment. Opportunities must be created for absorbing the services of such young men, who must also be encouraged to take to trade, commerce and industry. There must be a closer association between the State and the educational authorities, on the one hand, and representatives of capitalists, of trade, industry and commerce, on the other. The State must also pursue a policy of a fairer and more equitable economic distribution and strive for the utilisation of India's vast natural resources in the interests of the people of this land. Neither can our aspirations be ever satisfied unless we succeed in breaking through the barriers, which at present restrict our entrance to certain careers, such as the army and the navy, which absorb not a small percentage of the youths of other civilised countries.

Suggestions are now and again put forth to limit admissions to universities, either directly or indirectly, mainly with a view to alleviating the increasingly distressful problem of unemployment. While, as I have said, it is the duty of the State and the people to explore new avenues which could absorb our trained young men, I must affirm that it is a retrograde measure to seek to solve the problem by reducing the number of educated men. We must not forget that the percentage of university-trained men in our country in relation to our population is deplorably lower than in other civilised lands, and any attempt to reduce still further even this small number will bring about national deterioration. Crude and medieval standards of life yet prevail in most villages and in many towns and call for immediate redress at the hands of trained and skilled workers. With the development of electric power, broadcasting, cinema, to mention only a few, scientifically trained men can, with the help of the State, make themselves eminently useful to society. Cultural and political awakening due to the influence of universities still calls for their services. Educational institutions must not regard themselves as factories for the production of clerks and subordinate officers but they have also to supply the country with the leadership and skill in different branches of activity—economic, commercial and industrial, municipal, provincial and national—India stands in urgent need of university men, animated with the ideals of service, imagination, courage, catholicity of outlook and resilience of nature.

There can be no question of reducing the existing educational facilities on the plea that reorientation of education is vitally necessary. We do not believe that the present number of schools and colleges is too large for the requirements of the country. Those who urge their reduction on the ground that the education imparted by them is defective, must, in the first instance, secure the foundation of a sufficient number of institutions where the right type of training will be provided for the children of the soil. The schools and colleges may be enabled to adapt themselves gradually to the altered demands of educational reformers. The situation becomes extremely dangerous when a reduction in their number is advocated on the plea of educational reform. Let us not follow the path of destruction so easy of access until the materials for reconstruction and expansion are generously made available to us.

No far-reaching reforms, aimed at increased facilities for education, which will be varied in character, will ever be accomplished without larger financial assistance from the State. The central government recently distributed to the provinces a crore of rupees for rural reconstruction. For this, it has earned the gratitude of the people of India. The same government has just inaugurated a Central Advisory Board of Education for India; it rightly regards education not merely as a provincial concern but also as a national problem of supreme importance. Let us put forward a united demand that government should set apart at least a crore of rupees annually for several years in succession for distribution among the provinces, in proportion to what they themselves may raise, to be spent for the improvement of primary and secondary education, principally the latter in relation to the problem of unemployment. This expenditure will be productive of national efficiency and will yield results far more valuable than what some other departments of the State, which absorb not one but several crores of rupees from the public exchequer, can ever hope to achieve. This is the only practical way in which the government can realise the object it claims to have in view, namely, a wide expansion of sound education; and it can do it far more speedily and effectively than by the periodical publication of reports, resolutions and schemes, however exhaustive, elaborate and learned they may be.

Let me turn for a moment to the intricate problem of education of girls. One of the noteworthy features in recent times has been the rapid growth of female education. Our responsibility in this sphere becomes all the greater because it is left mostly to us, men, to discover the best methods for educating the future mothers of our race. We must not perpetuate the blunder of training them under the same system as governs the education of our boys. In these days of female emancipation, I do not urge that women should not be treated with equality, but it must be recognised, however insistent their demand for equal treatment may be, there are certain differences which cannot with any effort be obliterated. Our ideals should be, generally speaking, to give our women an education which will make them the mainspring of spiritual force in our society. They must be rendered fully qualified for discharging those sacred obligations which constitute the heritage of Indian womanhood. From them will radiate the great virtues of strength, of purity and devotion, of truth, joy and beauty of patience under suffering, reminiscent of the glorious past of India, which will constitute an irresistible force in the future development of our mind and character. From this, it does not follow that we should discourage women who may enjoy special aptitudes from following particular branches of knowledge or professions, now mostly the prerogative of men. It is, however, essential for us to remember that if our society is to be held together and not be broken to pieces, Indian women must be so educated as to enable them to take their rightful place in family and social life, peculiar to the traditions of this country, which with suitable improvements must in their fundamental features be worthily maintained in future.

Before I close, permit me to emphasise that true education consists more in the spirit it conveys than in the instruction it imparts. The question is, whether we have been able to strengthen those invisible bonds of understanding which unite man to man, irrespective of caste, creed and community, or whether we have betrayed this ideal and imposed artificial restrictions on natural sympathies and brotherhood. Judged by this test, I am sorry to have to say that many of our educated men are today often the victims of narrow provincial and communal feeling. Pray do not think for a moment that I am casting a reflection on any province or community in particular, it must make every teacher pause and think when he/she finds that uneducated men are often from these trammels and we, who claim to be educated, are trying to inoculate them with this severe poison. So long as the present environment of distrust and suspicion continues, we can never hope to attain our cherished goal of a united and regenerated India. It makes us sometimes despair of our future when we realise how our education often fails to check the growth of bitter communal feuds and increasing inter-provincial ill-feeling. I do not ignore that the present economic and political condition of the country is also responsible for this state of affairs. While the teachers have little to do with these aspects of the matter, I would implore them with all the emphasis at my command, to ask themselves every day whether the influence they transmit and the atmosphere they are likely to strengthen the separatist tendencies or to break them down. The success of their teaching will be judged not by the result of examinations or the careers which their students may obtain, but by the qualities of patriotism, self-sacrifice, courage, freedom from communalism and from sectarian instincts which they develop. If the members of this association, and through them teachers in general, interpret their functions in this more catholic and spiritual way and inculcate upon our youths, the masters of our future destiny, the right relation between their province and community, on the one hand, and their Motherland, on the other, they will be the true heirs of this great ancient land to whom we owe almost all that we know and live by.

Let us all be true to our salt, and let us so strive and so act in the sight of all men that if we fall, future generations might at all events love us and bless us as brave loyal souls that fought for the right. If we believe that culture is the essence of the best, that man toiling through the ages like 'an infant crying in the night, like an infant crying for the light with no language but a cry', has felt and said; if we believe that culture is the summation and harmony of things as they should be; that it is the divinely appointed principle of evolution forever dynamic, growing from more to more; that it ministers, unites, elevates and saves; if thus strong and radiant be our faith, it is still possible that we shall be able to get the better of communalism. And we shall do so, if sternly we resolve to honour men according to their quality and character, regardless of the sect or camp they come from, and to stamp our mint-mark on great thoughts and deeds as such, uninfluenced by the colour and creed of the thinker and doer. Communalism, cliquism, cabalism are but cultural nullities—from them come only freaking growths and perverted performances. May we be endowed with the strength and courage to regard ourselves, however humble and unworthy, as soldiers in the war of Liberation of Humanity, marching proudly for the promised land or the *swaraj of the intellect*, the mental emancipation of man!

Presidential address delivered at the Eleventh Session of All-India Educational Conference held at Nagpur on 27 December 1935

4

MEDIUM OF INSTRUCTION

Before I come to the problems themselves, may I ask you to bear with me for a brief moment while I attempt to hold out before you the picture of the ultimate goal which it ought to be our ambition to reach. In other words, the question which I take upon myself the responsibility to answer though I know imperfectly is what ought to be the aim of secondary education in Bengal? I know and you, gentlemen, all know as well that an answer to this question alone may require the lengthy discourse which is not permissible in today's proceedings. To my mind the system of secondary education should be so moulded as to produce young men who will have a thorough mastery over his vernacular, will know the history of his country and certain broad features of the history of the world at large, will have a training in mathematics and last, but not the least geography. Politically placed as we are, a working knowledge of English is essential for our future progress, but here English must be treated as a secondary language (and) not as the language which will be a vehicle of instruction and examination. The students will be taught various subjects through the medium of his own vernacular and he will learn English at this stage not so much from the point of view of a dignified scholar as from the point of view of a person who can express his thoughts in speech and in writing in simple and decent English. I cannot purposely include in the list of compulsory subjects a study of classics. I do not desire to open the doors of controversy so far the compulsory study of a classical language is concerned. I feel that the first claim should be that of the student's vernacular and in order to appreciate properly the vernacular language it may be necessary to have training in classics as well. I would much rather provide for such training in the early stage of a student's career than overburden the students by making it compulsory subjects at his final examination.

The importance of making vernacular the first language in the school curricula and also making it the medium of instruction and examination is becoming obvious every day. Nearly forty years ago, a proposal to recognise the vernacular as a compulsory subject for the university examination was turned down as retrograde and ridiculous but during the last twenty years we have witnessed changes of momentous character and our mother tongue has been placed side by side with English, French, Latin, Sanskrit, Arabic and Persian as a subject for the degree of master of arts in our university. These movements to give a recognised position to our vernacular deserve the gratitude of all Bengalis. But though much has been done, more still remains to be done. In spite of the recognition which our vernacular has received at the hands of the university, it is a fact which we cannot deny and neither does the university deny that the thousands of students who are reading in our schools and who after matriculation examination enter the university are not learning their vernaculars as well as we would have liked them to do. The reason is that the school courses are hopelessly artificial, if not lifeless altogether. The students are apt to regard themselves as more or less working machines who are somehow to go through the prescribed course, store them up in their minds and pour them forth in the examination hall. No doubt there is a compulsory paper consisting of 100 marks, 40 marks of which are assigned to questions taken from prescribed texts but so far as all the other subjects are concerned, they are largely to depend on the poor stock of their knowledge in the foreign tongue. The obvious result is stagnation. The students do not find themselves really interested in their subjects and their work amounts to a drudgery. The first step that is to be taken is to make vernacular the medium for instruction and examination for all subjects in schools except English and this experiment is bound to revolutionise the entire system of education.

Speech delivered at the conference of teachers of secondary schools [undated]

5

EDUCATION AND EMPLOYMENT

In recent times, no report on educational work is deemed complete unless it has some reference to the question of the future of university education in relation to the problem of unemployment. It is no wonder, therefore, that your principal has also referred to it. I have no desire to enter into a detailed discussion of this very complicated question today but I would like to make a few general observations. It is argued that the present system of education is bad because it cannot solve the problem of unemployment. The question assumes an acute form when despondency and disappointment follow the close of one's educational career. It is, however, a problem not peculiar to this country and exists in an abundant measure in other countries where the educational system is not equally defective. Many remedies are suggested by people who look at the question from different points of view. One school of thought urges a reduction in the number of educational institutions, a proposition which we must at once dismiss as narrow and short-sighted. Another school emphasises the need of institutions of a special kind which may divert the energies of students into different channels. I think it is now more or less agreed that the province stands in urgent need of special institutions, which would provide for training in varied pursuits so that our students may not be compelled to follow a course of instruction which is predominantly literary in character.

Here, however, there are certain considerations which we shall do well to bear in mind. In all education, the main cause of failure is staleness. Vocational or technical education also will be of no avail if we conceive of it merely as a system of giving our youth one specialised manual aptitude. We must guarantee that we do not take a mean view of technical training. It has been said that there are three main roads along which we can proceed with good hope of advancing towards the best balance of intellect and character: the way of literary culture, the way of scientific culture and the way of technical culture. Not one of these methods can be exclusively followed without grave loss of intellectual activity and character. A mere mechanical mixture of the three elements will not produce the desired end. The problem for investigation will be to devise means of retaining the dominant emphasis, whether literary, scientific or technical, and without loss of coordination to infuse into each way of education something of the other two.

I would emphatically urge that there should be no suggestion of curtailing the present educational facilities which are already limited, unless and until the reorganisation has actually taken place and the existing institutions have been remodelled or special institutions through State aid. We cannot afford to face the risk of losing the little that we have now, even though it may not be the best that we should have, on the remote chance of the province being supplied at some future date with better equipped institutions answering to the changing needs of the community. I would urge that this practical aspect of educational reform should always be kept in view in the discussion of future plans and policies.

I would also point out that even vocational or technical education on a large scale is not by itself likely to solve the problem of unemployment. The principal refers to this possibility and we share his apprehension. In recent years, we have come across brilliant young men who have received first rate training in different branches of science, technology or engineering in this country or abroad and it is pathetic how many of them still continue to add to the list of the unemployed. The main duty of the university is to impart the right type of teaching and training to its alumni. Such teaching and training should be as varied and complete as possible in accordance with the modern requirements of society. But it is quite a different thing to ensure that employers who stand in need of trained hands will absorb the products coming out of the university. Then again, there is the question of turning the eyes of our young men to fields of occupation other than service.

Influenced by these considerations, we have urged the university that an employment bureau should be established not as a purely university body but consisting also of representatives of government and of various commercial and industrial interests. We may fight the menace of unemployment only if the university is permitted to act in close cooperation with those bodies and persons whose privilege it is to give employments. Such cooperation will be of mutual advantage to all parties concerned.

The question of reconstruction of university education is at present engaging the attention of various authorities—official and non-official. I cannot possibly deal with the task of reconstruction; [it] presents far graver difficulties than the work of destruction. The end in view will never be achieved except with the cordial and trustful cooperation of all persons interested in the solution of this question. The State must also be prepared to spend more on education than what it has hitherto done; for no far-reaching reforms are capable of execution without generous financial assistance.

Standing in the presence of so many of my young friends, I cannot bring my remarks to a close without addressing a few words to them. Let me in the first place congratulate you on the success you have attained and the prizes you have won. I understand that although some of the prizes were available in cash, you preferred to receive books instead. This preference reveals a most praiseworthy tendency for which you deserve our special congratulations.

You are fortunate enough to receive your education in an institution which abounds in so many features of excellence; I hope and trust that you will make the fullest use of the opportunities which are offered to you for developing a healthy corporate life. I have no desire to hold before you a gloomy and despondent picture, but it is essential for you to bear in mind that we are now passing through a period of great strain and anxiety and we have to equip ourselves properly and efficiently for facing the battle of life. You have heard it often said that Bengal is lagging behind other provinces. I do not believe that, taking all things together, we are inferior in quality to any other province in India. The truth, however, is that while twenty years ago Bengal was the first in many spheres, in the field of politics and in education, other provinces had not come up to the forefront. The situation is altered today. In almost every province, we witness the growth of a new and vigorous life and a legitimate endeavour to improve its efficiency and quality. This only means that if we have to maintain our position as a first class province, we cannot afford to dream only of past achievements. We have to struggle hard and equip ourselves in the best possible manner. After all it is only the fittest who will survive. To you, my young friends, I would say, and say it with all the emphasis at my command, that it is for you to shape the future of your province. Take not the charge of inferiority lying down; accept it as a challenge to your sense of manhood and self-respect. The 'cram-book spirit' which dominates our academic system also looms large in our everyday affairs. Remember that success can never be achieved by any 'short-cut' process. You have to toil and work hard during this formative period of your career and you will find that it will turn into a profitable investment. Whatever work you undertake, do it seriously, thoroughly and well, never leave it half-done or undone, never feel yourselves satisfied unless and until you have given it your very best. Cultivate the habits of discipline and toleration. Surrender not the convictions which you hold dear but learn to appreciate the points of view of your opponents. Remember that respect for and obedience to your superiors constitutes no sign of weakness in human character. Abandon everything that is false, sham and hypocritical. Forget not that labour and social service form the two basic principles of life in society. Contempt for labour and indulgence in luxury make a person a parasite and perpetuate national subjugation. Use all in your power to assist others by doing at least one good deed every day, thus, paving the way for the more important work of national reconstruction. Remember that the blessed work of helping the world forward does not wait to be done by perfect men and you are fully equipped for this task. Form the spirit of love and charitable sympathy for your friends, neighbours and different communities, endeavouring to work together in righteousness and to cooperate to the best of your ability.

Pray do not misunderstand me while I am speaking to you in this strain. I am addressing you as the future masters of your country's destiny and it is the duty of each one of you to understand the position clearly and thoroughly. If you shoulder this responsibility in all earnestness and strive hard to restore our beloved country to its position of honour and freedom, the era of humiliation and hardship will cease, the glory of our race will be enhanced and this glory will be yours. Let me hope and pray that under the fostering care of your college and university, under the influence of your home, you will train yourselves physically and morally, widen your intellectual activities and capacities, develop the spirit of bravery and perseverance, inculcate noble ideals and patriotism; in short, mould yourselves into good citizens of a united and regenerated India.

Speech delivered at the Scottish Church College, Calcutta, on 7 December 1935

6

REVAMPING THE EDUCATION SYSTEM

I welcome the opportunity you have given me to associate myself with the proceedings of your conference. Although I have been rather out of touch with the educational affairs of West Bengal for the last three years, my interest in your cause has not in the least abated. The need for reorientation of our educational policy has become all the more obvious to me as I have looked upon the problem in a somewhat detached manner. One of the remarkable features of the development of secondary education in Bengal has been the support and patronage given to its cause by generations of private individuals. Hundreds of high schools sprang up within one generation through the sacrifice of devoted bands of teachers who regarded spread of knowledge as the noblest mission of their lives. If Bengal had to depend upon State support alone, education would have miserably lagged behind and the country's progress would have been greatly retarded. Whatever defects there might have been in the system of education imparted through our schools, we will fail in our duty if we do not acknowledge our gratitude for the solid work of national importance which was rendered by generations of selfless teachers and other promoters in all parts of Bengal. We are naturally reminded today of the network of high schools which functioned in East Bengal whose representatives still continue to be members of your association. The loss suffered by Hindus in East Bengal has been colossal. One's mind is naturally filled with indescribable grief and disappointment, when one thinks of the fate of the large number of private institutions, open to all communities, which were established mainly by Hindu influence and patronage and through which generations of scholars came out successful and spread their influence far and wide. Many of those institutions rekindle in our minds memories of the sacred association of diverse types of people, known and unknown, who never could dream of the tragic developments which have overtaken us today. Although the schools have, to all intents and purposes, disappeared from our thought, the fate of more than 1,000 teachers who have been uprooted from their sphere of work, has been of a tragic character and their future rehabilitation is a matter of grave urgency. The State has a definite responsibility in this respect. I am glad to find that this conference proposes to consider the possibility of establishing a colony for rehabilitating a large proportion of these teachers. I hope that whatever scheme may be agreed upon will be of benefit to the sufferers, as also to the society as a whole and will receive unstinted support of the State.

While speaking about rehabilitation of teachers, we have also to consider the future prospect of thousands of uprooted school-going children who are today scattered in different parts of the province in a most miserable condition. During the last three months, I have come across thousands of such young boys and girls. I have found them pathetically clamouring not even so much for food and shelter as for continuance of facilities for education. Their physical wants have not chilled their ardour for knowledge, and failure to satisfy their demand will be nothing short of criminal neglect of one of the elementary duties of any free State. Let us not forget that this will not only mean ruination of thousands—if not lakhs—of individual lives, but the shattering of the hopes and aspirations of an entire generation. I have discussed this matter with many unfortunate guardians and parents, who do not see any hope for their own future but who are eager to hand over the custody of their children to the State or any well-established organisation which is prepared to take charge of their future education. I see no reason why a scheme should not be formulated which will provide: first, for the opening of schools to be held in camps in different parts of the province and run mainly with the help of refugee teachers; and, second, for attaching suitable hostels to existing schools outside Calcutta, which will be specially meant for refugee boys and girls. This work should be entrusted to a special committee which should execute the plan speedily and efficiently under the direction of government.

Secondary education occupies a most important place in the educational system of our province. On its proper development and administration depend, on the one hand, the progress of higher education and on the other hand the implementation of any sound scheme of primary education, requiring the services of a large band of well-qualified young teachers and other workers. The Sadler Commission had recommended the establishment of a board of secondary education more than thirty years ago. The delay in giving effect to the proposal is due to a variety of causes which are well known. Only recently a bill has been enacted by the legislature and it is expected to come into operation in the near future. I hope and trust that this Act will receive general support from the educational authorities and also the public. Whatever criticisms may be levelled against some of its provisions, the Act will be judged by the way in which it is actually implemented. We have seen in the past how an apparently good legal enactment can be nullified by its imperfect working, just as an Act of the legislature, though defective, may be generally utilised for advancing the good of the community. Much depends on the individuals who are called upon to initiate reforms and to create sound and healthy traditions. There was a time when public opinion was acutely nervous of State control of secondary education. This opposition became all the more intense during the dark period of Muslim League administration of undivided Bengal. In those days, education was being openly utilised for narrow communal and political purposes to which the public resolutely refused to surrender. After attainment of political freedom, we have to examine this problem dispassionately and in a spirit of realism. The government of the day, which is responsible to the legislature, cannot absolve its responsibility for the planning and execution of a national policy of education, well suited to the needs and aspirations of the people. At the same time, we have to guard zealously against the possibility of education being made the plaything of party politics. The degree of governmental control may vary in relation to the different stages of national education. A university, whose administration is controlled by statute, can and should claim utmost possible autonomy, especially in respect of all academic matters. The right of government to intervene can arise only when it is proved to have failed to fulfil the sacred obligations entrusted to its care. So far as secondary education is concerned, the government must have a comparatively larger voice in its administration. At the same time, it will be fatal if high schools are made to function under a strict policy of regimentation, or there is official interference in their day-to-day working.

One of the main defects of our educational system lies in the paucity of scope and opportunity open to students with diverse tastes and aptitudes. Our education in high schools has been predominantly literary in character, and a large proportion of students are necessarily driven to stereotyped collegiate education which hardly helps them to earn their independent living. The chronic problem of unemployment amongst educated middle-class people is a grave social and political problem. No educational institution can solve the problem of unemployment. This falls within the sphere of State responsibility. But any educational system, worth its name, must not permit the mass production of unemployables. The training we impart must produce healthy and useful citizens, who will not shirk work and who, if given the opportunity, will be able to stand on their own legs. We need not be alarmed at the number of educated youths. Any artificial restriction of educational facilities does not offer any solution at all. I do not for a moment subscribe to the false notion that Bengal has encouraged an educational system which is an inverted pyramid. If we examine figures of other countries, such as France, Germany, America, United Kingdom and Denmark, we will find the higher stages of education here have not been unduly stressed. What is lacking is a diversified secondary system with facilities for every type of aptitude—general, technical, commercial, vocational, and agricultural—so that the really bright students might go for higher education. This needs a complete reorientation of the system of secondary education. It will require enormous funds—both capital and recurring. In no country has education prospered if it is made to depend entirely on fee income. In many countries, education, even up to the university stage, has been made free, either wholly or partially, at the cost of the State. At any rate, there must be generous provision for scholarships and free board, so that not a single deserving young student is deprived of facilities for education. The salaries paid to our teachers are ridiculously low. We often make public reference to the great national service that the teachers render at heavy personal sacrifice. I see no reason why a section of our community, on whose efficiency and integrity depends the future of the rising generation of our race, should be expected to carry on a miserable existence on the plea of adherence to noble idealism. Further, low salaries and bleak prospects often fail to attract men of talent and ability to the great teaching profession. No secondary education act would serve any useful purpose until abundant funds are placed at the disposal of schools for the improvement of the salaries and conditions of service of teachers, for opening new lines of training, for development of libraries, laboratories and gymnasia and for provision of hostels and free seats for the students.

I would also plead for a revision of the syllabus and curriculum used in our schools which seems to be too heavy a burden on the minds of the pupils and on the purse of their guardians. What matters is not the quantity of book knowledge that we can somehow thrust upon the students, but the choice and contents of the subjects and the manner and method of their treatment while imparting instruction in classes. We are often anxious that everything that a future citizen has to learn must be taught in our schools. Let us take languages alone. We argue that Bengali being our mother tongue is indispensable; English is inescapable; Sanskrit is basic; Hindi is expedient. Apart from languages, we regard history, mathematics, geography, and science as of fundamental importance in modern age. Then there is the list of optional subjects including fine arts, music, agriculture and vocational studies. If some knowledge of each of these languages and many other subjects is deemed essential, must they all be made subjects of study for the final examination? I know, psychologically, omission of a subject from the final list makes both the teacher and the pupil often neglect its importance. This is due to the faulty method of examination which dominates the entire educational system.

In any case, the need for revising the list of subjects and their contents is urgent and imperative. We must simplify the courses of study in relation to value and importance of the subjects, and also the capacity of the pupils to understand and absorb them correctly. I am not one of those who would like to exclude English altogether from our schools and colleges, but I would entirely revise the syllabus and the list of textbooks in English. It is enough for the ordinary student, who completes his high school career, or who reads for a university degree to learn how to read and write and express himself in simple English. The heavy course prescribed for the English examination at various stages is quite unnecessary and may be set apart for those who want to specialise in English. This step alone will greatly reduce the burden which falls heavily on our students. I would advocate the adoption of a well-thought-out scheme for encouragement of extra-academic activities including social service, sports, games and excursions, which will help in developing the pupil's body and mind. Re-establishment of intimate contacts between the teacher and the student is the best means for creating an atmosphere of regularity and discipline in educational institutions. There was a time when political struggles between the peoples' representatives and a foreign government affected the peace and normal activities of our schools and colleges. Today, after freedom, the situation has undergone a complete transformation. Whatever grievances one may have against the government of the day—and in no country can there be a system of administration which will be free from abuses or weaknesses—the remedy does not lie in merely appealing to the emotions and sentiments of the student community. According to their age they will no doubt study the great problems—economic and political—which are awaiting solutions. Let them, by all means, be conversant with the implications of these problems, according to their own capacity and judgment. As adult voters, they will even exercise their franchise. But in a free country, teachers and students, as such, must not be used as pawns in the game of party politics. They should be encouraged to devote their entire energy to the great task of strengthening the foundations of the institutions, of which they are members, and raising the standard and quality of their work. We are living in an age of intense competition today. We can only hope to regain for ourselves the position that we once occupied in this great land of ours, if we can truly and correctly build and administer our educational institutions free from all narrowness and partisanship. The future of our country lies in our devising and executing properly balanced scheme of national education which will represent the highest traditions of our culture and civilisation and at the same time absorb the best that the west can give. The crisis through which we are passing just now is bound to affect the working of our educational institutions. Still, on the maintenance of their correct standard and the facilities given to the teachers and students will depend our strength to meet the challenge that faces us today. I hope and pray that in spite of all obstacles and difficulties, you resolutely carry on your work, instilling in the mind of your pupils a spirit of dauntlessness, love for truth and knowledge, and reverence for their country and its culture, so that you may all play your part worthily in the great struggle that lies ahead of us.

Speech delivered at the annual session of the All Bengal Teachers' Association at Vishnupur on 16 July 1950 to the [illegible] kind of [illegible], if we use truly and [illegible] build and administer, [illegible] educational institutions free from all narrowness and partisanship. The [illegible] our country needs in [illegible] dignity and [illegible] a properly balanced [illegible] national education which will represent the [illegible] conditions of [illegible] [illegible] the crisis through which we are passing just now is bound to [illegible] of our educational institutions. Still, [illegible] and the facilities given to the teachers and students will [illegible] to meet the challenge that faces us today [illegible] and difficulties, [illegible] the minds of your pupils a spirit of [illegible] [illegible]

Speech delivered at the annual session of the All Bengal Teachers' Association [illegible]

Reorienting Higher Education

7

REORIENTING THE UNIVERSITY TO ITS GOALS

Time will not permit me to review in detail the activities of our university, to dwell on its achievements as also its failure during the last three quarters of a century. Broadly speaking, however, the university has passed through two main stages. Brought into existence during a period when India was passing through a great political upheaval, the first university established under the British rule in this country aimed merely at conducting examinations and affiliating institutions, which in their turn, prepared candidates for examinations. The university was started not mainly for promotion of teaching and research or for the conservation of Indian traditions and culture, but chiefly to test the fitness of Indian youths to enter the learned professions and hold appointments in the various services. The steady pursuit of this policy has left a deep impression on our national growth and has not been entirely satisfactory in its consequences.

The second period which commenced in an active form after the passing of the Indian Universities Act of 1904 marks the growth of a new ideal—the ideal of a great teaching and research university. During the last thirty years, we have witnessed remarkable progress in various departments of study and thought and in spite of our limitations and difficulties we are still attempting to follow that policy of advancement of learning which will bring glory to our alma mater and our Motherland.

We cannot also shut our eyes to some of the lasting benefits which have accrued to us through the agency of the university. This university has stood for the spread of education, has thrown open its gates to one and all irrespective of caste, creed and community. It has brought the east and the west together, opened new visions and awakened in us new ambitions. It has roused the political consciousness of the people and has contributed to the growth of national solidarity. It has called into its service distinguished representatives of all communities who have steadfastly worked together for its general welfare. While we can legitimately take pride in our past achievements, we must not be lulled into inactivity or allow ourselves to remain satisfied with what has been done. Inspired by the progress we have attained, we must be as anxious to conserve the best traditions of our university, as eager and fearless to remove its inherent weaknesses.

Ours has been the first university in India to sound the clarion call of progress at the beginning of this century. Since then, other provinces in this vast country have been making rapid advances in various fields of activity. We have to march ahead, in full remembrance of the fact that Bengal's great men have in the past stimulated work and thought in all parts of India, and in social, educational, religious and political spheres, Bengal has led the way; if we are to hold in future a position of pre-eminence, we must never be forgetful of the imperative necessity of reshaping our policy, of increasing our efficiency in all directions and maintaining a standard of work which will be second to none in any part of this country.

When we first thought of celebrating the foundation day, I was anxious that we should concern ourselves mainly with the activities of our students and bring them into closer touch with the university. It is a matter of disappointment to me that we have not been able to associate with today's function the students of the university outside the metropolis. To you who are assembled here today, I express my personal gratitude for the splendid way in which you have responded to the call of your alma mater. You have proved today that if you are given proper training and facilities, you can give as fine a display of organising ability and disciplined action as any band of university students can be expected to achieve. True as you are and as you must be to your own college, you have carried today through the streets of the city the new banner of your university, thus proclaiming your loyal adherence to the university to which we all belong and of which your colleges are vital and component parts.

One of the great needs of the hour is to build up a healthy corporate life in this university, to provide for our students the amplest facilities for the full exercise of their powers, so that the great qualities which lie dormant in them may shine forth in perfection; to help in the establishment of students' organisations with a view to equip them to face the battle of life; to develop them into men, strong and self-reliant, hard-working and fearless, proud of their national culture, but not narrow in their outlook, anxious to promote peace and happiness, felled with a lofty idealism, but not swayed by class hatred or unthinking emotion—men who will be the worthy leaders of a new Bengal and who will carry the torch of learning and freedom to the lasting glory of their beloved Motherland.

From every corner of this great province there rises today the anxious question, shall we live or shall we die, shall we rise or shall we fall, shall we unite or shall we divide, shall we strive to reconstruct or shall we follow the barren path of destruction. Let me gather in my own the voices of you all who are assembled here today and of those whom you represent and send back the response—we shall live, we shall rise, we shall unite and shall accept truth and service as the motto of our lives.

Speech delivered on the occasion of the University's Foundation Day Celebrations in Calcutta in 24 January 1935

8

AIMS OF UNIVERSITY EDUCATION IN INDIA

I yield to none in my conviction that through education, rightly planned and generously fostered, lies the salvation of our country, and that today in India, education offers a sphere of service and activity limitless in scope, challenging the lifelong labours of men of all creeds and communities. Is it not true that generations of men in this ancient land have cheerfully sacrificed their wealth, their comfort and even their life for the sake of spreading knowledge and implanting in the human mind that insatiable quest for truth which in every age and clime is the foundation for the attainment of freedom?

In recent years, university problems in India have received an almost superabundant measure of attention from people belonging to diverse schools of thought, both progressive and reactionary; and numerous and conflicting remedies have been proposed for our intellectual salvation. Though any suggestion for the curtailment of educational facilities must be resolutely opposed by the united voice of all lovers of Indian progress, we must not be slow to remedy the weak points in our system and, sinking all differences, readjust it to our changing needs and aspirations.

I believe opinion is unanimous today that the present system of university education in India requires thorough and immediate reorganisation. On the eve of reconstruction, let us leave aside comparatively minor issues and ask ourselves the fundamental question, what should be the aims and ideals of university education in India? Education is not static. Its course must change with the passage of time and with the altered conditions of the community it seeks to serve and elevate. It must always be closely related to the life of the people. Otherwise, it becomes stagnant and soulless and instead of uplifting society tends to retard progress.

Generally speaking, the Indian university must regard itself as one of the living organs of national reconstruction. It must discover the best means of blending together both the spiritual and the material aspects of life. It must equip its alumni irrespective of caste, creed or sex, with individual fitness, not for its own sake, not merely for adorning varied occupations and professions, but in order to teach them how to merge their individuality in the common cause of advancing the highest traditions of human civilisation. That constitutes the perennial ideal of a university, rooted in Indian soil and expresses one of the greatest needs of the hour.

While it will raise the average quality of its alumni and influence the steady march of progress and freedom, the university will not neglect the supreme task of giving protection and privileges to its brilliant teachers and advanced students, whose sole duty will be an unceasing search for truth and the pursuit of learning for its own sake. A university is not worth its name which does not provide for both teaching and research of the highest order in diverse branches of knowledge. India must produce her own band of discoverers and conquerors of new realms of thought who will help to raise the intellectual level of the country and call forth the spontaneous homage and respect of nations far and wide. There is indeed no limit to the scope of such investigations which must be conducted in an atmosphere of truth and freedom, unhampered by worries and anxieties. They must also be closely related to Indian conditions and constantly aim at their betterment.

Let us examine briefly how universities may make their contributions towards national advancement. The preparation of the nation's youth for the diverse professions which commonly absorb their energy and intellect will continue. New vocations and avenues of useful and honourable employment which are but partially open to the Indian youth, such as the army and the navy, trade, commerce and industry, will receive adequate attention. Scientific and technical knowledge of various kinds and grades will be generously imparted in full remembrance of their supreme value in the making of a new India, capable of standing on her own legs. An army of leaders and workers, not a band of narrow specialists, is to be created whose aim will be to foster India's economic and industrial development. It will be for them to devise ways and means for conserving and utilising the rich and inexhaustible raw materials in which this country abounds, not for individual profiteering but for the benefit of its toiling millions, and for providing them with food, clothing and shelter, thus stabilising national efficiency and wealth and preventing their continued exploitation. Problems of health, sanitation, hygiene and diet will be investigated and the conditions for the alleviation of suffering and malnutrition carefully analysed. Agriculture must form a distinctive part of the work of the university and the possibility of increasing the productive power of land with the aid of science explored and explained.

Neither will cultural pursuits and the study and investigation of arts and letters be discontinued or discouraged. Philosophy, literature, archaeology and architecture, fine arts including music and painting, the Indian languages, classical and modern history and polity will be carefully nurtured and the correct interpretation of the manifestations of the genius of India in the realm of thought and culture will be faithfully and courageously given. These studies will not be a mere catalogue of past achievements. The modern Indian scholar must have the training and the vision to connect our ancient history and civilisation with our present needs and condition and to suggest rules of conduct and formulate an outlook on life which the Indian society of today can worthily accept. Economics and banking, particularly the position of this country in relation to foreign trade and competition, and the conditions of a prosperous and an economically free India, must be critically examined, especially the fundamental aspects of the government and constitutions of countries which are attempting to rehabilitate themselves on the ruins of their former existence. Education and psychology will form the subjects of active investigation. A department of educational research will devote itself to the study of local problems, as also of great experiments, made in countries far and near, particularly in Russia and Japan. Important languages of the east and the west will be studied by our rising generations. Indeed, while the Indian university will maintain the great characteristics of India's past culture and civilisation, omitting all that is pernicious and anti-progressive, it must not summarily reject what the west may give us. If western ideas can be assimilated into our system without detriment to its national character, we shall welcome them. If such acceptance denationalises us, we shall reject them without hesitation.

A great problem which Indian education must face sooner or later relates to the place which should be given to religious education. Religion has played a dual role in the evolution of mankind. While it has done enormous good to humanity and has introduced order and solidarity in critical periods of man's history, it has at times been utilised as a convenient excuse for senseless oppression of mankind; Indian education was deliberately made secular according to a policy of religious neutrality pursued by a foreign government which would hardly have acted otherwise. This has had in some respects devastating effects on the Indian mind.

One feels doubtful, however, of the practicability of including religious education as a subject for study in our schools and colleges, open to youths belonging to various religious faiths. The danger lies in the fact that this instruction is likely to be impacted by men who will lay greater emphasis on the seeds of exclusiveness and fanaticism, ruinous for the growth of Indian nationhood. Religion must, therefore, be left mainly to home influence, the standard of which must be appreciably raised. But I would at the same time earnestly urge a regular and well-balanced study of the great truths and beauties underlying the different religious faiths, presented in a manner which will not seek to proclaim the superiority of one to the other, nor emphasise minute differences among one another. The text which will require most careful preparation, will record the ultimate triumph of truth and righteousness, lay stress on the essential unity of all religions and aim at the foundation of a common sympathy, a just and equitable understanding and a sense of universal brotherhood.

A vast field of service that is open to the Indian university relates to the enrichment of our national languages. We must make them the vehicle of our instruction and through them spread knowledge far and wide in diverse branches and in forms both scholarly and popular. Another paramount need is the supply of thousands of university-trained youths, inspired by the best that a university can give, for directing the work and activities of elementary schools in India. There have no doubt been illuminating instances of scholarship, of high artistic attainments, of intellectual achievements in the spheres of letters, science and administration. But who will deny that all this has been limited to a very small circle beyond which there is a state ranging from twilight to total darkness? Who will deny that much yet remains to be done to dispel the clouds of ignorance, fear and superstition that cover the Indian horizon today? That more than 90 per cent of the Indian population should continue to be illiterate even after 175 years of British rule in this country is an intolerable situation which calls for immediate action. A new race of university-trained youths must go forth, and fired with a spirit of zeal and sacrifice, undertake the duty of directing the affairs of schools, throbbing with life and energy, to be opened at every village from one corner of the country to the other. The school will be the centre from which will radiate the joy and glory of knowledge, applied to the needs and conditions of every grade of society, not treated as separate units but as living parts of one organic whole—knowledge that will liberate the latent abilities of the children of India and enable them to know themselves and the heritage that is theirs. It is thus that the university will carry its banner of progress and liberty into the very heart of India, will cease to be characterised as the producer of small groups of men, ease-loving and self-centred, and will awaken a spirit of sympathy and support, nationwide in extent, in furtherance of the noble mission it will have made its own.

Our object is to give to the Indian youth an education which will be a true preparation for life and this cannot be achieved by fostering intellectual activities alone. We have to raise the physical standard and efficiency of the rising generation and must aim at creating a sound mind in a sound body. Physical education must be made compulsory in schools and colleges. For this purpose, there must be an abundant provision of playing fields and gymnasia; there must be a regular supply of skilled teachers who will instruct our youth in daily habits of physical welfare and will consider individual needs and capacities; there must be an organised system of free health examination and a network of after-care centres. Closely connected with physical instruction is the supreme question of supply of cheap but nourishing diet without which physical culture is meaningless if not harmful.

Addressing the university of the province that claims Dr Moonje as its own, need I emphasise that military training also should be made compulsory in our colleges? Its object will not be to proclaim the doctrine of 'might is right' but to instil into the minds of our students a sense of discipline, alertness and organisation so essential for building up a character. It will also serve to show that, given adequate scope, Indian youth may worthily form the foundation of a national force, capable of defending our hearth and home; this will deepen a sense of self-respect and self-confidence in the minds of our people and remove an unjust stigma on our capacity and character.

I have been hitherto speaking of some of the major activities which should form part of the programme of every Indian university. We must not overlook, however, the need of altering the methods of imparting instruction and knowledge. We must re-establish that close and intimate relationship between the teacher and the student which was one of the features of ancient Indian education. The system of mass lecturing and formal communication of information which is not often properly assimilated must obviously be modified, giving place to a more intensive system of tutorial and seminar work which will stimulate the growth of right and independent thinking. For this purpose, we must be enabled to employ a much larger staff than at present and to pay our teachers adequately. Nothing is more important to the success of an educational scheme than the selection of the right teachers, men of character and learning who will regard their task as a sacred mission—men who will inspire the respect and affection of their students and will act as their guides, philosophers and friends.

A thorough revision of the system of examination is also urgently called for. The predominance of examinations in university education in India has seriously affected the march of progress. Whether in schools or colleges or in the universities, the goal ordinarily in view before one and all is success at the examinations. This aspect of educational organisation is not peculiar to India and has recently been receiving considerable attention in other countries. We have to explore the conditions under which we can dispense with the rigours of the examination system and secure a more satisfactory recognition of the work done during a student's career in educational institutions.

We must also provide for a more intimate relationship between student and student and for this purpose generously equip our universities and colleges with halls, unions and common rooms. This contact, this free and frank exchange of ideas and ideals, will help to lay the foundation of true and lasting comradeship; this will build up character, knock down angularities, create wider interests and enable youths to know themselves truly and well. A mere pursuit of knowledge in the lecture room, the library or the laboratory cannot make a man worthy of his life's mission.

I have today spoken of some of the fundamental problems of educational reconstruction which will take years of ceaseless, determined and patient toil to solve. Before I conclude I must, however, enumerate the primary conditions which require to be fulfilled in an adequate and satisfactory measure before any scheme of reorganisation, truly national in character, can be undertaken with success. First and foremost, a system of education, consistent with the genius of the people of India and suited to modern life and conditions, cannot be fully achieved unless and until India enjoys a political status which will give her the liberty to decide for herself what constitutes her national needs and how best they can be satisfied. Call it dominion status, responsible self-government or swaraj—I am not concerned with the nomenclature; I am concerned with the supreme fact that the constitution must give us real and not shadowy rights and powers and enable India to be the mistress of her own destiny. Secondly, there must be less of degrading poverty and less of disease and pestilence, now nationwide in extent, which are sapping our vitality and energy and shutting out the inrush of joy, light and beauty into this land of proud and ancient civilisation. Thirdly, the State must spend far more adequately and generously on education, in all its grades, than what it has done in the past. All schemes for reconstruction will remain unrealised until this paramount condition is wholeheartedly, fulfilled. Fourthly, there must be an elaborate system of elementary and secondary education which will form an enduring foundation on which the great structure of university education will be built, shining like a crown of purposeful achievement, drawing inspiration and strength from the abundance of materials which the lower stages will bring to its doors. Fifthly, education at every stage should be as cheap as possible while its quality will be maintained at a high level. Even in a rich country like Great Britain more than 40 per cent of university students receive concessions and aid, the total value of which is about Rs 17,800,000 excluding the contributions of private trusts and corporations. In Russia, education is free in the lower stages and 80 per cent of her university students are not required to pay anything. Sixthly, while expressing our deepest gratitude to our past benefactors, let us emphasise that universities must inspire private benefactions on a much wider scale than they have hitherto done. In every country, we witness today a conflict between class and class. We witness the unjust and inequitable distribution of wealth and the existence, side by side, of proud and abject poverty. But this disparity is nowhere more staggering than in this unfortunate land of ours. If our wealthy men who have amassed fortunes, whether through personal efforts or through the accident of birth or otherwise, make up their minds to allot a portion of what they possess for the uplift of their brethren, for the wide diffusion of knowledge and culture, for the alleviation of suffering, they will be uprooting feelings of hostility and antagonism and will inspire the affection and confidence of the masses whose prosperity and improvement they will thus have helped to stabilise. Seventhly, there must be a close and honourable connection between education and trade, industry and commerce, so that men trained in different branches of practical skill and knowledge will have a natural scope for their talents. Mere technical education, divorced from such association, can never solve the problem of unemployment. Lastly, universities must be given the amplest freedom to work out their salvation. We must free education from the undercurrents of political and communal strife. Let each university have a constitution judiciously planned on academic considerations and truly representative in character. Let the men chosen for their administration be of the right type inspired solely by the idea of training youths who will be an asset to the cause of Indian progress.

Fellow graduates, let me make it clear that while I am anxious that the university-trained youth should be saturated with the highest ideals of Indian life and culture and imbibe the best elements of western science and knowledge, I do not want him to grow up as an aggressive nationalist utterly forgetful of his ultimate loyalty to the spirit of humanity at large. Neither do I minimise the value of his attachment to his community and province. Let us, however, constantly bear in mind that the introduction of communal and sectarian factors in the field of Indian politics is sharply dividing her peoples into warring sections, each distrustful of the other. For the sake of our very existence, let us not forget the supreme need of discovering a proper synthesis between apparently conflicting interests.

To you who are about to enter the arena of life, I plead with all earnestness that whatever spheres you may work in, let your banner be a symbol not only of knowledge and enlightenment, of liberty and balanced judgment, of clean thoughts and actions, but also of unity and service. Let us remember at every step that we who call ourselves educated, exist not primarily for our own sake but for adding our individual contributions, however humble to the advancement of national prosperity. Let us learn to identify ourselves wholeheartedly with the cause of the suffering millions of our countrymen. Let no fear come to us because we have been born in an age not of peace and comfort but of restlessness and adversity.

Fortified by a supreme belief that the cause of Indian progress and freedom is just and legitimate and that India has an ennobling message to give to the rest of humanity, let us equip ourselves truly and well, and march collectively and courageously towards our cherished goal. Let us all solemnly and humbly pay our tribute of homage to the eternal spirit of our Motherland and pledge ourselves to her service in the words of the warrior poet, words which were uttered in his last convocation address by my revered father fourteen years ago and which are still ringing in my ears:

'I vow to thee, my country,
all earthly things above
Entire and whole and perfect,
the service of my love

The love that asks no question;
the love that stands the test,
That lays upon the altar
the dearest and the best;
The love that never falters,
the love that pays the price,
The love that makes undaunted
The final sacrifice.'

Speech delivered at the Nagpur University Convocation in Nagpur on 5 December 1936

9

FUNCTIONS OF A UNIVERSITY

In the sphere of academic work, in our efforts to serve the cause of intellectual advancement, we have striven to introduce gradual changes in our system, some of which are capable of far-reaching consequences. Our greatest handicap is want of funds but there can be no question that we must resolutely combine our resources to extend the facilities of education from one corner of the province to the other and also to endeavour to raise its quality in every possible manner.

While the university must always help in spreading the bounds of knowledge and also in other ways strengthen the intellectual life of the country, one of its primary duties must be to devote itself directly and indirectly to the progressive welfare of the student community in general, acting in close cooperation with schools and colleges under its jurisdiction. The university has steadily continued its policy of helping and coordinating the corporate activities of the colleges. Of the new projects already approved is the scheme for the promotion of military studies among its students, which though limited in extent, will lay the foundation for training in a sphere of activity capable of vast possibilities in building up national life and character. May I not express the hope that at no distant time our scheme will develop and

Bengal will have a fully equipped institution for imparting military training to our youths who will obtain more extensive opportunities for efficient training in this direction?

Among the schemes of expansion for the improvement of the conditions of our youths which are now engaging the attention of the university, I must mention the development of the students' welfare department which with its limited resources is now doing splendid work. We want to see established within the university a well-equipped organisation devoted entirely to the welfare of our students, which will act in cooperation with schools and colleges and with local branches created throughout the province. It must, among other things, organise after-care centres, arrange for free medical examination and treatment, supply teachers for physical training and maintain a central institute for physical training and for general promotion of health, character and efficiency. It must foster the establishment of students' organisations within each college, pledged to their own corporate welfare and controlled and managed by themselves, for which they must be genuinely encouraged to undertake responsibility. Let me emphasise that no student movement has succeeded in any country, nor will it succeed here, unless it guarantees to the students themselves all reasonable facilities for free and unrestricted development on lines best suited to their needs and to the needs of the nation. Again, we want to see established in this city special hostels, as cheaply managed as possible, open to all classes, which can accommodate an appreciable number of many of those hopeless youths who, pursued by a burning zeal for education, move about helplessly from place to place or succeed in securing shelter sometimes under humiliating conditions. These and other projects of expansion cannot be carried into effect without substantial endowments and donations; and to the State and public-spirited citizens, I earnestly appeal to come forward and help us with generous assistance.

Closely related to the welfare of the students is the recent scheme for providing practical training in the technicalities of trade and for helping our youths in other directions. Let me say at once that the university has never claimed that the problem of unemployment with which are closely connected many social, political and economic factors, can be solved single-handed by the university. What we are trying to achieve is to direct the attention of our educated youths to the supreme fact that if Bengal is to live and grow as a self-respecting province, her children must discover how they can be best prepared for and employed in various vocations in life, many of which are now closed to them, and not concentrate on jobs and services. This change of mentality and outlook will never be realised by mere advice, however wholesome. From all directions, we must start taking action no matter how modest the beginning may be. Of the various conditions which the State and society must fulfil, the university is attempting to achieve one and that is by seeking to establish a definite contact between itself and the world of business, trade and commerce, which may serve as basis for future cooperation and understanding.

I have been recently asked questions regarding the form of our celebration. We are not pledged to any particular programme. We ourselves have been making changes and any reasonable proposals for future expansion of our activities will receive due consideration by the university. But let me emphasise here once again that it was never the intention of the university that the students display that we witness here this morning should be confined to a show or demonstration organised only for the purpose of the celebration. What the university has always aimed at is that each college under its jurisdiction should steadfastly carry on a programme of corporate activities for the benefit of its students and strive to equip them for active service in different spheres of useful and constructive work. Such activities must obviously include an intensive programme of games, drills and other physical activities conducted throughout the year to which will be attracted all students of the college. At this annual celebration, friends and well-wishers of the university assemble here and witness the performance of the chosen representatives of each institution who will spontaneously come and gather under the protecting banner of their alma mater. If with the cooperation of the principals and professors and the students themselves, a scheme of work, aiming at simultaneous growth of intellect and building of health and character, steadily continues and develops, if this can gradually sow the seeds of unity, organisation and discipline even among 50 per cent of 30,000 youths who read in the colleges today, we shall be helping to create a new Bengal, a Bengal that is destined to lead and not be led, a Bengal that will produce at a moment's notice thousands of able-bodied intellectual youths—Hindus, Muslims and Christians—trained and brought up according to the highest ideals of service, capable of responding to the call of the nation and ready to unfurl the flag of truth and sincerity, of progress, unity and freedom. That was one of the principal ideals which lay behind this part of the programme of our celebration to which you, my young friends, have so nobly responded today.

If the university is to be true to its salt, if it is to fulfil its mission in awakening a true national spirit and the consciousness of the people, it must contribute in every possible way to the building up of the youth of the country and train them in all spheres of useful and constructive activity. Our resources are limited, our difficulties are formidable and the task of reconstruction that faces educational institutions is gigantic.

Though the ideal will never be reached except by united effort and tireless work, we shall never desert our post. If Bengal is again to play her part in the remaking of India, she must produce through her educational institutions a race of men and women, strong in body and mind, true, resolute and self-reliant, burning with lofty patriotism and idealism, not carried away by emotions but capable of exercising critical and reasonable judgment, trained both to be leaders and soldiers, amenable to discipline—discipline imposed by the combined will of themselves—devoted to duty, determined to work not as a class or community but in a spirit of corporate service, and ever willing to place their services in all capacities, humble and great, for the good of society and for the advancement of the highest interest of the nation. Let us not for a moment consider the attainment of this ideal to be an impossibility. Has not Bengal produced generations of men who nobly played their parts in the regeneration of their Motherland? Let the sacred memories of such men ever permeate the atmosphere of the university and its educational institutions, and let them serve to remind the university, its teachers and students, that we who work in this sphere of national activity are charged with a tremendous responsibility which we can never shake off.

I pray from the bottom of my heart that the university may now and forever be the national home of progressive culture and enlightenment, the torchbearer of knowledge and freedom and bring to its doors all classes and communities, who may be willing to join us in serving the cause of education and sow far and wide permanent seeds of national development. If the university's band has opened today's proceedings by playing to tune the opening lines of a celebrated national song or if you are ready to sing in chorus a song specially composed by Rabindranath, all this serves a deep and significant purpose. That purpose is nothing more or nothing less than to invoke, in the performance of our daily duties of reconstruction, the sacred name of our Motherland, to sound the clarion call of unity to one and all—Hindus, Muslims and Christians—make a fervent appeal to them to place the interest of the country, whether it is theirs by birth or adoption, above every other interest or consideration, to bow their heads in the deepest loyalty and reverence to her unconquerable spirit and pledge themselves to her eternal welfare and prosperity.

Speech delivered at the foundation day of the University of Calcutta in 30 January 1937

10

UNIVERSITY EDUCATION AND OUR DESTINY

In recent years, occasions like the present [annual convocation] one, have been utilised with remarkable zeal for discussing problems of educational reconstruction in India. I am inclined to think that public attention has been sufficiently stirred by such utterances and by the publication of numerous reports, pamphlets and addresses. And the time has now come for initiating a new policy of education, suited to our needs and aspirations and consistent with the best traditions of our past. That the aim and outlook of Indian universities should be altered in many respects in the light of our changing conditions is acknowledged by all schools of thought. The future policy in respect of Indian universities must, however, be one of progressive expansion and not of short-sighted curtailment.

Those who advocate restriction either of a direct or of an indirect nature, base their suggestions on two main grounds. They argue that a large number of university men do not find suitable employment for want of either opportunities or necessary training; further that the universities admit many into their portals who are not fit to receive higher education. Even assuming the criticism to be partially correct, the remedy obviously is not artificial restriction of the number of university students, but the provision of sounder preliminary training, the introduction of an improved system of education, varied and diversified in character, the creation of fresh opportunities for work and the opening of new avenues of employment to absorb the constructive energies of the youths of the country. Surely, the existence of seventeen universities with a little above a lakh of students receiving training under their influence is not an alarmingly large number for a country like India which has a population of more than 300 million. Instead of merely criticising the policy pursued by the universities, let our critics help in introducing a new era of constructive efforts towards the establishment of special institutions and departments, technical, industrial, agriculture and commercial, for imparting a thorough training to youths for varied occupations in life and for national service.

Let me, however, emphasise that the mere production of such trained youths will not solve the problem, that it will be the bounden duty of the State and other authorities so to readjust and modify their policies affecting the economic and political conditions of society as fully to utilise their services in a useful and productive manner. Such a policy of educational reconstruction, enunciated and carried out solely for the advancement of India's interest, requires a very large expenditure of money from the public exchequer. It is futile merely to talk of defects and shortcomings, of ill-equipped schools, colleges and of universities with their ill-trained alumni. No reforms of a far-reaching character are possible so long as out of the total revenues of British India only 5 per cent goes to education, 34 per cent being reserved for defence, for police and jails. It is to be hoped that with the inauguration of the new constitutional changes, education and other nation-building departments will receive their legitimate shares out of the revenues of the country.

The universities in India today are threatened with attacks from two classes of critics. One, as I have said, urges artificial reduction in their number and in the sphere of their influence, justifying its policy on the plea of academic efficiency, though some of its champions are consciously or unconsciously impelled by the fear that education may break down the barriers of superstition and slavery and lead men along the path of equality, liberty and progress. The other, often unthinking and short-sighted, regards higher education as an unnecessary luxury benefiting a comparatively small number of people and of doubtful value to the largest interests of the nation.

We have to guard against both these classes. We must boldly assert and prove that a university if properly conducted, can be the home of progressive thought and culture; it can be the mouthpiece of national hopes and aspirations; it can be the recognised medium for conserving and advancing the bounds of knowledge, and for preserving and raising the intellectual life and thought of a nation, breathing an atmosphere of freedom and truth, drawing together men and women of all castes and creeds, inspired by a zeal for devoted and unselfish service. Indeed, there should be no question of conflict between the different stages of education: primary, secondary and university; and each should receive the unstinted support of the State and the public.

Students of the university, let me now address a few words to you directly and through you to others who are still pursuing their studies. You are about to enter the arena of life and whatever trials and responsibilities you might have had to face in the past are nothing in comparison with what await you in the days to come. It may be that some of you will achieve success from a worldly point of view and attain fame and wealth in your respective professions; there may be others amongst you who may pursue the path of scholarship and learning or follow other walks of life, beneficial to society but not highly lucrative; there may be still others who may have to spend their days in comparative obscurity or may not attain worldly success at all. Some of you will become leaders and issue commands; others will learn to carry them out, all acting for the common welfare.

But whatever may be your lot in future, are you carrying away with you any special traditions, do you feel inspired by any ideals, which will mark you out as men and women different from those who have not passed through the doors of universities? Apart from imbibing information and knowledge in the special subjects of your study, do you not regard yourselves as messengers of a new hope, faith and courage, which it will be your duty to instil into others to whom the gates of knowledge yet remain closed? Inspiration comes not from books and study alone. Your determination to serve the cause of your people cannot come merely from reading stories of similar efforts made in other countries.

Your faith in truth, simplicity in life and uprightness of character and conduct is not to be derived from any dry and academic theories. Your striving after intellectual supremacy or your exertion in the cause of economic and political freedom is not of men with no history or civilisation of their own.

Has not your own province for centuries past been a scene of activities of eminent persons, whose names are remembered with gratitude and affection throughout the country, names which will never be blotted out from the memory of any self-respecting Indian? They stand out as illustrious workers in diverse fields of activity, in the pursuit of culture and knowledge, in the study of literature and languages, in art and architecture, in social, educational and humanitarian work, in commerce and industry and last but not least in the great movement for India's struggle for the attainment of swaraj. If Shivaji coined the expression *swaraj* 300 years ago, Bal Gangadhar Tilak brought it back to the minds of the sleeping millions of modern India and roused their energies to constructive work which has had far-reaching effects on the destiny of our country. Let us pay our unstinted homage to and draw inspiration from such names as Dadabhai Naoroji, Pherozeshah Mehta and Gokhale; Agharkar, Namjoshi and Apte; Telang, Bhandarkar and Bhagwan Lal Indraji; Ranade, Wacha and Chandaverkar; Mandlik and Badruddin Tyabji, Rajwade and Chiplunkar; Jamshedji Tata and Jeejeebhoy, Wadia and Thackersey, names taken at random of persons who are no longer in the land of the living, names which recall loyalty to duty, persistent constructive activities, fearless advocacy of truth and justice, steadfast devotion to culture and scholarship, honesty and sincerity of purpose, sufferings and triumphs in the cause of national progress and prosperity. Of those living, the name of Mahatma Gandhi naturally comes uppermost in our minds as one whose greatness and goodness have given India a new position in the eyes of the world.

Traditions such as these should fill you with both pride and responsibility. Of what practical value will these traditions be if you do not mould your own lives and activities in accordance with the ideals of your chosen hero? What will these traditions be worth if you do not link them with the changing needs and aspirations of society and hold them in correct perspective before the people at large who do not always know what their true heritage is?

You have drunk deep at the springs of western knowledge. While you will not hesitate to absorb for your benefit and for the national good the best elements in western culture and thought, you will not in any case permit the destruction of the vital elements of your own civilisation. As true sons and daughters of Bombay, you will of course strive for the increasing greatness of your presidency and be loyal to her in thought and action; but never disown your allegiance to the spirit of your beloved Motherland and whenever the occasion needs it, do not hesitate to proclaim yourselves as Indians first and anything else next. One feels distressed to find the recent growth of communal and provincial feelings, which unless checked are bound to retard the progress of Indian nationalism. I need not enquire into the origin of these differences, but it is true that if the idea of Indian unity is to grow permanently, it can do so mainly by the determined efforts of the youth of the nation. And who else can sound this call to unity than you who are entering into the fields of public activity after a full intellectual preparation, ready to face the struggles of life?

Let us unreservedly stand by our conviction that whatever our detractors may say, Indian universities are bound to play a large and noble part in the emergence of a new India which will be the mistress of her own destinies, the proud inheritor of an ancient civilisation, rebuilt and reshaped with the changing requirements of the age. Let us stand united to make our universities centres of culture, and independent thought nurseries of honest and open-minded teachers and scholars pursuing and advancing knowledge, from which will go forth manly and useful citizens, brave and self-reliant, patriotic and fair-minded, capable of making sacrifices and judging issues and problems critically and fearlessly. Let Indian universities mould their activities in full remembrance of the fact that the progress of a nation, if steadily maintained, can alone prevent degeneration, that there must be new life and purpose or there will be weakness and decay. At this crisis in the history of human civilisation, when cherished doctrines of liberty and democracy are often discarded and freedom of thought and opinion suppressed, let Indian universities and their sons and daughters proclaim the noblest ideals of Indian teachings and thought, which may once again secure for her that supremacy in the world of intellect which is truly her birthright. And let the Indian universities prove to the world that India can achieve this simultaneously with a progressive and systematic pursuit of western knowledge itself. Let Indian universities be the worthy participators in a constant movement towards a higher and nobler civilisation, a civilisation that will make its conquests without resort to war or oppression and achieve its greatest victories pursuing the path of peace and justice.

Friends and fellow graduates, let a fervent prayer go forth from every member of this assembly in the soul-stirring words of Rabindranath Tagore that we may face our duties and responsibilities with courage and fortitude and make our contributions, however humble, to the cause of national welfare:

'Let honour come to me from Thee
Through a call to some desperate task
In the pride of poignant suffering.

Lull me not into languid dreams,
Shake me out of this cringing in the dust
Out of the fetters that shackle our mind,
Make futile our destiny,

Out of the unreason that bends our dignity down
Under the indiscriminate feet of dictations,
Shatter this age-long shame of ours
And raise our head
Into the boundless sky,
Into the generous light,
Into the air of freedom.'

Speech delivered at the annual convocation of the University of Bombay on 17 August 1937

11

ROLE OF THE UNIVERSITIES IN MAKING THE NATION

You will forgive me if I do not make educational reconstruction the main theme of my disclosure today. So much has recently been said on the subject that it may perhaps be more useful if we cease for a while from speculating on theories and concentrate on carrying out our declared policies, keeping in view the cardinal truth that India stands in need of a wide and progressive expansion of educational facilities from the lowest to the highest stage and not their curtailment in any form whatsoever.

As I stand in the historic city of Patna, the ancient Pataliputra, I feel tempted to trace some of the fundamental features of our civilisation in the majestic march of Indian history, not with the knowledge of historian—for I lack such qualifications—but as a layman, a humble worker, who takes pride in the glories of our past history and longs for the day when this great land of ours may again claim her rightful place among the nations of the world and provide for the millions of her sons and daughters a higher and nobler life in all spheres—social, political, economic and cultural.

India has been styled on epitome of the world. This city, which was the capital of the imperial Mauryas and the Guptas, the scene of the activities of Bhadrabahu and of Sher Shah and the birthplace of Guru Govind Singh, may well be described as an epitome of the land of Hindus and Muslims, Jains and Sikhs. From time immemorial, it has been known for its toleration and catholicity, its love of learning and love of men. From the region where the waters of the Sone unite with the mainstream of Ganges, issued those messages of overflowing love towards the men and even dumb animals which made the name of Asoka immortal. His edicts carved on rock and pillar throughout his vast empire served as a source of inspiration to rulers, statesmen and philanthropists. To the city of Pataliputra flocked merchants, diplomats, savants and sages, students and enquirers from all quarters of the civilised world.

The welcome extended to the visitors from distant lands was only equalled by the solicitude shown for the material comfort of the humblest among men. The free hospitals for the metropolis were open to all, irrespective of caste or creed. Toleration and concord were the watchwords of the rulers; benevolence and righteousness inspired their subjects at large. The province that boasted of Pataliputra included within its boundaries Uruvilva and Nalanda, Uddandapur and Bikramasila, the centres of Gautama's enlightenment, of Shilabhadra's discourse, of Gopala's piety and of Dharmmapala's charity. The massive towers and fairy like turrets of Nalanda and her sister cities were visible symbols of that solid learning, high aspiration and conspicuous talent for which those great seats of the spiritual and intellectual life of India were justly famous.

India has had a splendid past. Many were the epochs when she lay safely anchored in a heaven. But at times storm and wind battered her masts and threatened to throw her precious burthen overboard. Nature, while impressing on her the stamp of unity by encircling her with lofty mountains and rocking seas, left gaps through which successive waves of invasion swept into the interior and brought ideals and ways of life that did not always fit in with her environments. In the interior itself, the hand of nature has drawn lines by rock and wood that proved serious impediments in the way of developing a common national life. But in spite of these, our forefathers did not despair of their country and we have had brilliant epochs in the history of India when she could justly claim respectful attention from the civilised world. There were times when the political unification of the country ceased to be a mere dream of poets and patriots and came near a historical reality, resulting in an outburst of activity in the domain of religion, literature, science and art, comparable to that of Greece of Pericles or the England of Elizabeth.

That splendour was by no means ephemeral. Indian culture has retained its vigour and vitality and has found a worthy place among the civilisations of all ages. The pyramids bear mute testimony to a vanished civilisation on the banks of the Nile, the winged bulls are but lifeless relics of another culture that once flourished on the banks of the Euphrates and the Tigris, the ruins of Persepolis and Susa are today but subjects of antiquarian interest. Greece has achieved her political independence but the old Hellenic civilisation has disappeared for good like the Medusa and the Minotaur.

Here in our land, however, the Hindu still chants the Vedic hymns on the banks of the sacred rivers, the Buddha, sangha and dhamma are still invoked by millions of devotees from the mysterious heights of Fuziyama to far-off Adam's Peak. The civilisation of India is still alive; its philosophy and teachings still inspire millions of human beings, although Indian culture no longer finds its stimulating support from an independent nation state. We must attribute its success to its catholicity and universal sympathy.

The ancient Aryans did not revel in destruction for its own sake, they believed in assimilation and improvement. The Macedonian and the Greek, the Saka and the Kushan came to conquer and slay but remained to wonder and pray. It has been often asserted that the polytheistic Hindu failed to establish a spiritual kinship with the monotheistic Muslim who held much that is Indian in scorn and still seeks his spiritual inspiration abroad. How can we say that India ignored the teachings of Islam when we find saints like Nanak and Chaitanya, Namdev and Tukaram preaching the brotherhood of man and the futility of caste in matters spiritual? Although attempts on Hindu cultures and institutions fill the pages of Indian history, how can we assert that Muslims ignored the appeal of Hindu culture when we find Muhammad Jayasi weaving a beautiful romance to illustrate the teachings of Hindu philosophy, when we read the simple devotional hymns of Kabir and Sheikh Farid, who refused to recognise the barriers of caste and creed on the high road to God's kingdom? 'Utter not one disagreeable word,' said Farid, 'since the true Lord is in all men.

Distress no one's heart for every heart is a precious jewel.' In the same strain did Kabir proclaim, 'There is the same God for the Hindus as for Muslims.' A rejuvenated India found an Akbar to put an end to political chaos and social disharmony and a Shah Jehan to dream a dream in marble the like of which is not to be met with in the world.

India did not confine her attention to her adopted children alone. Whenever the stranger stood in need of spiritual solace, she ungrudgingly gave of her best. Did not she send a prince and a princess from this very city more than 2,000 years ago to the land of the Yakshas to teach them the supreme truth that the only way to happiness lies in non-violence and renunciation? Did not the imperial ascetic send the same message to the far-off lands of Egypt, Asia Minor and Greece? Did not this country spare her very best Dipankara, when Tibet and Sumatra stood in sore need of him? That tradition is not altogether dead even now. Only the other day, Swami Vivekananda bore the message of Paramhansa Ramakrishna and of India's storied past and taught the true path to peace and happiness to a struggling materialistic world, suffering from the evils of its very greatness. And today every civilised country in the world finds in Mahatma Gandhi a new messenger of peace, an embodiment of truth and non-violence who can brave the wrath of the mightiest and suffer nobly and patiently for the sake of its ideal. Do we not find again in Sister Nivedita and Mira Ben the representative of those pilgrims who have been coming to us all through the ages in search of the truth eternal?

It may be asked that if such has been the greatness of India as a home of culture and thought, why is it that she lost her political independence and has become a subject nation? Would it be true to say that the catholicity and universal sympathy which contributed so much to the everlasting freshness of India's civilisation, concealed in them the germs of her political downfall? Did they engender that other-worldliness which spelt ruin to the prospect of India's freedom? History supplies the answer. Did not India produce Chandragupta and Samudragupta, Pratap Singh, Shivaji and Ranjit Singh, in spite of the pacific teachings of our ancestors? Did not the nameless but illustrious heroes, the Indian Argonauts, who explored the mysteries of the unchartered seas and spread Indian culture to the furthest east, prove that Hindu pacifism did not eliminate enterprise and love of adventure? Indian sages and philosophers never suggested that cowards and weaklings would ever be the torchbearers of India's great heritage. *Naymatmabalhinenlabhya*: None but the valiant can achieve salvation. India's culture has not been responsible for India's bondage. That culture transplanted to the Himalayas and beyond has not taken the edge off the martial spirit of Mongolian races.

Is it then her climate that deteriorated the sturdy Aryan, Turk and Afghan in turn? If this were so, how are we to account for the rise of the Marathas and Rohillas, the Jats and the Sikhs? How are we to explain the resurrection of Rajputs? How could Hyder Ali of Mysore hold his own against the Marathas and the English? It is not the climate; it is not the culture; we must seek the cause of our downfall elsewhere.

India fell mainly because her people were at the critical hour divided and disorganised. Her influence waned when the forces of disintegration, political and social, were at work. If we left our neighbours alone, we revelled in internal strife which ceased for a time when great kings like Asoka and Akbar ruled over the destinies of India—mighty men, who sought to unite the teeming millions of this vast subcontinent by the bond of a common aspiration and a passionate longing for the eternal code of righteous conduct, charity and understanding. A strong and united India fearing none and loving all, brought the message of peace and goodwill to a distracted world. But as soon as the sceptre dropped from their hands, when their grip over the country was loosened through weak and short-sighted successors, when narrow selfishness and mutual jealousy and distrust overpowered our souls, when local feuds and religious strife raised their ugly heads giving rise to social exclusiveness and moral decadence, unity was lost; freedom, man's priceless treasure, disappeared; the country broke into fragments and relapsed into a state of conflict and struggle. While the national and political unity of India was successfully achieved by great individuals, the masses did not at all times feel an abiding interest in its preservation. Thus although all culture has survived the storm and stress of time, we find ourselves in the strange and tragic position of the representatives and exponents of an ancient civilisation, yet alive but in bondage.

We may pertinently ask ourselves at this stage whether the forces of disruption that have effectively blocked the path of Indian progress in the past, have reacted more satisfactorily to their present environments, social, political, economic. It is obviously not possible for me here to deal with the history of the British connection with India except to make some very general observations. The English came to India as traders and ultimately remained as masters of an empire. During the last century and a half, we have witnessed the progress of India in various directions. Stability, peace and order have been generally restored. The benefits of science, which have revolutionised civilisation and have affected the lives of men and nations to an unprecedented extent, have penetrated into this great and ancient land, leading to considerable material progress. Western education has helped to broaden our outlook, deepen the sense of patriotism and lay the foundation of consciousness. Ideas of liberty and equality have slowly but steadily percolated from one corner of Hindustan to another and we witness the ever-increasing vitality of Indian nationalism. A spirit of inquisitiveness has captured the minds of Indians who have proved their worth in various domains of thought and activity. Many social evils have been uprooted and there is a general desire for uplifting the masses so that they may live more useful and noble lives.

While the progress of Indians on such lines is attributable to a large extent to western influence, no self-respecting Indian can ignore the vitals defects and limitations of our national life. We must boldly take stock of the things that we have lost and yearn for. We find a general decay of the creative Indian arts which once triumphantly flourished in this land, and produced the frescos of Ajanta and the Taj of Agra. Indian music, Indian art and architecture, and Indian literature were not systematically and adequately patronised and that they have not entirely disappeared today is due mainly to the persistent efforts of individual workers. We witness the decline and disappearance of the indigenous industries of India which mainly thrived in her own towns and villages. Such cottage industries, if they are to be revived, developed and saved from foreign competition require the unstinted support of the State. We find also deplorable neglect of the health and welfare of the villages of India which are today but shadows of their former affluence and happiness. Indeed much of India's poverty and distress is traced to a systematic pursuit of an economic and industrial policy which has not been prompted and administered in the sole interest of India and her inhabitants.

One of the most staggering features of Indian life of today is the illiteracy and ignorance of more than 90 per cent of the people and for this no plea or excuse will ever be accepted by any impartial historian. One other vital weakness about which Indians feel bitterly is that they have not been adequately trained to defend their own hearth and home. An autonomous India is unthinkable without a national army and a national navy controlled and manned by Indians themselves. It is not correct to assume that many of the peoples of India are devoid of military or naval traditions. Indian history gives ample evidence of collective courage and heroism. If there are parts of the country where youths have today become feeble in health and energy, surely the remedy lies not in condemning them for eternity but in training them up for competent services.

I do not forget that in recent times efforts are being made to meet some of our vital needs. But no reforms of a radical character in any field of activity will ever be possible, nor can India rise to her full stature spiritually and economically, until and unless she takes her rank among the free nations of the world. No material gain, no earthly possession can ever compensate for the loss of man's liberty. The conflict of ideals and interests between a subject race and the power that wants to hold it in its leading strings is as old as history itself; it can be solved peacefully and amicably only if the latter accords to the former the same treatment as it demands from others in respect of its own rights and privileges.

In defining freedom, I can do no better than follow the language of a British peer, a statesman and a philosopher, who has dealt with the question with remarkable lucidity in one of his recent books. What, he asks, is the ultimate goal of enlightened man? The answer is that one of the aims is that the nation should be free from alien domination. What, he asks, should be the pattern set for civilised mankind? The answer is, within the nation individual should be free, free to think, worship, speak and act as he would, subject to the similar rights of others, free under the protection of the equal justice to pursue his lawful business as he chooses. Men should no longer be bound down from birth to death by the hampering restrictions that come from bondage, poverty, overwork and environment. Freedom consists not only in the absence of restraint but also in the presence of opportunity. Liberty is not a single and simple conception. It has four elements—national, political, personal, economic. The man who is fully free is one who lives in a country which is independent; in a State which is democratic; in a society where the laws are equal and restrictions at a minimum; in an economic system in which national interests are protected and the citizen has the scope of a secure livelihood, an assured comfort and full opportunity to rise by merit.

This freedom, so truly and courageously defined, is not ours today and until this condition is reached, India will never achieve true greatness or happiness, based on the glorious features of her past civilisation.

The Indian universities, if they are to play their role in the rebuilding of a new India, must not regard themselves as exclusive institutions which exist apart from the currents of the country's life. Let them train their alumni in a worthy manner, saturate them with the lessons of Indian history and civilisations, instil into them unity and reason, strength and dauntlessness, inspire them with skill and knowledge and teach them to apply themselves devotedly and unselfishly to the service of their fellowman. Let the teachers of the universities consider it their sacred duty to be the interpreters of India's heritage, the seekers of truth and knowledge, and prove to the world that Indian scholars are second to none in their efforts to serve the cause of the humanities and the sciences in relation to the unfettered progress of India and of human civilisation itself.

Speech delivered at the Patna University Convocation on 27 November 1937

12

FORGING THE FUTURE THROUGH UNIVERSITIES IN INDIA

Your university cannot claim a long history bearing marks of the toil of generations, but within the short period of its existence, it has secured fame and a reputation peculiar to itself which have justly won for it an abiding place in the hearts of millions of our countrymen. Yours is a great seat of learning that has sprung into life amidst surroundings which reminds of all that is best in Indian civilisation. Your renowned city was the metropolis of a philosopher king of the Upanishadic age and the home of Parsvanatha, the celebrated Tirthankara of the Jainas. It stands in the vicinity of the holy steps where Gautama Buddha preached his first sermon, where Shankaracharya distinguished himself in dialectics and philosophy, where Tulsidas wrote his immortal songs, and where Shri Chaitanya distributed the nectar of divine love to high and low. Indeed, that great son of India whose name will forever be enshrined in the hearts of his countrymen, not only as the most illustrious of your founders but also as one of the makers of New India, could not have selected a more appropriate site for the Hindu University of Hindustan. May your university produce sages like Silabhadra and ardent missionaries like Dipankara who made this country the intellectual centre of the east and carried the torch of Indian civilisation beyond the heights of the Himalayas and across the shores of the southern sea. Advancing years have now left their mark on the health of Pandit Malaviya, and I voice the sentiments of all sections of Indians throughout the country when I pray that he may yet be spared for a long number of years to see the ever-increasing development of his beloved university as an active and progressive seat of learning dedicated to the service of the nation. The present distinguished occupant of the office of vice chancellor commands universal respect and confidence and the destinies of this university could not have been entrusted to a worthier person, whether from this country or from abroad.

I shall not attempt to analyse in detail the activities of your university but I must pay my tribute to the solid progress you have made in diverse branches of knowledge—literary, philosophical, scientific and technical. Scholars have flocked to your portals from distant parts of India, attracted by the richness and variety of facilities offered by you. The reputation of some of your departments, especially in the domain of science and engineering, has gone far beyond the limits of this province. If large and generous benefactions have enabled you to erect imposing and commodious buildings which have helped to create a beautiful city of your own, you have also been able to attract to your halls a long line of devoted teachers who have considered it their sacred duty to dedicate themselves to the cause of knowledge. I know financial difficulties have often been a matter of deep anxiety to the authorities of the university, and it is all the greater reason that one should gratefully acknowledge the spirit of sacrifice that has animated the members of your staff who have cheerfully carried on their work, often in spite of great financial uncertainties. I hope the State will do its obvious duty towards this great national institution and, by giving you the necessary financial relief, will enable you to march along, with vigour and courage, on the path of progress and expansion.

Your university has paid and will pay due homage to the cause of spread of knowledge in its diverse branches, but I would also ask you to fulfil in an abundant measure your obligations for the revival of the glory of Hindu culture and civilisation, not from a narrow or bigoted point of view but for strengthening the very root of nationalism in this country. In this great land of ours where twenty-eight crore of Hindus live, the word Hindu sometimes stinks in the nostrils of many a son of India. A reorientation of Hindu culture and ideals, of which your present vice chancellor [Sarvepalli Radhakrishnan] is one of the ablest exponents, will not only help to bring back to India that political freedom which she has lost but will also raise the soul of mankind throughout the earth to a higher level of thought and action.

As a university you have a great role to play in reshaping the destinies of the people of your country. We must bear in mind the cardinal principle that we want to see developed and trained through education the whole nature of our alumni, intellectual, moral and physical, not merely for the purpose of qualifying for any special calling but to bring up good citizens, useful members of society, men, true and fearless capable of bearing their part with credit in public and private life. Such university-trained men are needed in rich abundance in India today.

Interested persons often try to raise a controversy about the relative claims of elementary education and higher education in India forgetting the fact that the university expresses the corporate longing of the people for the higher things of the spirit. As university men, we want that elementary education should spread from one part of the country to the other and that provision should be made for this purpose in a liberal and unstinted manner. Indeed, the failure of the government, which has remained in dominant authority in India for more than a century and a half, to discharge this obligation is regarded as one of the black spots in its administration. Let us not, however, forget that eminent thinkers in countries where elementary education is both free and compulsory have felt that such an instruction unless crowned by something which is higher, is not only barren but may even be dangerous. It is not enough to teach our democracy to read unless we also teach it to think. It is the ignorant and unthinking mind, with its trivialities, its uncertainties, and its clouded vision, from which we have most to fear.

Another class of critics in our country often advocates the curtailment of university education in view of the increasing acuteness of the problem of unemployment. The universities of India have on their rolls a little over one lakh of students, which constitute an insignificant proportion of India's population of thirty-five crore. It is not feasible for the university to find employment for all its alumni, although the university should do all it can to establish close contact with those men and institutions that control the fields of commerce, business and industry. These must know and understand one another and work in harmony for the larger welfare of the community. It is indeed one of the primary duties of the State, more than that of anybody else, to solve the problem of unemployment. In a country such as ours, where so much still remains to be done, where more than thirty crore of people are still illiterate and the task of spreading the light of knowledge alone may occupy the energy of tens of thousands of educated youths, where raw materials still remain in perpetual abundance and are often at the mercy of exploiters and adventurers, where industrial expansion absorbing the valued services of thousands of skilled technicians yet receive only half-hearted recognition from the State, where the vital agencies of national defence such as the army, the navy and the air force have yet to expand on an all-India basis, thrown open to all classes of people, free from artificial restrictions—in a country such as ours it is amazing that unemployment should stare ardent educated Indian youths in the face and that unpatriotic demands should be made for arbitrary restriction of higher education. It is true that no country can have a truly national system of education unless it enjoys the blessings of freedom. But let the universities within their limited sphere do their duty with courage and foresight and so readjust and reorganise their courses of study that they may worthily meet the manifold requirements of our country in diverse fields of public service—social, industrial, economic and political.

An important subject to which I should like to refer is the progress of science and industry in this country. Faced as we are with international conflicts of gigantic proportions, it does not require much imagination to see that the scientific and industrial development of a country is essential not only for its prosperity but also for its very existence. In this sphere, the universities in advanced countries, backed by liberal and active support from their governments, have played a vital part. The industrial development of a country is, however, conditioned not only by research but also by the all-important questions of finance and national policy. In Germany, as is well known, the intimate cooperation among the government, universities and the industrial organisations resulted in a very rapid development, although the industrial revolution came to that country considerably later than in Great Britain. Both in Japan and in Soviet Russia, it is the driving force of the government, mobilising and coordinating all the resources of the countries that has led to their phenomenal industrial progress in recent years.

In this country, by contrast, we have a tragic story to tell. The universities and the industrialists with their limited means have been ploughing practically lonely furrows. The university laboratories, particularly, have worked under great handicaps, which have been only partially lightened by the generous donations of a few benefactors. It is absolutely clear that unless the government of the country pursues a settled and irrevocable policy of industrialisation and adopts coordinated measures for furtherance of this object, industrial progress in this country can at best be only fitful. The danger of this industrial backwardness does not require any emphasis today. Even the Famine Commission of 1880 recognised that the problem of the dreadful poverty of the Indian people could not be tackled by improvement in agriculture alone, but required also the improvement of industries. The war of 1914-18 again threw into relief the pathetic industrial helplessness of India and the Indian Industrial Commission was appointed in 1916 to make remedial recommendations. But this commission was specifically debarred from entering into the question of tariffs or any other aspect of the fiscal policy of the Government of India. 'The part of Hamlet must be totally omitted,' Sir Frederick Nicholson honestly declared in his statement to the commission. The commission, nevertheless, made some fairly comprehensive recommendations within the province allotted to it. Although the able minute given separately by Pandit Madan Mohan Malaviya showed that even these fell short of public expectation and had some serious defects, there was no indication that they were going to be implemented by the government. A series of conferences met, but the situation remained practically where it had been. It was indeed clear that the government had no heart in a policy of industrialisation, and it has required the war of 1939 to quicken the government again to some semblance of action. The Board of Scientific and Industrial Research, which was long overdue, has been set up with a grant of five lakh rupees, which is all too meagre for research in government laboratories and universities. The corresponding organisation in Great Britain was set up in 1916 and it now enjoys an annual grant of a crore of rupees. Even the National Research Council in Canada, which has a population of only a crore and a quarter, has got an annual grant of about thirteen lakh rupees from its government.

It is not yet clear whether the government, in the midst of this deepening crisis, still realises that the industrialisation of India is the sine qua non for the safety of India, that the rejection of a full-fledged policy of industrialisation would be tantamount to a betrayal of the people of this country. Our universities have their brains, their laboratories and their workshops, and in a very large measure they can deliver the goods. Benares has amply demonstrated this in her own limited sphere. But where is the evidence that the government is eager or even prepared to mobilise these resources for a policy of industrialisation, which, in order to be effective must not be confined to munitions industries alone but to all heavy and light industries necessary both in peace and in war? Are we sure that the Eastern Group Conference will assist this all-round industrialisation of India? Or is India going to supply chiefly the raw materials, and perhaps steel, for industries to be built up in countries other than India? And is this going to be done in the name of rationalisation and coordination of war effort? The other day the leader of an important delegation to this conference suggested, with reference to the aircraft industry, that since it was already developed in Australia, the best rationalisation of war effort would be affected by the expansion of that industry in Australia and not so much by the creation of aircraft industries *de novo*. There is a genuine apprehension that the industrialisation of India may still be prevented by vested interests and by the inertia of the old policy. Great things can yet be achieved if only the Government of India would realise the danger of adhering to the policy of retaining India as only a market for manufactured goods, of exploiting her raw materials for the benefit of foreign capital, and of regarding Indians as only hewers of wood and drawers of water. If the government, universities and industrial organisations are made to participate in a national policy of intensive industrialisation, none can resist the early attainment of India's economic freedom. Deputation of a few hundred Indians for training in British factories can hardly meet our need and aspirations.

If the State policy hitherto pursued has hampered industrial progress on rational lines consistent with our vast resources and national requirements, there is another direction in which much fuller cooperation is possible, and is indeed essential, between the State and the Indian universities, and this relates to the preparation of our youths for efficient and adequate military training in accordance with the needs of modern warfare. It is not for me to stress here the history of the control of the Indianisation of the so-called Indian army. But I believe there is none today who will deny that the policy of keeping Indians unarmed and unprepared for national defence has not only put this country in a highly perilous state but has practically emasculated the manhood of India. Indian universities should demand with one voice the provision for compulsory military training fully related to mechanised warfare. The existing arrangements for the University Training Corps constitute a most niggardly acknowledgment of the rights of Indian youths. Only the other day, one of the able representatives of your province in the Council of State raised the question of reorganising the University Training Corps as mechanised units. The characteristic reply of the Defence Department was 'heartfelt sympathy' with the proposal but 'great practical difficulties' in accepting it.

It is not want of funds or want of resources that constitutes the stumbling block. Such difficulties are not insuperable. It is the absence of the will, it is that old deep-rooted distrust and apprehension of possible repercussions that stand in the way of taking effective steps for militarising the youth of India. What has England not done for her own sake in her home territory since 1939? Are not stupendous difficulties melting away before the call of national service and solidarity? Today, the European War threatens the destruction of civilisation itself. Whatever the merits or demerits of the respective combatants, philosophy, logic or reason will not weigh with any of them at a time when moral forces have almost ceased to function, and that power will be the ultimate victor which has at its disposal the largest supply of brainpower and those forces of defence and offence which the knowledge and skill of man can invent. We are repeatedly told that India may become a part of the war zone sooner than many of us expect. If that be so, it is essential that the defence of India against foreign aggression and from internal chaos should be well-organised and broad-based on gigantic efforts of Indians themselves. Some progress has been made recently, but we are satisfied neither with the extent of the arrangement nor, what is more vital, with the policy behind them. The Indian universities should, within their limited sphere, be taken into full confidence and the youth of India should be thoroughly trained to defend their hearth and home just as the children of every free country claim to do.

A good deal of confusion prevails today about the ethical doctrine of ahimsa. There is no doubt ahimsa is one of the cardinal virtues taught by Indian thinkers of all denominations throughout the ages. 'Dharma' consists in ahimsa, proclaims the Mahabharata:

Ahimsa Lakshano Dharma
Iti dharmavido viluh.

'Ahimsa confers immortality,' declares the Code of Manu. The doctrine of ahimsa is a necessary corollary to the Hindu belief that the supreme spirit pervades the universe (*Sarvam brahmam idam jagat*), that everything is strung on the Blessed Lord as rows of gems upon a thread *(Sarvamidamprotkam sutra mani gananaiva*), and that welfare of all beings (*Sarvabhutahita*) is a sacred duty. Ahimsa doubtless implies abstention from selfish and aggressive violence. But does it signify inertia and pacifism under all circumstances? Did not Shri Ramachandra, so kind to righteous men and women, including even *Nishadas* and *Savaras*, wage a war to punish the arrogant evil-doer who insulted womanhood and violated the sanctity of the peaceful hermitage? Were not *"Panchajanyasyanirghosho gandivasya cha nisvanah"* meant to strike terror into the hearts of those whose pride and conceit would not allow them to do justice and repair wrongs? Did not Shri Chaitanya roar like Narasimha to restrain the bigot and the oppressor? Did not the great Asoka himself lay as much stress on *Parakrama* (prowess) as on ahimsa and declare in one of his rock edicts that there was a limit to his forbearance? 'Should anyone do him wrong, that must be borne with by his Sacred Majesty so far it can possibly be borne with.' Even Buddhist theologians prescribed condign punishment for treachery and mischief-making, typified by the career of Devadatta.

Readers of the Chachnama need not be told what pusillanimity masquerading as religious quietism may do to endanger the life and liberty of a people and destroy its morale.

If I have understood the history of my country aright, a pacifism that refuses to take up arms against injustice and makes one a passive spectator of oppression and aggression does not represent the real teaching of India. Let us not forget that valour was greatly esteemed by the sages and free rulers of India in olden times; when valour languished, the entire polity weakened. When the sword and the book of knowledge [were] kept together, justice, equity and liberty ruled the affairs of the State. We want to see the reappearance of the ancient spirit of valour tempered with a spiritual wisdom consistent with our genius and present needs, which alone can recover civilisation out of the chaotic condition of the modern age.

We live in an age when the need of *parakrama*, ceaseless exertion, courage and valour in all spheres of activity affecting the public weal, is more imperative than ever. The menace of invasion from without is within the bounds of possibility. Disruptive forces are at work within the country itself. A nation can only save itself by its own energy. But energy and strength hardly come to a people that do not enjoy the blessings of unity and freedom. Unity need not imply uniformity in every respect. In a country like India, with its huge extent, teeming population and diverse culture, a dull uniformity is not to be encouraged. India is traditionally a land of village republics, and local autonomy has had many noble champions whose patriotism and public spirit are beyond question. But accentuation of differences cannot make for strength. A divided India was always a prey to the foreign invader from the days of Alexander and Mahmud of Ghazni to those of Vasco da Gama, Duplex and Clive. There is much disharmony and disunity in India today. Communal differences have taken such an acute turn that fantastic claims for the vivisection of our Motherland are widely asserted, backed by tacit encouragement of the powers that rule the destinies of India today.

Political and social justice requires, not the disintegration of a country and destruction or humiliation of a class which shows initiative, intelligence and drive, but equality of opportunity for all, genuine freedom for self-fulfilment, in which all men irrespective of caste or creed may share. Slavery withered in the atmosphere of England when Catholic and Protestant, Anglo-Saxon and Jew, Northumbrian and Kentishman obtained equal citizenship. Can freedom flourish where religious and racial groups are encouraged to clamour for separate existence as segregated communities, and majorities are set up by statute unalterable by an appeal to the general body of citizens? We have to sweep away the cobwebs of mistrust and the miasma of hatred if India is to fulfil her destiny and play her part worthily in the Commonwealth of Free Nations.

We are passing through momentous times and situated as we are, we know not what the future has in store for us. There are obvious limitations within which the universities of a country such as ours have to function. At this critical period in the history of India, it is our duty, first and foremost, to give that training to our youths which will fit them to uphold, with dignity and courage, with faith and fervour, the flag of Indian liberty. Let the universities hold aloft the torch of learning and make their students devoted to those subjects of study which will make them useful citizens and amply widen their horizon. Let our students become physically strong and morally unbreakable, never forgetting the eternal teachings of our great masters that, even when the body of men is chained, his soul may still remain free and unconquered. Let Benares bring together twenty-eight crore of Hindus, not for the purpose of professing the weak and the depressed, but for uniting the Indian people and laying the foundations of the spirit of that true democracy which signifies a government of the people, for the people, by the people. Political subjection has not yet completely destroyed the soul of India, but the perennial truths of Indian religion and philosophy have to be saved from the clutches of fear and superstition which dominate the popular mind, and the hearts of all, the rich and the poor alike, have to be blended together so that love for truth, righteousness, justice and equality that constitute India's great heritage may once again reign supreme.

Today nations intoxicated with power claim to justify their international endeavours and actions, especially in relation to their conduct, towards weaker countries which they desire to dominate, on self-deceptive grounds of either

God-gifted trusteeship or of elevation to a higher level of thought and achievement. Let us declare without fear and hesitation, that to us, justice and liberty as propounded by them are meaningless if they do not include their willingness to do justice and honour the liberty of other men and other nations. It is not so much what our students learn, not so much what they know, as what they are which should concern us. Do they love liberty, love it so much that they will fight for it, die for it and will accord it to others as well as claim it for themselves? Do they love their country, and not merely say they love it; do they love liberty and justice with a fervour that transcends their desire for ease and wealth and position? Let us remember that nations live or die according to the character of the people. Wealth, arms, munitions, disciplined armies and navies are of splendid service, but the character of the people, the character into which the youth is growing, determines the life or death of the nation. An Indian politician of repute, in answer to the question as to what would happen if England lost the war, observed the other day that God who has so long protected India would then have to protect both England and India. But we do not wish to treat the Almighty merely as a useful palladium. Heaven helps only those who help themselves. History affords us examples of great peoples who fell but rose again out of a sheer determination to win back their lost freedom, without which they thought life was not worth living. 'Liberty,' says Manu, the great law-giver of our race, 'is happiness and dependence is misery'. *Sarvamparavasamduhkham, sarvamatmavasamsukham.* Do we share the same feelings with equal intensity and devotion? With our ancient heritage, with the spirit of India still ennobling the mind of man, with our vast resources of manpower and buried wealth, let a supreme effort be made by all classes of our people to organise themselves effectively for the liberation of our country, and in this task of mighty reconstruction let the trained youth of India heroically play a conspicuous part, not by mere surrender to emotions but tempered by a keen sense of practical wisdom and a thorough and efficient preparation—physical, moral and intellectual.

Let us pledge ourselves, body and soul, to the preservation of the noblest ideals of our race and culture and a lifelong devotion to the cause of that enlightened liberty, which a great seer has worshipped in words worthy to be written in gold that will remain engraved in the heart of mankind for all ages to come:

> O Liberty, thou art the god of my idolatry! Thou art the only deity that hates bended knees. In thy vast and unwilled temple, beneath the roofless dome, star-gemmed and luminous with suns, the worshippers stand erect; they do not range, or crawl, or bend their foreheads to the earth. The dust has never borne the impress of their lips. Upon thy altars mothers do not sacrifice their babes, not men their rights. Thou askest naught from man expect the things that good men hate—the whip, the chain, the dungeon key. Thou hast no Popes, no priests, who stand between their fellow-men and thee. Thou carest not for foolish forms, or selfish prayers. At thy sacred shrine hypocrisy does not bow, virtue does not tremble, superstition's feeble tapers do not burn, but Reason holds aloft her inextinguishable torch whose holy light will one day flood the world.

Speech delivered at the Banaras Hindu University Convocation on 1 December 1940

13

REORIENTING THE UNIVERSITY EDUCATION SYSTEM TO CHANGING INDIA

Universities in British India owed their foundation mainly to a desire on the part of the authorities to secure the loyal services of administrators and service-holders that could keep going the complex machinery of a bureaucratic government in an orderly and efficient manner. There was also the idea of spreading in a conquered territory, through the agency of the universities, a system of western education which in those days of benevolent despotism was regarded by the rulers as a path of duty and the sure means of elevating India to what they thought to be a higher standard of life. Universities were not established as seats of learning, nor was education attempted to be organised for the highest development of Indian culture and civilisation. Nearly half a century after the establishment of the first university in India, the ideal of a teaching university where scholars might meet for the dissemination and advancement of knowledge was first formulated. But the general system of education was not even then closely linked up with those essential problems which called for early fulfilment, so that India might reach her destiny through education and regain her supremacy in the domain of culture and enlightenment as also in the social, economic and political spheres of activity.

While I shall be the last person to minimise the value and importance of the work which Indian universities have done to advance educational progress in the country, to spread wholesome ideas among the people, to widen the outlook of millions of men, to instil in their minds fundamental ideas of progress and liberty, and to rouse the national consciousness of the citizens, I shall yet say that the time has come when a reorientation of university education is urgently called for in order to suit the changing condition of our country. Our universities should no longer continue to be regarded principally as training grounds for the professions and services. The professions are overcrowded and recruitment to public services is now based on a variety of considerations where merit does not always play the most prominent part.

The colleges should provide at the base what has been known for generations as a sound liberal education, that is catholic, expansive, free from narrowness and bigotry in ideas or doctrines, appropriate for a broad and enlightened mind. That education should be imparted through the medium of our own languages. The acceptance of this principle may raise initial difficulties but such difficulties have been overcome in free countries and India must also face and surmount them. In Eire, the Irish language once said to be unsuited to the needs of modern civilisation has been introduced with success. This is of fundamental value in the true building up of national life. It is more than a mere means of communicating ideas; it is the expression of the national spirit. The other day a vigorous attack was launched on the Nazi policy of attempting to destroy the language and literature of some of the countries over which Hitler holds his sway today. The critic rightly expressed his abhorrence of what constitutes a deathblow to the culture of those countries. In India also, for more than a century, education imparted through the medium of a foreign language has unduly dominated its academic life and it has now produced a class of men who are unconsciously so denationalised that any far-reaching proposal for the recognition of the Indian languages as the vehicle of teaching and examination up to the highest university stage is either ridiculed as impossible or branded as reactionary. But I plead earnestly for the acceptance of this fundamental principle not on account of any blind adherence to things that I claim as my own but out of a firm conviction that the fullest development of the mind of a learner is possible only by this natural approach, and also that by this process alone can there be a great revival of the glory and richness of the Indian languages.

A problem that has presented difficulties in India but which to my mind is certainly avoidable, relates to the recognition of different Indian languages by the universities. In my university, elaborate provisions have been in existence for more than thirty years for the recognition of all the important Indian languages. At the post-matriculation stage, a candidate coming from outside Bengal is encouraged to offer his own mother tongue at his examination. Important Indian languages other than Bengali have been included for the MA examination also. At the matriculation stage, non-Bengalis are not compelled to accept Bengali as the medium of their examination. Hindi, Urdu and Assamese are recognised as media along with Bengali and have been given the same importance as the language of the province itself. Others are allowed the option to offer English as their medium. I do believe that the question of the study of important Indian languages should not present any difficulty whatsoever in any Indian university, only if we remember the cardinal point that, in whichever corner of the vast country we might reside, we are bound to one another by ties of brotherhood and comradeship; and in generally helping one another in the field of education we are but strengthening the foundation of that great Indian nationhood, the full attainment of which has been the dream of generations of Indians irrespective of caste, creed or community.

While I plead for the due recognition of our own languages, I recognise that English should remain a compulsory second language and that it should be taught to all, mainly for the purpose of a correct expression of ideas and assimilation of knowledge to be gathered from books written in that great language. Provision should also be made for the study of other important languages, both eastern and western.

A thorough examination of the syllabuses and the courses of study, not from the standpoint of any one individual subject but in light of the requirements of the entire educational structure, is also called for. We are pressed by our expert advisers, each speaking with unconcealed loyalty to his own special subject to store the minds of our youths with knowledge. But what is sometimes forgotten is that the capacity of their minds is limited and knowledge that would be useless or superfluous in after-life must make room for that which is necessary and useful. Well did a distinguished scholar once observe that we would not be able to apply our stock of knowledge with that readiness which the exigencies of life demanded, if our mental storehouse was like an ill-arranged lumber room.

We have, therefore, to keep in mind the need for a liberal and useful education, on which will be raised the superstructure of such departments of study as will produce men and women trained in diverse branches of knowledge, theoretical and practical, which will make them fit persons in the service of the nation. The question has been and will be how far and how best we can combine education, that is, the bringing out of the faculties with instruction, that is, the imparting of valuable knowledge. If we can induce the right mood, achievement of the purpose will not be difficult. Each university should adequately reflect the peculiar needs of the country and the area it specially serves and should produce men who will not add further to the waste of human materials but possess both knowledge and culture so as to be absorbed in worthy occupations. To put it differently, we can say that true education should include the local idea, the national idea and the international idea.

A problem that has recently agitated the minds of persons interested in education relates to the relationship of student with colleges and universities. In our country, from time immemorial, the teacher and the student stood in the same relationship as did a father and his son. In modern days, the atmosphere in educational institutions does not always lead to the formation of a healthy social life between the teacher and the student. This is all the more conspicuous in non-residential institutions, where opportunities for mutual contact are necessarily limited. The situation often becomes embarrassing to educational authorities when exciting political questions agitate the minds of students and directly influence their conduct within the colleges, although the authorities have no responsibility whatsoever for such situations or developments. My intimate association with the student community makes me assert unhesitatingly that we should miss no opportunities of discussing with them all those problems that agitate their minds, even though they may have no direct connection with their academic work. This close association and frank exchange of ideas soon melt away feelings of shyness and aloofness from their minds, and whatever their ultimate viewpoint, it creates an atmosphere of mutual trust and confidence whose value cannot be overestimated.

Unfortunate disturbances, such as strikes and noisy demonstrations, are becoming a common feature in educational institutions and this tendency should be discouraged in the interest of all concerned. If the controversy relates to a matter affecting the internal affairs of an institution and cannot be amiably solved by the college itself, the final decision should be left to a representative university board. I see no reason why the university regulations should not make the decision of such a body binding on the parties concerned. I know this interference on the part of the university may not always be welcomed by all educational institutions. But let me impress upon them that I would gladly accept, first and foremost, any satisfactory solution by the college itself without inference from anybody else. If this is not possible, I would much rather leave the decision in the hands of an impartial body of academic men than permit the disturbance to spread and be exploited by persons who may be least concerned with the welfare of the institution or of the students affected.

As regards disturbances due to extraneous reasons, I would beg of the students not to make the educational institutions the forum for expressing their disapproval of questions of public policy which might deeply stir their minds. I am not one of those who favour university students remaining aloof from the burning questions of the day. I would not, however, like them to be engrossed in party politics, for I believe they should maintain their independence of outlook and zealously cultivate that spirit of clear and critical thinking, that free power of reasoning, which should be their main asset as they enter upon public life on the completion of their educational career. But nothing should prevent them from an active study and discussion of all important political questions of the day, and even, should they so desire, sympathising with particular schools of thought which they individually or collectively might choose to support. With goodwill and understanding on both sides, the university and college unions should prove a healthy training ground for future citizenship. Frankly speaking, occasional outbursts of youthful feelings should not worry educational administrators. But when they are allowed to interfere with the regular routine of academic work, or create deadlocks on issues, small and insignificant, they become a disease which, if unchecked, will destroy the very foundation of that strong disciplined character which must be an essential possession of all young men and women anxious to dedicate their lives to the cause of their country's liberty.

I have noticed recently a notification issued by a provincial government laying down severe penalties for the maintenance of discipline amongst students. One threat held out is that such students as may come under the purview of the order will be debarred from government service. To my mind, threats of punitive action will defeat the very object which the authors of the order themselves allege to have in view. Besides, this particular threat is an idle one. For today admission to public services is controlled by various non-academic considerations and in any case it absorbs only a fraction of university-trained youths. Again, no words can be too strong to condemn any policy of espionage which encourages secret reports of the activities of students to be supplied by teachers themselves. Any attempted transformation of the free and sacred temple of learning into a branch of the Intelligence Department is a sure method of destroying the soul of India's manhood.

Enforced discipline, such as these processes imply, must make room for discipline from within. Modern psychology tells us that mind of man cannot be built up by superimposed ideas and instructions without regard to its own living impulses. We shall be untrue to our work as teachers and administrators if we fail to make the right appeal to the student community to make them realise that the maintenance of sound discipline in educational institutions is a duty not cast on officers and teachers alone but must readily be shared by the students themselves. The mass student mind is sound and pure. In every country, the youth adores the spirit of patriotism. The time of youth is the time for initiative and enthusiasm, for that disregard of consequences which makes men willing to undertake great things, the time when a man can do great things that the mass of men cannot believe to be possible. 'Adore enthusiasm,' says Mazzini, 'worship the dreams of the virgin soul, and the visions of early youth, for they are the perfume of paradise, which the soul preserves in issuing from the hands of the creator.' In a subject country such as ours, the patriotic impulses of youths are apt to be all the more fervent and outspoken and it will be the height of folly if thoughts and ideals that vibrate their minds and make them feel restless are not fully appreciated by us. The academic atmosphere can retain its sanctity and freedom, only with the loyal assistance of students. We must do all that lies in our power to awaken them to the realisation that national problems have not been solved in other countries, and cannot be solved in India, by such childish methods as students' strikes and demonstrations within the colleges, that the best way of helping to cope with a national crisis that faces India today is for them to combine with the universities in securing for themselves better education and better preparation for life.

For us who are responsible for shaping the policy of the universities, it would be well to remember the prophetic words of a great thinker that it would be a most deplorable thing to make the price of education for our youths the surrender of the years of the greatest initiative and enthusiasm and of the hope and capacity for great deeds to rigid surveillance or to the work of acquisition alone. Let us keep our students at work getting knowledge out of books but not while the enthusiasm of youth is ebbing away and the capacity of doing things is being gradually lost. Learning itself is not always of the greatest value. The man who is made is the great thing and the work of doing is the great thing in the man. But it is not the man alone that the university is to make. Let us teach our students and let us ourselves demonstrate that no man lives to himself, that no task can be more patriotic than that of binding the whole community together by common association and aspirations. The object of education is not the construction of a single man who dies and is forgotten. Benefits to the community, to the nation, to civilisation, are all that are of value, and the production of the individual man whose influence shall live forever in the weal of humanity—that is the great object of every university. Let us lift up the mass of our countrymen from hard conditions of poverty and ignorance and let us produce the individual man framed and trained in our universities who will worthily participate in that majestic progress. All our students may not become very learned, all may not even go very deeply into any one subject. But what is our education worth if we have not been able to push back their horizons, to remove their vision from the little concrete objects that fill a narrow and isolated life and to make them realise, however vaguely, the existence of a vast field of human life an interest, of history and science, of achievement and failure, of examples and warnings outside of themselves, beyond the period of their lives and even the limits of their province and country?

The need of a broad outlook and a clear vision was never so imperative as at the present moment. We meet in a time of storm and stress. Kings and crowns are tumbling down and countries that have long been the citadel of freedom are today the ruthless victims of superior force. India appreciates, more perhaps than any other country, what it is for a people to lose their political power and independence. Battling nations and warring ideologies contend for mastery in the east and the west. The roaring tide of partisanship and passion threatens to sweep away many of the institutions we hold dear, and, who knows, may even destroy whatever remains of the integrity of this ancient land of ours. Distrust and prejudice invariably associated with the doctrine of overlordship, still cloud the Indian horizon. In the words of a keen observer of modern times, racial and religious prejudices, which we had fondly believed to be the outcome of ignorant reaction, have been made the basis of national policy and learned men have been found able to reconcile the defence of this barbarism with their conscience.

Agra faced problems of serious import in the past when it first emerged to full view from the mist of antiquity. It found an India divided against itself—a prey to internal chaos and external aggression. The central government whose power had once been felt from the Himalayas to Madura had collapsed. Rival princes and barons fought for supremacy in the various provinces. The spectre of foreign domination loomed large on the horizon. Buccaneers from neighbouring continents were already intercepting pious pilgrims and peaceful traders, and trying to establish their lairs on the defenceless seaboard of India. How did the eminent men of Agra deal with the situation in the sixteenth century? They realised the supreme need of the country's unity. India, according to certain bureaucratic administrators and myopic politicians, is not one country or nation. But was not the unity of the land and its people emphasised by ancient writers? Did not the poet sing of the whole country as:

Mera sone ka Hindustan
Tu hi mere dil ki roshni
Tu hi meri jaan.

It is to the task of the unification of this land of Hindustan that a long line of rulers, Hindu and Muslim, directed their energies in the past. In the work of political unification in the sixteenth century, Akbar was ably seconded, among others, by Todar Mal and noblemen of the house of Jaipur. Your city became the metropolis of a united Hindustan and retained that proud position for well-nigh a century. The Rajput and the Pathan, the Mughal and the Audhi Khetri retained their individual culture. But they cooperated to establish an edifice carved in granite and hewn out of the rock of liberalism, toleration and a broad-mindedness that did away with the artificial barriers raised by racial and religious prejudices. The structure stood till the recrudescence of intolerance and arrogance levelled it to the ground, to the eternal misfortune of our country.

With unity had come freedom from the foreign menace. The kings of Iran and Turan came to acquire a wholesome respect for the government of Hindustan, and the sea rovers from the west were content to send pious missionaries and peaceful ambassadors to the Imperial Court. The quiet teachings of medieval *bhaktas*—apostles of ahimsa—useful as they were in imbuing the people with ideas of catholicity, national organisation and solidarity would not have sufficed to save the country from chaos and aggression, had they not been reinforced by the valour of the horsemen of Akbar, the spearmen of Man Singh and the cohorts of Todar Mal. Will the lessons of the past be lost on us? Shall we encourage movements that threaten to disrupt the unity of this country? It should not be forgotten that if Indian history teaches a lesson, it is this—that political disruption due to tribal jealousy and religious antagonism has been the harbinger of foreign damnation.

If Indian unity is a desideratum, its essential prerequisite is a broad toleration in every sphere of life. Racial and religious prejudices have often, throughout the ages, turned Europe into reeking shambles and disintegrated nations and 'ramshackle empires', which, had they remained united, would have been better able to withstand the shock of external invasion. A loud lament has gone forth from an Anglo-Saxon statesman that his navy bears a heavier burden through lack of ports in a Celtic land with a predominantly Catholic population, which was once united to his country by stronger political ties. Perhaps the Catholics and Celts still remember Drogheda and Wexford, the penal laws and coercion acts. Our Motherland has to be saved, if necessary, without lifeblood, from Droghedas and Wexfords, and their inevitable corollary—an Ulster in an 'Emerald Isle' and a sullen Eire within a frowning Commonwealth.

Let men and women trained in Indian universities of today unite in their efforts for the remaking of their Motherland. No country has attained greatness or liberty except through loyal and disinterested service of her children. The spirit of the New India must be born of struggle and arduous labour and sacrifice, of noble scorn of ease and luxury, of thirst for knowledge and its widest application to the alleviation of human misery and suffering, of a broad-based toleration and justice affecting the rights of the vast multitude of the Indian people, of a burning and unalterable faith in the political integrity of the country, of loyalty to truth and faith in God. Let us proceed on the path that leads to the home of liberty, of justice, of righteousness, undaunted by obstacles or failures, gaining courage and strength from the everlasting truth that even if the present generation comes to its journey's end before the goal is reached, our ceaseless efforts will inspire those who follow us, and they will carry on the unfinished duty with unabated energy and determination and know no rest or peace till victory is achieved.

Speech delivered at the Agra University Convocation on 23 November 1940

14

THE PURPOSE OF HIGHER EDUCATION

This is my first visit to this great seat of learning which we feel proud to regard as a national asset. Let me pay my tribute of respect to the memory of your illustrious founder and his renowned successors, who had not only the courage and vision to propound new educational ideals but also the capacity and determination to translate them into practice by the establishment and development of institutions dedicated to the cause they held so dear and sacred. Today we stand at the crossroads of history. Our beloved Motherland, rich with an ancient heritage, struggles for the attainment of that free status which is her birthright. It is through education that the ultimate battle of Indian freedom will be won. The gigantic task of reconstruction—cultural, social, economic and political—can be rendered possible through the coordinated efforts of bands of trained and disciplined Indians. Armed with the knowledge of India's past glory and greatness, her strength and weakness, it is they who can place before their country a programme of work, which while loyal to the fundamental traditions of Indian civilisation will be adapted to the changing conditions of the modern world.

If the history of education in British India is traced by an impartial historian, the record will be hardly creditable to our ruling class. We have suffered not for want of zeal and devotion for the cause of education on the part of the children of the soil, but on account of the colossal blunder made by our rulers while formulating their educational policy a little over a century ago. That policy, determined in the days of Bentinck and Macaulay, was influenced not by considerations of the welfare of the Indian people but of the advancement of the interests of the ruling class. In no country has education properly developed unless it has drawn its inspiration from the fountain of its own national life. Education with its roots cut off and superimposed by the edicts of an alien power is doomed to ultimate failure. Applied to a subject race which has not entirely lost its intellectual curiosity and virility, such a system may for some generations foster an artificial growth; it may even produce a race of able imitators but it can never inspire or elevate the people as a whole, far less advance their permanent welfare.

When Bentinck decided to concentrate State aid and support on European education alone, he started an era of cultural conquest of the Indian people. Afraid of the possible dangerous results of the spread of knowledge among the masses of the people, Macaulay and his co-workers chose to favour a select class of Indians and train them on western ideas, not with a view to help them develop into self-reliant and patriotic Indians, but as Macaulay himself said, to form a class of persons, Indian in blood and colour but English in taste, in opinions, in morals and in intellect. Contemporaneous records of those days disclose a lamentable lack of knowledge of our masters of the greatness of India's past civilisation. They indeed portray a remarkable over-emphasis on the so-called virtues of western culture and an unconcealed contempt for everything Indian. What we deplore is not that the gate of western knowledge was thrown open to Indians, but that such knowledge was imported to India at the sacrifice of our own cultural heritage. What was needed was a proper synthesis between the two systems and not neglect, far less destruction of the Indian base. India's chequered history amply demonstrates that during a period when many of the European countries remained steeped in ignorance and barbarity, our great seers, savants and sages, backed by royal support, had attained an intellectual eminence which might well be the envy of any highly civilised nation. In this country was developed a state of society which encouraged not merely scholastic learning, philosophy and religion, but also art, architecture, medicine, science, astronomy and engineering. Education must be nourished by ideas and thoughts consistent with the traditions of the country which it claims to serve. The sustaining force of western education in India was chiefly the glamour of state service. Education was encouraged not for its own sake but for opening avenues of employment essential for the successful functioning of a bureaucratic machinery.

I have no desire to trace here the growth of the educational system in India in detail. Macaulay's prophecy was partially falsified by the results that followed its adoption. The national consciousness of educated Indians could not be suppressed and far from being blind supporters of an alien rule, they themselves became the torchbearers of revolt. The education of the masses was neglected in a manner unprecedented in the history of any civilised administration. The educational system failed to serve the real needs of India and its defects were soon manifest to patriotic Indians. Attempts have no doubt been made from time to time to introduce far-reaching changes into the educational system in accordance with the needs and aspirations of the people. In the field of higher teaching and research, in arts and science, it has been demonstrated that the power of original thinking of Indian scholars has not been extinguished and they are capable of holding their own against any foreigner. Partial success has been achieved in some spheres of thought and activity but a general dissatisfaction is evident suggesting a thorough overhauling of the entire system.

The problem of education can never be fully solved in a manner acceptable to self-respecting Indians until and unless it is left in the hands of a government representing the national will and freed from foreign domination. We move indeed in a vicious circle. Without education properly outlined and directed, we cannot easily attain our freedom. Without freedom and full control over our own destinies, we cannot reshape our educational policy entirely according to our will and requirements. So long as the present situation continues, however, it is obvious we have to make the best use of the existing machinery and by constant efforts and agitation secure changes and improvements which will bring us as near our goal as possible. Acceptance of our national languages as the media of instruction and examination up to the highest standard is a fundamental condition which is yet to be fulfilled. You have rightly adopted this course in developing your activities. Each province has its own major language and this should be accepted in its own educational sphere. If there is another language which has a substantial number of adherents, this may also receive recognition under suitable conditions, although the multiplicity of languages within the same provincial zone may lead to obvious complications. A bureau should be set up in each province under the supervision of well-trained scholars and working in close cooperation with government and universities, it should undertake the preparation of books in all subjects of study in the provincial language. A working knowledge of English at the post-elementary stage is sufficient for our ordinary purposes, except in the case of that limited number of scholars who may choose to study the English language and literature as part of their academic training. Similarly, a working knowledge of Hindi is essential so that direct contact among peoples of different provinces may be maintained. The study of different subjects has to be reorganised in a manner suited to the conditions of our country. Subjects like history, economics and social science have to be dealt with in relation to Indian environments. With regard to science which knows no geographical boundaries, the nomenclature should not be divorced from what is in use in other parts of the world, for only thus can we keep ourselves in touch with world progress, and retain contact with co-workers outside our own sphere of activity.

While we cannot but emphasise the need for well-equipped libraries and laboratories, seminars and museums in any system of national education, we have to keep down unnecessary expenditure on buildings and hostels. In a poor country such as ours we should aim at minimising expenditure in every possible manner so that money thus released may be utilised for the progressive expansion of education. The conditions of living and training of our alumni should be such as to render it possible for them on the termination of their studies to identify themselves without any pang with the environments amidst which they had been previously accustomed to live. Nothing is more ruinous to the cause of our country's progress than to create a separate class of so-called educated Indians, entirely out of touch in outlook and mode of living with the vast millions of their less fortunate fellow countrymen to whose service they must dedicate their lives.

Education can hardly be separated from the social and economic surroundings of the people. While those responsible for imparting education cannot guarantee employment to all students, the system should be so regulated that the training given is a help and not a hindrance to them in their struggle for existence. For this reason, education must be many sided and institutions of various types must grow up so as to train people in manifold directions suited to the economic and industrial progress of the country. It is in this sphere that a national government will deem it a supreme duty to coordinate effectively the activities of academic institutions with trade, commerce, agriculture and industry. There can be no clash of interests among these agencies only if all strive to achieve one ultimate end—the service of the nation as a whole.

Relation between the teacher and student must be such as between a father and son. It is only by the fulfilment of this condition that a correct standard of education can be maintained and its objects properly fulfilled. Obedience that grows out of spontaneous loyalty and affection is permanent; enforced discipline born of the fear of rules or rods fails to mould the character of the students. Your basic concept of *gurukul*—the home of the teacher—is a gift of the ancient Indian mind and has seldom penetrated into the artificial atmosphere of residential schools, copied for the western pattern in many parts of India. An Indian *gurukul* cannot separate education from the mainsprings of Indian dharma, interpreted in its broadest sense. The heritage that belongs to an Indian youth must be clearly and boldly held before his mind's eye. The eternal value of the teachings of the ancient seers must be explained to him—not for lowering his vision or choking his spirit of inquisitiveness, but for making him judge for himself their fundamental values. Civilisation in our society meant progressive socialisation of our lives by developing all the finer feelings which helped us to realise our own selves in others and others in our own selves. This is why our social life had been dominated more by moral consciousness rather than political. If today we suffer from divisions and disruptions, the fault lies with those interpreters who for historical reasons clung to form and practices and narrowed the base of the original structure of our society striking at the root of service and equality, so manifest in the teachings of our ancient seers. Pride in one's national heritage such as ours which transcends all barriers of race and creed must be implanted in the heart of our youth, for by this alone will he shake off an inferiority complex and lack of self-confidence, fatal to the cause of our progress. We claim that instead of turning westwards we can rebuild our society fundamentally on our own model. In a country such as ours with people following different religions and faiths, we must so adjust our movements as to permit full scope for intellectual and cultural developments to all essential units, each remaining loyal to its creed, helpful to and trustful of each other, and all owing allegiance to the imperishable spirit of Indian unity.

Today the world is faced with a crisis unknown in the history of human civilisation. Western civilisation has failed to give the world peace and freedom. In spite of material advancement and scientific and industrial progress, the ruling classes in Europe were dominated by the triple forces of power, prestige and possession. The future happiness of the world will depend on the outlook of the men who control the destinies of the stronger and more powerful nations. Whatever lip sympathy they may pay to the doctrine of equality, democracy and freedom, if in their actions they allow themselves to be dominated by a policy of aggression and exploitation of weaker or less fortunate countries, they can never hope for the inauguration of a better world order. The future of the world lies in a federation of free countries where each will have the scope of developing its national life in accordance with its best ideals and traditions. If this goal is acceptable to all, the educational system in all parts of the world must be so moulded as to encourage the growth of correct international behaviour and understanding. Among the fundamental moral qualities, man must have a deep concern for the good life of his fellows. Every person should be given a fair chance of growing up sound in mind and body and making the best of his natural faculties. He must have a sense of social responsibility and the will to sink his personal interest and that of his class in the common good. He must be a man of independent judgment, respect the individualities of others and be tolerant to opinions in conflict with his own. He should realise that he has responsibility not only as a citizen of his own country but also as a citizen of the world, that there must be equal justice for all, that government should be based on general goodwill and support rather than on brute force.

One of the urgent problems confronting us is replanning of a system of national education suited to our needs and aspirations. We do not yet know when political conditions will permit us to give effect to such a reformed scheme. But this must form a major part of post-war reconstruction. We should lose no time in setting up a competent machinery, fully representative of all interests, which should explore the lines of our future educational programme. The matter will not be an easy one. Problems relating to languages, traditions, needs of different communities and employment will require the closest examination. The aim of education has to be defined with clearness and precision. Briefly put, our object should be to develop every Indian child as completely as possible so that he may feel himself consciously at one with his community, share in its traditions of the past, its life and action in the present and its aspirations and responsibility for the future. A vast country like India will present problems peculiar to particular provinces. Our aim should be to inculcate in the mind of every child a passionate loyalty to the spirit of Indian unity and so to regulate his daily work that he may become aware that what he is doing is for the advancement of his nation and through his nation of humanity at large.

Your great institution will contribute in no small degree to the solution of the Indian educational problem. Regimentation of rules and adoption of a rigid pattern in the sphere of education virtually give it a death blow. They strike at the root of its life and lead to deadly stagnation. You have demonstrated that education in this country can be organised by a correct synthesis between the fundamental aspects of Indian civilisation and the true requirements of a scientific age. The influences for the good which alone can save human civilisation from the destructive forces of an arrogant and selfish materialism have been steadily nurtured by you in spite of grave obstacles. In the task of reconstruction of Indian society, you are bound to play a dominant part and your experiences will influence in no small measure the future course of educational policy and administration in this country. India amidst all her diversities presents a unity of thought and action which is indeed remarkable. In spite of political bondage, we have been able to keep our heads erect because of the inherent power of assimilation that the Indian mind has shown itself capable of. The aim of our culture has been the complete realisation of life. Nature, man and God make for life's entire knowledge; and service and love are the materials which go to the making of man complete. In the firm belief that the cause of Indian advancement is just and righteous, and standing at the foot of the Himalayas and near the Holy River that have from time immemorial witnessed the mighty career of Indian civilisation, which no alien power can crush, let us draw inspiration from the glorious past, sustain fortitude and strength to face the trials and tribulations of the present and fearlessly contribute our humble share in the rebuilding of a free and united India of the future. Let us gather in our own the voices of India's oppressed millions and proclaim in the words of our beloved poet our determination to march along the path of truth and justice and to consider no sacrifice, no preparation too great for the emancipation of our Motherland.

'Where the mind is without fear and the head is held high:
Where knowledge is free; Where the world has not been broken up into
fragments by narrow domestic walls:
Where words come out from the depth of truth:
Where tireless striving stretches its arms towards perfection:
Where the clear stream of reason has not lost its
way into the dreary desert sand of dead habit;
Where the mind is led forward by Thee into ever
widening thought and action—
Into that heaven of freedom, my father, let my country awake!'

Speech delivered at the convocation of Gurukul Vishwavidalaya, Kangri, Haridwar, in May 1943

15

UNIVERSITIES IN POST-INDEPENDENCE INDIA

I feel grateful to you for having given me an opportunity to associate myself with the first convention of university teachers from all over India. Coming so soon after the attainment of our political freedom, this convention is in some respects a unique occasion. It has been summoned for the purpose of organising all over the country an intellectual and educational movement connected with the universities and their teachers. It signifies a new awareness on the part of the universities and their teachers at once of their special mission in our national life and of their ability to play their distinctive role with courage and firmness. You would recall that last summer the International University Teachers' Association held a conference at Brussels to organise the university teachers on an international level so as to enable them to discharge their functions in a worthy manner.

I find you have chosen three main topics for discussion and the convention will be divided into three sections for the purpose, namely, (i) The place of university in society and national life, (ii) Teaching and research in universities, and (iii) Problems of finance and administration. After the inaugural session, the convention will go into these sectional sessions and deliberate on these weighty topics. I have no doubt that the eminent sectional presidents you have elected will be able to guide your deliberations along fruitful lines and indicate the lines of future policy of educational administration and expansion.

It is not my purpose to trace the history of the growth of universities in India nor to discuss in detail how India suffered on account of university education at the initial stages being linked up with the principal object of supplying the needs of the British administrative system in India. In spite of all their defects and shortcomings, Indian universities have served a great and useful purpose. They brought India into intimate contact with the culture and civilisation of the rest of the world. They opened up new avenues of thought in literature, history, philosophy, science and technology. They quickened our moral sensibilities to a certain extent and gave a healthy stimulus to our ideals of nationalism and liberty. Nonetheless, deriving as they did their origin from foreign inspiration and ideals, Indian universities, in spite of their best efforts have not been properly related to our national life and needs. With the dawn of independence in India, our university teachers must come forward and be prepared to think courageously and plan energetically to reconstruct our educational system. They must claim for themselves their rightful place not only in the sphere of academic administration but in shaping the policy of education as a whole. Theirs must be the primary responsibility to serve as the connecting link between the people at the bottom and the legislators and administrators at the top. There need be no conflict between university education, on the one hand, and secondary and elementary education, on the other. Expansion and not curtailment must be our watchword. There must be a rational adjustment amongst different types and spheres of education. None need function at the sacrifice of the other and all must develop so that our country may be broad-based on a truly national system of education which will respond to the economic, cultural and social needs of our society.

Hitherto our educational system has been predominantly liberal as opposed to vocational in bias. It has produced a strong intelligentsia markedly unrelated to our economic and political form. Today not only have we achieved a free political state but we are also about to enter a period of rapid industrialisation.

Our educational system, therefore, must adjust itself to answer to the new requirements of our nation. We must at the same time recognise while a university has obligation to social order, it must not be assumed that it will always satisfy only the demands which society can make or articulate at any time or period. A university must seek to make society aware of what it ought to want as well as to satisfy those wants it readily says it has. It must provide not only the technical personnel required to serve a particular cultural, economic and political order but also make available the elite in thought and leadership so that society may outgrow itself along lines of tenable development. While it pursues abstract truth for its own sake, no university can stand aloof from the tension and pains from the modern society striving to adjust itself to technical development as well as to new thought pattern.

The university, thus, occupies an integral place in our society and national life. It must address itself wholeheartedly and unreservedly to the advancement of knowledge, the study of problems, from whatever source they come and the training of men—all at the highest level of possible effort. Teaching and research constitute its twin functions—teaching to train up the personnel of our society and research to seek out new forms and relationships both of man and matter. Extension of facilities for higher teaching and research is an urgent national need, if we are to make maximum utilisation of our own resources and not depend on foreign support for every big scheme of national advancement. To perform these high functions adequately, the university would need two things above all others—freedom and finance. Let me speak of freedom first. We all know of the frightful results of lack of freedom creative though is stunted and it speedily leads to doctrinism and degeneration. Let us not forget what happened in the fascist countries as soon as political control was installed on the universities. The latter lost their autonomy and became a handmaid of the political party in power. Education—creative education—was replaced by dogmatic indoctrination. We have seen the spectacle of a whole nation being indoctrinated and led by the political party to action, with apparent initial success but also ultimate chaos.

After all the State is in practice a coercive instrument in the hands of a predominant political party. Such a political party naturally has a desire or inclination sometimes to silence the voice of its opponents and it will not hesitate on occasions to impair or to restrict the academic freedom of university teachers or invade the autonomy of university administration. This will be indeed fatal. The government in this country must set a salutary example in this direction and not allow the autonomy of universities to be curbed in any way, once their constitution is fashioned according to well-recognised principles consistent with the needs of the country. In the advanced countries of the west, the cry has been raised that the all-powerful modern omni-competent States should on occasions voluntarily abdicate some of its functions, that there should be in the body politic some portion or some sphere of liberty which must be exempted from the interference of the State. This voluntary withdrawal of the State again is only possible if the university teachers or the leaders of the enlightened thought in our country can create conditions or bring about a situation in which the State will, of its own accord, retire from the arena of interference. All this is the task of liberal education. And it is my firm conviction that university teachers in India can promote this liberal education if they become sufficiently aware of their powers and responsibilities.

Political interference may, however, take another shape as well. Take our university finances. About 45.8 per cent of the expenses of Indian universities are met from fee income. The income derived from endowments covers another 15 to 20 per cent. For as much as 35 to 40 per cent of their budget, therefore, the universities are dependent on the year-to-year favour of government. This is a pre-eminently unsatisfactory position. The State pays too little and the student too much for the maintenance of our universities. Thus, a university has to depend not only on the political party in power, but is also subjected to a standing temptation to lower its standard in order to attract students so as to increase the fee income. This again means a perverted scale of valuation whereby the teaching profession in India has come to be the least remunerative. If we are to increase the standard of education and research, the universities must have more freedom and more finances on a secure basis. Let there be periodical surveys made of university activities by a body of impartial and well-reputed educationists but each university must be provided with adequate statutory grants which will extend for a period of five to ten years, so that they may live and grow in an atmosphere of peace and freedom. Take the case of Britain. In the budget last March, the chancellor of the Exchequer announced a vast increase in grants to universities on a quinquennial basis so that the universities may plan five years ahead. The increase in grant is so great that it is estimated that universities may not be able to spend during the year all the money they have been allowed. In 1938-39, the total exchequer grant to the universities was [Pound] 2.4 million including a limited non-recurring grant for capital expenditure. The grant has been increased over the next five years to the level of [Pound] 12 million for recurring expenditure and [Pound] 7.5 million for capital expenditure. In other words, the universities have no further financial problems to worry about and they have been asked to increase their activities to the limit of their physical capacity. They are not dependent on the annual doles of the political party in power. That is a scheme of national investment which India may well emulate within her available resources. The amount of money other advanced countries spend on research is simply staggering. I am not thinking of the two million dollars or Rs 600 crore which the USA spent on atomic research. I am only thinking of the normal expenditure on scientific and industrial research in other advanced countries. The total expenditure comes up to as much as one-half or one per cent of national income. If we assume that our national income is of the order of Rs 3,000 crore, we should spend Rs 20 to 30 crore on research alone. The mere mention of this figure would show where we and our universities stand today.

Medium of instruction is another problem which has long exercised the minds of our educational reformers. When Macaulay wrote his famous *Minute on Education* in 1835 or when Sir Charles Wood sent his Despatch on Education in 1854, we Indians, without any sufficient awareness of the consequences that might follow, became involved in the curriculum of English education. This education has undoubtedly benefited certain classes in India; it has given us, as I said before, a good deal of healthy political consciousness. But the masses remain, for the most part, neglected and despised under this system of education. It was difficult for the illiterate and depressed Indian peasant or worker to acquire the rudiments of education through a foreign tongue which he could not easily master. The result was that our schools and colleges remain, for the most part, exotic in the land. They could not cater to the needs of the people at large. Education can most usefully be imparted through the medium of the mother tongue, but due to our subservience to foreign domination for more than one century, we attempted the impossible task of imparting education to our people through the medium of a language which is not theirs. At the present moment, fortunately, in almost all the provinces of India there has been a movement to give instruction to our boys and girls through the medium of their own mother tongue. There is also a move to establish regional universities. While our provincial languages must be enriched and encouraged by all possible means, we must from now decide how we would maintain coordination and exchange of ideas in academic spheres on an all-India basis. We cannot allow any trend towards linguistic autonomy to lead towards the linguistic fragmentation of India. Such cultural and academic disruption will also hamper the growth of the political unity of India and may prove disastrous to our national welfare and progress. I am only suggesting that this vital question may be kept in view from the beginning in shaping our future academic policy. The only balanced solution will apparently be to encourage simultaneously the adoption of Hindi as a common spoken language which will be the medium of inter-provincial contacts. Here again we must carefully decide the place of English in our academic system, not from any political standpoint but purely in relation to the needs of our own national development and international contacts. In fact our universities must provide fuller facilities to our students for learning the great languages of the world so that they may readily gather the highest treasures of thought in the domains of letters and science.

In discussing the responsibilities of university teachers, I must also refer to the problem of unrest in our student community. Students have taken their legitimate share in all popular movements or upheavals in our country. They have not been behind any other community in bearing the burden of persecution, sorrow and suffering. On many occasions, they have acted as the spearheads of attacks against foreign administration, and many of them have patiently and cheerfully laid down their lives on the gallows. Such a community has undoubtedly the right to express their views on important national questions. I do not want to suggest that students with immature minds, or with no training, should be allowed to dictate policies to our teachers and administrators. But students sufficiently grown up, students who have become adults and students who have obtained a sufficient amount of higher education, should be permitted to deliver their considered opinion on important political, social, economic and educational problems confronting the country, without becoming partisans in active politics. For this purpose, we must favour the growth of university unions and of giving unfettered freedom to such unions. We need not be afraid of such unions if they are guided along healthy lines and properly handled. These unions will be able to focus on the considered views of the student community, and it may very often happen that the views of the student community will ultimately be found acceptable to the leaders of thought and action in our country. But our university teachers have got an important responsibility in regard to the growth and encouragement of such students' unions. Students, by themselves, cannot possibly have any interest in creating indiscipline, disorder or confusion. Being misled, they sometimes do things which are bad, but when they do anything bad, it is their error of judgement and not their crime. If our teachers can exercise tact, and if they sympathetically try to understand the legitimate grievances of the students, then, I think, the problem of indiscipline among the student community in our country will be a thing of the past. The test of a good teacher undoubtedly is that he should be able to inspire the confidence of his pupils. 'The true object of education,' said one great German philosopher, 'is to form tastes and not to impart knowledge.' A good teacher should be able to form healthy tastes in his pupils. He must try to build up his character by the example of his personality, character and erudition. If a teacher fails in this endeavour, then I must say that his mission as a teacher has been frustrated to a great extent. Of course, I do not say that in all controversies between students and teachers in our country the teachers are guilty of dereliction of duty; there are other factors also which complicate the situation. But I want to emphasise that university teachers, guided by the best of motives should be able to find a solution for this problem of unrest among our student community. Research in educational problems is one of the primary and essential duties of university teachers. We are bound to search after fresh principles if we desire to lay firm foundations for a progressive practical life. In our relations with the student community also, we must search after such fresh principles.

The old relationship between the teachers and the taught has perhaps vanished for good. If that relationship cannot be revived, we must strive for a new integration, a new synthesis. In such a synthesis, the university teachers by their vision and courage may perhaps show the way to a better and more enduring understanding between the teachers and the student community in general and may act finally as the moral guardians of our society.

I have abundant hope and faith in the future of Indian universities. It is only four months since we attained our political liberty. Although partition of India has created gigantic problems affecting our peace and prosperity, we are determined to meet the situation with courage and realism and do everything possible to maintain and enhance our national solidarity and efficiency. In the remaking of a new India, based on a progressive social and economic order, consistent with our noblest traditions, Indian universities are bound to play an active and distinguished role. We are now in the difficult stage of transition from the old to the new. I hope and pray that during this critical period, it may be given to the teachers of universities and colleges in India to adopt a standard of work and service which will correctly influence the minds of the rising generation and also of the people at large, so that our country may regain its power and position among the free nations of the civilised world and worthily contribute the fruits of her ancient and glorious heritage to the lasting benefit of mankind.

Speech delivered by Syama Prasad Mookerjee as president of the first All India University Teachers Convention in Allahabad on 24 December 1947

16

UNIVERSITY FOR SPIRITUAL REBIRTH

It is difficult for an ordinary individual to realise in full the significance of the message of Sri Aurobindo's life and teaching. His philosophy forms an integrated system of thought created out of the highest and most sustained efforts of the human spirit. It is given to very few of us to attain that level of spiritual effort, for it demands a thorough discipline of the body and the mind, and what is still more difficult, the sacrifice of the immediate for the ultimate. Once upon a time, the rishis of ancient India rose above the calls of the present, the clash of arms, the rise and fall of empires, to contemplate the eternal verities of existence. In the words of Matthew Arnold:

She let the legions thunder past
and plunged in thought again.

Coming much nearer to our own times, when the favourite disciples of Guru Govind wanted him to lead them in the affairs of the world, he declined and warned them not to tempt him with ephemeral offerings.

Similarly, when in 1922, Mr CR Das [Deshbandhu Chittaranjan] asked for Sri Aurobindo's help in the political struggle in which Deshbandhu was engaged, the sage declined on the ground that he had not attained the fullest realisation of the spiritual reality, without which efforts to seek the salvation of mankind would only create an illusion.

These spiritual efforts of the great masters often defy common understanding. Yet, the call of the times was never so imperious as it is now. What India is suffering from today is not so much the poverty of the means of material existence. She is suffering much more from the bankruptcy of her spiritual resources. The government moves in the same vicious circle. Moral standards are at a discount. High purpose is reserved exclusively as an adornment of pontifical pronouncements from high offices. The scene is virtually littered with the debris of the spiritual achievements of a people that was once great.

The fact is that we have lost track of our real culture. The culture of a people, as Sri Aurobindo tells us, may be roughly described as the expression of a consciousness of life which formulates itself in three aspects. 'There is,' he explains, 'a side of thought, ideal, upward will and the soul's aspiration; a side of creative self-expression and appreciative aesthesis, intelligence and imagination; and a side of practical and outward formulation.' Philosophy and religion belong to the first of these three aspects of culture; art, poetry, literature to the second; and society and politics to the third. In India, however, the master idea that has governed the life, culture and social ideals of her people has been the seeking of man for his true spiritual self and the use of life. We have lost track of this noble idea. A base hedonistic view of life seems to inform all our activities today, even where they belong to the realm of the first two aspects of culture. As a result of this, philosophy becomes propaganda, or is prostituted to suit the so-called materialistic interpretation of history; religion is sacrificed at the altar of secularism; literature becomes pamphleteering; the artist becomes a mere artisan. This is the tragedy of the age to which we belong. Even where moral issues as such are involved, we go in for compromise or appeasement and call it diplomacy.

It is, thus, that the things of the mind permit the possibility of a spiritual self-expression to a greater extent than the outward institution of social life. Even in ancient India, social life, in its attempt to reflect the aspirations of the soul, suffered from the obvious limitations due to what Sri Aurobindo calls 'material exigencies' and 'the externalities of political and social construction'. But the dominant idea—the seeking of man for his true spiritual self—has never been forgotten even under such stress, even though it was no more than symbolically represented through the institutions of her social life. Such expressions as '*dharmarajya*', '*Ram rajya*', '*dharma yuddha*', '*rajarshi*' gave a character to the social and political institutions of ancient India to which even common people did not fail to respond. Today, those spiritual moorings seem to be utterly broken, and the spirit of man lost, given to the devil.

It is, thus, that the establishment of a university where the eternal verities of life will be taught and re-taught to a stricken people becomes supremely relevant. This is the task of an international university and it is in the fitness of things that the university should be dedicated to the sacred memory of Sri Aurobindo. It is in the fitness of things that along with its sister university at Santiniketan, named after another great Indian, this university should also be located in India where so many peoples and so many cultures have met and found their home. The Upanishads have expressed this synthesis and harmony by the three words—*Santam*, *Sivam*, *Adwaitam*.

Sri Aurobindo has also taught us the same truth. He even goes further and says that this synthetic turn of India's spiritual vision 'is not peculiar to the mystic or the literate or the thinkers, nourished on the high sublimities of the Veda and the Vedanta, but permeates even the popular mind'. It is here, on the sacred soil of India, where the call for synthesis first went out to the world and it is here that at the proposed university, scholars from the different parts of the world would assemble and inaugurate a new era of cultural renascence for India and the world.

I have so far dwelt on the spiritual call of Indian culture, even though the call may be going unheeded today. As Sri Aurobindo says, it is a spiritual, an inner freedom that can alone create a perfect human order. But this freedom does not ignore, cannot ignore, the evolution of man's lower physical, vital and mental nature. Progress to the age of the spirit must pass through the three conceptions—Annam Brahma, Pranam Brahma, Mano Brahma—each regarded as a reality, the third leading to the subjective age of mankind.

We cannot skip over any of the intermediate stages without peril to mankind, though such an adventure may succeed in the case of particular individuals. Body, life and mind, all these must assume significance in man's adventure of the spirit. The highest achievements may yet elude all except a few. But the disciplines they indicate are meant for the upliftment of mankind as a whole, their ascent from the ignorant nature with the spiritual existence. This great adventure is characteristically typified in the life of Sri Aurobindo. It began in an urge for the political liberation of India. It paved the path for a miracle, the great revelation that came to him in 1909 in his prison. The window that had been closed flew open and the Divine stood revealed before him. With the same abandon with which he had struggled for India's political freedom, he began his long patient quest for the freedom of the spirit. The two Aurobindo's merged with each other, the political fighter and the yogi. Even then his earlier patriotism was tinged with a spiritual penumbra. He was thus a true Indian. When we read of his books, he seems to appear out of the pages of our ancient sacred lore, the representative of all their wisdom made dynamic by an awareness of the present spiritual crisis. I am sure the proposed university will symbolise the world's urge for a new spiritual rebirth; it will stand out as an oasis amidst the barren tracts that breed jealousies, suspicions and petty conflicts.

Presidential address at Sri Aurobindo Memorial Convention in Pondicherry on 25 April 1951

The work that is about to be undertaken is a mighty one. No doubt, there will be support throughout the world that has not minimised the difficulties and complexities of the task. We propose to work this University for imparting training to men and women in accordance with the highest standards for the purpose of participating in the great task of reconstruction of humanity. Institutions of this type are bound to fail unless we can gather men and women who will not only feel on the lines that Sri Aurobindo lived, but also act up to them. This place has already within its resources such men and women who will be able to undertake this gigantic responsibility. It is our hope that men and women from all parts of the world will be attracted by the ideology for which this institution will stand.

Men and women selected for training must be carefully chosen because they must be able to absorb cent per cent the ideology for which this institution will stand. We need not pay attention to the quantitative aspect of the problem, because we have many universities where thousands of students pass out and we do not want to see any replica of such institutions.

The policy of our government should be to encourage experiments of the type being made here so that the work may be carried on without hindrance or difficulty.

Any institution, if it is to function must be under proper discipline and be conducted in a manner which will lead to smooth and efficient work. At the ashram, we see abundant evidence of the great organising ability of the Mother, who is the presiding deity over this place. Everywhere there is regularity, smoothness and efficiency; there is no hue and cry. This is a remarkable feature which, obviously, is an asset to any institution of the type we propose to develop. And with the Mother here, we have not the least doubt that this institution will grow from strength and will be the pride of not only India, but of the entire civilised world.

India has a mission and a destiny to fulfil. Some voice will rise from this land to which the world has to listen. It will not be the voice of conflict or chaos but the voice of peace where self-respect and honour will be kept. That voice was discovered by Aurobindo and the people all over the world will come to tread Aurobindo's path.

Concluding speech on the same occasion

17

REFORMING HIGHER EDUCATION FOR NEW INDIA

The University of Delhi, though of comparatively recent origin, has certain unique features of its own which strengthen its possibility of development and of service to the nation. Situated in the capital city of our country, it naturally receives special attention at the hands of the central government and no less a person than the President of our Republic is its Visitor. One can venture to express the hope that this association may lead to generous State aid so as to enable the university to carry on its plans for progressive expansion. Proximity of a university to the seat of the central government is sometimes fraught with the danger of unnecessary and irritating State interference which, it is to be earnestly hoped will be avoided. Delhi attracts people from all parts of India, and this university, therefore, can well develop into a seat of learning which will seek to harmonise diverse elements of the inhabitants of this great land, whose sons and daughters may assemble together to receive their training in different branches of knowledge. Further, a number of all-India institutions have sprung up in and near Delhi which is fast becoming the centre of useful studies and research in the domains of arts, science, technology, medicine and agriculture. These may well afford to the teachers and advanced students of the university opportunities for collaboration which will be of lasting benefit to all. Momentous problems arising out of government's policies in respect of administration and of passing of laws are constantly coming up, affecting the welfare of the entire nation. Sometimes they may even have international significance as well. Teachers and advanced students of the university and its colleges in Delhi have thus a great opportunity to study these problems at close quarters in a spirit of critical analysis and non-partisanship. Delhi is also often the centre of all India and even of international activities in such fields as sports, athletics and drama and thus holds out before its alumni various models of superior performance which are bound to act as healthy and powerful incentives to them. If full advantage is to be taken of all such varied opportunities for self-development and national service, the university and its colleges, their staff and students must receive generous aid from the State and the public. With the limited opportunities available today, the university has succeeded in making its mark in such departments of study as economics and science, thanks to the zeal and devotion of the distinguished staff associated with them.

Since attainment of Independence, the role that the universities in India are destined to play has been emphasised by both official and non-official spokesmen. The Radhakrishnan Commission has submitted a valuable report dwelling on the need for a planned and thorough reorientation of university administration and teaching. Unfortunately, like other distinguished commissions that had previously reported on Indian universities, this report also is in danger of being pigeonholed on account of want of financial resources. It is not through changes only in the external pattern of the administrative machinery of universities that we can expect to see the ushering in of a new era of reform and expansion. Their vital needs relate to improved methods of teaching and research and abundant facilities, both academic and extra-academic, to the staff and the students for performing their essential duties. This can hardly be fulfilled without adequate State aid. A university that has to depend for its existence principally on its fee income can never meet its obligation, however much it may compromise with sound academic principles for artificially raising such income.

A Universities Grants Committee appointed by the central government serving not only the central but also the state universities is a most urgent necessity. The committee should be so composed as to command the confidence of the universities as well as the public. It must have at its disposal adequate funds for distribution amongst the universities in accordance with a planned and systematic development on a national basis. There is a general tendency to believe that grants and control necessarily go together. The need for maintaining the autonomy of the universities and not making them subservient to the State on the plea that they receive State grants must be emphasised by all well-wishers of the country. We can generally accept the standard adopted by the Universities Grants Committee in Great Britain which has evolved a sound and efficient system of work, earning the praise of enlightened public opinion not only in Great Britain but in other advanced countries as well.

No external authority set up by the government can ever hope to secure coordination of work or enforce a common standard among all universities in India. It will thus become a super-university by itself, developing an extremely complex machinery, deadening the soul of all universities in India and making them rigid and stagnant. If such an authority is to enjoy executive powers, it will lead to a regimentation of university education which even totalitarian countries or autocratic regimes dared not experiment in. I do not ignore the need for coordination. I do not minimise the importance of maintaining adequate standards of university instruction and examinations. I appreciate the urgency of avoiding wastage and unnecessary duplication. All these necessary reforms have to be undertaken, first by each university acting in a rational manner, balancing regional requirements with national progress; secondly, by the inter-university board which, though having advisory powers, must be helped to develop healthy conventions and whose well-considered recommendations cannot be easily flouted by any university; thirdly, by well-informed deliberations in state legislatures and Parliament at the time of voting of demands on grants and lastly, by the Universities Grants Committee, which, functioning on the model of the British Grants Committee, can always exercise a healthy and decisive influence on both the administrative and the teaching activities of the universities concerned.

The universities of modern India have very little in common with ancient or medieval centres of learning. It is well known how the British authorities planned the establishment of universities in India about one hundred years ago mainly for their own administrative purposes. Western education itself was then visualised as the only passport to service and the learned professions, and also the means through which enlightened knowledge could elevate the people belonging to what was said to be rusty and backward civilisation. The very system of education which was deemed essential for forging bonds of unbroken alliance with the British power succeeded in unleashing revolutionary ideas and thoughts, which ultimately helped to throw off the yoke of alien rule in India. If we take a dispassionate view of what happened during the last one century, we must acknowledge that this has been an era in which good has been mixed with evil. The contact between the Indian mind and western thought and civilisation did not enslave the soul of India. In every domain of thought, in arts and architecture, in science, in history, philosophy and letters, in social services and in religious thought, great Indians gave their best, maintaining their stamp of originality as well as imbibing and assimilating fruits of western skill and knowledge. Though the number of Indians affected by such spread of knowledge was comparatively small, many of them assumed a much-needed political leadership and became the instruments of agitation and mass movements, leading ultimately to the political liberation of their country. The cultural renaissance preceded and created the silent political revolution. We must not, however, overlook the debit side as well. The masses were neglected. Villages where stagnant. Poverty reigned supreme. Elementary education remained in the background. Our languages were undernourished; specially neglected was that great storehouse of Indian knowledge and wisdom—the mother of most of our languages, Sanskrit. The aims and purposes of education were inconsistent with national aspiration. Respect for the noblest features of our great culture and civilisation dwindled away due to ignorance and disbelief. The pattern of society based on equality and justice, on contentment, and self-sufficiency that true education must foster and strengthen hardly took shape. Can we honestly maintain that after freedom we have been able to uproot these and other salient defects in our educational system?

Education must be examined from an organic standpoint. Free India must be able to cater to the needs of all stages of education as parts of one comprehensive national system. There need not be any conflict amongst primary, secondary and university stages, nor amongst literary, scientific, technical, vocational and agricultural courses of study. A national system of education must conceive of a balanced structure where due and proper emphasis will be laid on every section so as to maintain its harmony, its strength and solidarity. Today after freedom the universities must be conscious of much wider conception of their duties and responsibilities than before. There is an urgent need for adequate leadership in the professions, in commerce and industry, in politics and administration. Millions of teachers and workers are needed for institutions of various types. There awaits the solution of the problem of freeing the masses from want, disease and ignorance. There still remain untapped and hidden the vast natural resources and raw materials of India and it will be for the universities to create knowledge and to train minds which could bring together material resources and human energies which lie latent today.

I lay great stress on the need for developing the research activities of our universities. No doubt the importance of scientific study and research in modern ages must not be overlooked. It may not be possible for every university to specialise in every department of science; indeed want of resources and manpower will debar this. Yet the basic sciences must be a common factor and specialisation may be shared region-wise. Every university should offer facilities for study and residence to deserving students coming from other regions where similar facilities may not be available. There is a great need for encouraging research on subjects which have special relation to the Indian problems of today or to the basic conception of Indian culture and civilisation. Indian history, Indian thought and philosophy, Indian art, architecture, music, and Indian sociology afford field for laborious work by hundreds of scholars. The fruits of their study and investigation are bound to produce new light which will help us in remodelling the structure of our society and the pattern of our lives in a worthy manner. Information on these subjects is widely sought for today by people coming from distant lands and we fail to give them a correct and coordinated answer regarding many problems affecting our civilisation. To unearth the hidden wisdom of our country is not to seek benefit for ourselves alone, enabling us to appreciate our heritage, but also to share it with the rest of the world. Similarly, the gigantic problems relating to our social and economic reconstruction based on a comparative study of what exists here and the successful experiments made elsewhere have yet to be tackled. Political freedom, if not followed by social and economic emancipation, will be utterly meaningless and the guidance for this purpose must emanate in an appropriate measure from our teachers and advanced students, untrammelled by any dogma as such. It has been truly said that the main motif in India's history is her unity amidst diversity. What serious study, I ask, has been made of the urges, habits, outlook and modes of life of millions of men and women, of diverse castes and tribes, living under varied conditions, in plains and hills, in towns and villages, speaking a multitude of languages, but all cheerfully owning themselves as the sons and daughters of mother India, and swayed by common spiritual impulses? Some British administrators and experts and later on some renowned Indian scholars have no doubt dealt with some aspects of Indian sociology and anthropology, but much yet remains to be done before we can formulate a sound and progressive basis of true national consolidation. No country has ever spent too much on research either in the domain of arts or science. It matters little if we do not get a quick return, for we can never render a commercial account of research and investigation. Let our universities provide for basic training according to approved standards and maintain fellowships and scholarships on a well-planned basis. Let research for truth and knowledge be carried on in a spirit of harmony and cooperation, under the guidance of enlightened Indian teachers selected for their merit and efficiency.

A controversy faces us in respect of languages. While Indian languages must be fostered and developed in the widest possible manner, we need not and we must not take a hostile attitude towards English. Up to the secondary stage, the medium of instruction should be the mother tongue of the students or where it is not feasible, due to the paucity of numbers, the regional language should be the medium, with full facilities given to them to study their mother tongue. In many states, the regional languages will be rich enough to be the medium of instruction at collegiate and university stages also. By such an encouragement of the Indian languages will they be endowed with creative force and be able to compete with each other, and enrich the heritage of Indian literature. Hindi, which has been accepted as the official language of India, should be learnt by all without any hesitation. It will act as a powerful unifying force. The teaching of English should be revised so that less emphasis may be given on the compulsory study of English literature and more on current and spoken English, using it as a vehicle for general study and expression of views. We should have no prejudice against the English language as such. It no longer represents the language of our rulers. It is one of the greatest languages of the world through which we can make ourselves familiar with essential knowledge and information, to exclude which would render our education imperfect. Without lowering our sense of patriotism in any way, we can well utilise our two-centuries-old acquaintance with the English language to our best national advantage, increasing our capacity to compete with the rest of the world in spheres of higher education and international contacts. I similarly urge the systematic study of at least some of the important Indian languages at each university centre. A comparative study of Indian languages will be greatly facilitated, if under State patronage a scheme is formulated for bringing out well-known publications from different Indian languages in their original texts but printed in Devanagari script. I would urge also the revival of the study of Sanskrit and granting of special facilities for this purpose. I am not suggesting for a moment that these linguistic studies should be made compulsory, but the existence of such facilities is bound to attract the intelligent curiosity of a large number of our students and also to create a healthy foundation for proper appreciation of our cultural unity and heritage.

I would plead for exchange of university teachers on a planned basis along with programmes for visits of teams of university students from one centre to another. While our universities must be so equipped and administered as to make it unnecessary for Indian students to go abroad for studying ordinary subjects, our scheme for foreign scholarships and fellowships should be more liberal than at present. Care must be taken to ensure that we send abroad only those advanced students for whom facilities for specialised training do not exist in India. Such a rationalised scheme will save wastage of time and money. The system of examinations now in vogue also needs thorough revision. The increasing percentage of failures in the examinations of many universities is a matter of deep public concern. I do not wish to enter into a controversy and discuss how far it is due to the faults of students and how far to the prevailing system of study and examinations. In any case, we are accepting as inevitable the colossal wastage of human efforts and energy followed by deep frustration and sullen discontent amongst a large section of our youth. The rigidity of our university examinations can be removed only if we can provide for a more extensive tutorial system and make the final results dependent not on one examination but the performance of students during the entire session. This matter has been examined in detail by many foreign countries and no final and satisfactory solution has been periodically made. This has also to be examined in relation to our courses of study, our syllabus and methods of teaching. I do not ignore that any large-scale provision for tutorial work involves increased staff and hence additional expenditure which the educational authorities cannot by themselves meet without extra State aid.

No university can exist unless it can evoke a spirit of affection and loyalty in the minds of the students. Such an atmosphere of goodwill and cordiality cannot come into existence merely by means of extraneous rules and regulations of discipline. Our country was rightly proud of the traditional relationship of deep understanding between the teachers and the taught in days gone by. The present system of education and modern conditions of living are not always helpful for the maintenance of this relationship. The training that we give to our youth must be purposeful. If our goal is liberty and democracy then we must undertake the responsibility for teaching them the arts of being free and of governing themselves. If we teach them instead, the art of bullying and passive obedience, we will not achieve liberty and democracy at which we are aiming. Today the economic sufferings of the majority of our people are reflected in the attitude and outlook of our students. Grants of scholarships must be more liberal for the backward sections of our people and we must ensure that poverty does not stand in the way of any deserving youth from receiving the highest education. Many of our educational institutions are so large-sized that it is impossible to look after individual needs. Want of books and of guidance and half-hearted participation in sports and physical activities, want of food and nourishment depress the minds of the students. Want of aim and purpose in pursuing a particular type of education darkens their future. They also cannot but often share the sense of general frustration that dominates people's outlook today. Over and above these considerations, sometimes a wave of agitation, perhaps born out of a minor event, sweeps them away and they may lose valuable weeks or months. The contents of our education have yet to be remodelled so as to give them sufficient impulse for facing the perils of life with greater courage and success. The steadily increasing number of women students in our colleges and universities is bringing to the forefront the special claims of women's education and the role they may play in the service of the people. It is a supreme task for university administrators and teachers today to read into the minds of the youth of reawakened India and to place before them not only well-regulated courses of studies and well-thought-out programmes for extracurricular activities but also rousing in them a true scientific spirit and a deep impulse for devoted service to the cause of national well-being. A compulsory provision for three months of intensive social work for at least every intending graduate may narrow the gulf that divides the so-called educated class from the illiterate masses.

The great task of reconstruction is in front of us. The army of selfless and patriotic youths that must take up this challenge is also standing by. The only task is to link the two together, by giving the youth the training that they and the country deserve and to channelise and enthuse their selfless efforts in the noble task. Today, unemployment has become one of the curses of free India. Apart from millions of our countrymen who continue to remain in the dark abyss of ignorance, disease, poverty and superstition, we have thousands of educated youths who have passed out of colleges and universities and even received much coveted degrees and diplomas in science, engineering and medicine or have been otherwise qualified, who for want of work and opportunity are slowly withering away. They feel neglected, sullen and frustrated. No university can solve the problem of unemployment. Its main task is to impart a system of education that will not produce a race of unemployables. I admit even in this respect, much yet remains to be done by our universities. But the main task is for the State to see that they may be absorbed in employments and occupations made available to every son and daughter of India according to his or her ability. Economic depression chills the soul of man. What contribution can our educated youth make to serve society or to revive the glorious aspects of our culture and civilisation in accordance with the needs of the modern age if we cannot provide for them a decent standard of life?

Let the universities be the mouthpieces of that liberty of thought and expression which a true democracy must uphold. Let our students sweep away the cobwebs of mistrust and of the miasma of hatred from the minds of the people. An eagle alone can train an eagle. If teachers themselves are partisans and swayed by dogma, how can youth be expected to uphold free thought or righteous conduct? Let us declare that to us justice and liberty are meaningless if they do not include other men and other nations. It is not so much what our students learn, not so much what they know, as what they are which should concern us. Do we love liberty, love it so much that we will fight for it, die for it and will accord it to others as well as claim it for ourselves? Nations live or die according to the character of the people. Wealth, arms, munitions, disciplined armies and navies and air forces are of splendid service but the character of the people, the character into which the youth is growing, determines the life or death of the nation. 'Liberty,' says Manu, the great law-giver of our race, 'is happiness and dependence is misery.' With our ancient heritage, with the spirit of India still ennobling the mind of man, with our vast resources of manpower and buried wealth, with our undoubted capacity for assimilation of new ideas, let us, irrespective of all differences, make a supreme cooperative effort to raise our Motherland to a high and a nobler life of existence, bringing joy and contentment to all and making her a mighty instrument for the maintenance of world peace and freedom.

Speech delivered at the University of Delhi convocation in New Delhi on 13 December 1952

On Advancement of Education

18

ON SCIENCE EDUCATION

During the last twenty-five years, India has made noteworthy progress in the domain of higher scientific study and research. On an occasion like this, we cannot but recall with pride and pleasure that this has been achieved mainly through the efforts of Indian scholars who, after assimilating the best that their own universities could bestow, travelled abroad, equipped themselves with new knowledge and experience and came back to their Motherland, trained for national service. In this great movement, Calcutta has played her part with far-seeing vision and courage and has produced a band of capable and enthusiastic workers who have by no means remained confined to their own university—scholars whose contributions in the different branches of science have elicited admiration of eminent scientists in other and distant parts of the world. The splendid work which the University of Calcutta has been fortunate enough to accomplish has been possible as much on account of the far-sighted policy initiated by Sir Asutosh Mookerjee, your first president, as through the munificence of two of our illustrious countrymen, Sir Taraknath Palit and Sir Rash Behary Ghose, and later of the Kumar of Khaira. Outside the university, the three institutions which have added most to Calcutta's fame and prestige are the Asiatic Society of Bengal, the Bose Institute and the Indian

Association for the Cultivation of Science. Much valuable work has also been done in several scientific departments under State control which have been adorned by officers renowned for their ability and attainments. If Calcutta was the pioneer, other provinces have not lagged behind and the presence here of this distinguished galaxy of talent from all parts of India bears ample testimony to the progress which has been already achieved.

It will, however, be unwise for us to assume that we have reached our goal or have even come near it. Indeed much more remains to be done if India is to contribute her legitimate share to the scientific knowledge of the world. It is not for me to discuss here in detail the form your future activities should take. But, if you will permit me, I shall mention for your consideration only two problems of outstanding importance which must be solved if we are to enhance our national efficiency and prosperity.

It has been said that the future of civilisation depends upon the widening spread and deepening hold of the scientific habit of mind and it becomes an urgent duty with you, who represent science in this ancient land of ours, to think out and promulgate practical methods for affecting this. It is for you to indicate how to develop 'that questioning, impartial, problem-solving attitude of mind, which must obtain if truth and sanity are to rule the world'. It should be as much your duty thus to contribute towards the making of the Indian citizen as your privilege to closely relate science to our everyday life; to regard it not as the special field of work for the gifted few but to make it the inheritance of the many. Poets are often said to be the guides of mankind in the realm of thought, for they give shape and form to men's ideas. The same is no less true of men of science, with this difference that, while poets may draw inspiration from the limitless fountain of imagination, science, though not without its romance, cannot deviate from accuracy and truth. It is for you to raise the standard of education; to enrich its quality by interpreting the manifold discoveries of science to the lay public in non-technical language, preferably through our vernaculars; to unfold how the secrets of nature have been brought to light, how resolutely darkness has been chased away, how science, like sunshine before mist, has cleared away doubt and superstition and opened up a never ending vista before despairing humanity. This is one of the problems to which I venture to draw your attention. The other is concerned with the possibility—nay the imperative necessity—of an increasingly closer connection between the institution you represent and the development of Indian industries. While it is true that by your original researches you have attained individual eminence, and some have acquired international reputation, inspiring others to follow your examples, it is time for you to consider what contributions you can make for the industrial regeneration of your country; for the proper utilisation of the inexhaustible raw materials in which India abounds and which are at present being but partially utilised and that also not always to India's best advantage. Modern India asks you, have you considered the problem of helping the cause of our national progress not from the political platform where differences of opinion are bound to exist but from your quiet and peaceful laboratories and from your organised workshops? Have you considered how science should be applied towards the alleviation of poverty and sufferings of millions of your countrymen? It is for you to undertake a systematic and scientific investigation of India's industrial problems, the solution of which would result in the improvement of our economic condition. Who are better fitted for this great work than you, who are expected to act inspired solely by the lofty motive of serving your country and humanity not for personal gain or profit? What nobler return can you give for all the facilities which you have been privileged to enjoy and for the confidence which your countrymen have reposed in you?

Your responsibilities are indeed immense. You have taken upon yourselves the sacred task of widening the boundaries of knowledge. Your contributions are subjected to searching examination by the master minds of other countries which offer opportunities to their scholars on a scale which we have yet to attain. On you rests the maintenance of India's prestige and reputation as a home for scientific and technological study and research. You cannot remain satisfied with academic achievements only. India expects you to utilise your attainments in such a way as to benefit your country and humanity at large—to regard science not as a powerful instrument of destruction but as a vital factor for promotion of the good of mankind. To enable you to fulfil this noble mission, you are justly entitled to unstinted assistance from the people and from government. As trustees of the precious heritage of knowledge, may you use your gifts in a manner which may not at any stage be marred by petty jealousies or unprofitable friction; may you extend the usefulness of your organisation from more to more, cementing all differences and raising higher and higher the mighty fabric of the Temple of Truth and Service whose doors will be thrown open to all seekers of knowledge irrespective of caste, creed or colour!

Speech [welcome address] delivered at the Indian Science Congress on 3 January 1935

19

ON ADVANCEMENT OF SCIENCE

It is my proud privilege to offer a warm welcome to the delegates and other members who have assembled here as representatives of different universities and various academic bodies from all over the world. We, of this university and of this city of Calcutta which witnessed the inauguration of the Indian Science Congress, whose jubilee is being celebrated this year, feel honoured by their presence. We are particularly gratified that this should be a joint meeting of the Indian Science Congress and the British Association for the Advancement of Science which has done so much for the promotion of scientific knowledge not only in Great Britain but in the British Commonwealth of nations as well. This joint meeting which has brought together distinguished men of science from various parts of the world bears testimony to the spirit of fellowship which binds together the scientific workers of the world. It heartens us in these depressing times to think that at least in the realm of science and scholarship, there is a unity of outlook and activity which has immense possibilities for moulding the future destiny of the human race.

The prevalent idea that Indians are metaphysically minded and their contributions to positive science are inconsiderable is not based on a full and correct appreciation of historical facts. India has not been a mere dreamer.

In her great days, her missionaries went abroad to spread her culture and her civilisation far beyond her bounds. Charak and Susruta, Nagarjuna and Bhashkaracharyya, Aryabhatta and Lilavati and many others who explored the secrets of nature, made definite contributions to knowledge which succeeding ages have profited by. There has, unfortunately, been a long period of stagnation, but today India is again forging ahead and beginning to contribute to the world's stock of knowledge. Some of her illustrious sons have achieved international fame and eminence. There are many others, less known, who are quietly pursuing their activities in the domain of science, undaunted by adverse circumstances and sustained by remarkable zeal and devotion. It is perhaps a matter of justifiable pride for us to recall that this university was the first in modern India to foster the pursuit of higher scientific knowledge on an organised scale with the help chiefly of Indian scholars, trained here and abroad. We owe it mainly to the vision and constructive ability of Sir Asutosh Mookerjee, its vice chancellor and first president of your Congress, and to the munificence of two of Bengal's illustrious sons, Sir Taraknath Palit and Sir Rash Behary Ghosh. Today, this movement has spread to all parts of India and a steady growth of scientific activities is evident at different centres in the country.

If we are to achieve satisfactory results, it is imperative that larger freedom and ampler facilities should be given to universities and other bodies interested in scientific work. The problem of coordinating their activities and of ensuring unity and harmony among them is an urgent one. The conditions leading to a successful solution of this problem should engage the earnest attention of both scientists and administrators who should possess the right vision of temper.

More and more throughout the world science is being harnessed to the service of men. While specialists must necessarily labour in their chosen fields, the interconnections between the various branches of science are being increasingly stressed, and the distinction between pure and applied science is becoming less and less marked. While research in the pure sciences without any utilitarian object in view must continue to provide the fundamental basis of discoveries on which the application of science is to rest, the conscious collaboration between pure and applied science is being steadily fostered everywhere. Let this joint session, historic in its composition, give a clear and definite lead to future activities in India in the direction. India is a country where the vast body of scientific knowledge already gathered, has not yet been utilised to any appreciable extent for the daily life of man. The practical application of scientific knowledge to problems of industry and agriculture, of sanitation and nutrition, all contributing to the steady increase of the prosperity, joy and happiness of the people, is a question of paramount importance in a country where millions are yet sunk in poverty, disease and ignorance.

The fact that science and technology have been used and are likely to be used in future for destructive purposes has raised doubts in many minds about the utility of science itself. Indeed the harm that has been, can be and is being daily inflicted throughout the world by engines of destruction, scientifically devised, is incalculable. Science is being used for the purpose that no one who believes in humanity can contemplate with unconcern. There have been people, honest and well intentioned, who have been stampeded by this fact into a denial of science itself. A halt has been cried in many quarters to the march of science and technology. Yet, it must be clear on a little consideration that the blame must attach not to science but to those men and nations who call themselves civilised, and are shamelessly putting science to an inhuman use. Science, like fire, is capable alike of good and of evil and like fire it needs to be used with discretion and care. The good that science has done is obvious and immense. If used exclusively for the good of mankind, it is capable of promoting peace and happiness in this world and of conferring benefits beyond imagination.

What is wrong with the world is not the spirit of science but the moral and social failure of the peoples who handle science. Science in a comprehensive sense provides us with the material appliances of life. It is the spirit of man who uses them that requires to be educated. The view of science should be supplemented by the vision of beauty and truth. It is of no little significance that this congress is presided over by one who has proclaimed to us that the world of science reveals the mind of the Supreme One and it is men of his type who should be able to contribute towards the establishment of peace on earth and goodwill towards men.

In spite of political, national and racial prejudices, devotees of knowledge can and should collaborate and become the harbingers of the new era that is to be. Freedom and unfettered division to truth must be the supreme condition of their activities. Here in this gathering are assembled men and women from distant parts of the world who, while differing from one another in many respects, visibly demonstrate a fraternity that is truly human. When the clouds of distrust and oppression that hang over the world will lift, things will come out in clear perspective and matters that seem important at the moment will appear inconsequential. Humanity will then proceed in a spirit of common brotherhood to higher and still higher reaches of knowledge and happiness. Let India and her scholars play their part in this noble remaking of man's destiny. Rich with traditions and thoughts and endowed with strength and validity, India claims the right of being treated as a companion with equal rights in the world's march towards a higher and nobler civilisation. Let this international meeting mark a definite stage in this collaboration on a worldwide scale, based on justice and fair play, leading towards the triumph of truth and of righteousness, of freedom and of peace.

Speech delivered at the opening ceremony of the joint session of the British Association of Science and Indian Science Congress Association on 3 January 1938

20

SCIENCE EDUCATION AND RESEARCH IN INDIA

The world became conscious of atomic energy after the unfortunate atom bombing of two Japanese cities nearly three years ago. This incident unfortunately received such great publicity that it overshadowed the great peacetime applications of atomic energy which promise to cause a transformation of the world just as the steam engine did 150 years ago. We are told by the competent authorities that atomic energy may work out the following miracles:

- It places in the hands of man a source of power limitless in quantity, transportable to every region of the world and usable for every need of mankind. With this gift we can create conditions of paradise on a scale undreamt of by seers and saints and certainly impracticable in spite of good wishes with the power and technique at the disposal of man in earlier times. It will thus, relieve mankind of much of the drudgery which is responsible for the creation of societies composed of slaves and lords or capitalists and labourers.
- Atomic research places in the hands of man new weapons for study, control and treatment of diseases.

- It gives new and very powerful means of studying how plants and animals grow. This will open the way for better food production and nutrition.

India cannot, therefore, remain a mere spectator in this grand drama of human achievement, particularly when she has all the raw materials in plenty for the development of atomic energy. It may be that within our own lifetime, we may find the results of atomic energy research affecting all the phases of human life. At this dawn of the atomic age, we find ourselves very nearly in the same position as the first man who produced fire. The fire was used for cooking, heating and lighting and very often for burning one's enemies and their belonging. But the first fire makers could not imagine that one day fire would be used for steam engine, locomotives, turbines and for central heating. Hundreds of years elapsed between the first discovery of fire and its large scale industrial application. The same may happen with respect to atomic fire; but the USA, England, France and Soviet Russia have set up huge organisations for fundamental as well as developmental research on atomic energies, in order to shorten the time period between the first scientific discovery of release of atomic energy and its peacetime applications. Even small countries like Sweden, Holland and Norway have mobilised their scientific talents and resources for atomic energy research.

The Government of India has, of late, been conscious of its duties in this respect and an Atomic Energy Bill has been passed in our Parliament. An Atomic Energy Research Board was also set up nearly two years ago.

It is a matter of satisfaction that the University of Calcutta has been the pioneer in India in recognising the importance of atomic energy research. It is nearly seven years that the university took the first steps in this matter, thanks to a gift obtained from the Tata Charities of Bombay through the efforts of the present Prime Minister of India. In spite of conditions created by war, famine and the apathy of the government, then in power, our workers have been actively engaged in building up the laboratory and contributing their share of research, some of which have received international recognition.

I am sorry to note that post-war conditions have made the continuance of the work undertaken still more difficult, for India has to import all her scientific instruments and machineries from abroad. Some of the sources of our supply of scientific instruments like Germany, other European countries and Japan have gone totally out of the picture while England and the USA require all the enormous expansion of their own scientific activity during the post-war period. The USA has even gone so far as to put a ban on the export of all instruments and scientific apparatus used for atomic research.

Free India has to take up this challenge of post-war world conditions. The Government of India has appointed a committee under the chairmanship of GR Paranjpe of Bombay for giving them plans for a Scientific Instruments Establishment which will be capable of producing all the scientific apparatus and instruments needed by India's scientific men, technicians and industrialists. Further, we may well regulate the export of such materials in which India is in a position of vantage, that is, manganese, mica, monazite, beryl, finished jute products and tea. Export of these materials should be regulated on a barter system for such of our immediate necessities as petrol, machineries and scientific instruments.

We must remain fully alive to the needs of fundamental research on every branch of human knowledge particularly in atomic energy. I am told by the competent authorities that in spite of the spectacular effect of the atom bomb, they know very little of the laws of the atomic nuclei, and the processes leading to the release of atomic energy. Fundamental discoveries in this line may revolutionise the whole technical procedure and make all our present machineries obsolete. For this reason, America and European countries are spending colossal sums of money on fundamental research in nuclear studies.

I am glad that the University of Calcutta has now taken the bold step of organising a full-fledged Institute of Nuclear Physics devoted to teaching and fundamental research. Thanks to the fact that it started a theoretical and practical course in nuclear physics seven years ago, we have now a number of young men with suitable training who are eligible for appointment in any atomic energy establishment which may be set up in the near future. I am also glad to hear that about a dozen of the scholars of the University of Calcutta have gone abroad for further training in nuclear physics in the best research centres of the world.

I hope that with this nucleus and after the completion of the Institute of Nuclear Physics, the University of Calcutta will be able to provide arrangement for teaching and research for a larger number of students every year. The total amount of money spent both on the capital and recurring heads are extremely modest when we remember the huge sums spent in similar establishments in the USA and England. I am glad to know that the government of Bengal has already given Rs 2 lakh for the building and I hope they will provide the balance needed to complete the building and its equipment which may come up to Rs 3.5 lakh, in the supplementary budget.

The Government of India is already considering the question of assuring continuity of the grant which this institute has been receiving from the Council of Scientific and Industrial Research for the last two years. I hope our industrialists and capitalists will also come forward with offers of permanent endowments for the creation of research fellowships at the institute.

In closing, let me express the hope that the Institute of Nuclear Physics may form the nursery of nuclear scientists for the service of India and may continue to make contributions of a fundamental nature in the near future.

Speech delivered while laying the foundation stone of the Institute for Nuclear Physics, University of Calcutta, in 1948

21

TECHNICAL EDUCATION AND ECONOMIC DEVELOPMENT

As we are all aware, the year following our attainment of Independence was one of great economic and political stress. Not only was the Government of India beset with a number of complex political problems on the morrow of Partition but also our economic machinery was creaking and slowing down as a result of the aftermath of the World War as well as the new economic strains imposed by the immediate effects of Partition. Today our industrial production is slowly looking up from the low level reached in 1947 but this means no more than that we have just been able to avert a crisis, if only for the time being. Our economic position is still precariously poised. The food position is as acute as ever and even in regard to industrial production, for example, in regard to textiles, our largest single industry, the position depends unfortunately on the uncertain supply of cotton. To put it generally, although we have attained our political freedom, the task of economic reconstruction has yet to be tackled effectively and on a national scale. No political institution can be of permanent benefit to the country, or even in itself of a stable character, unless the basic foundation of a contented people, having a reasonable standard of living is assured in that country. The economic safety of the vast masses of the people—their economic security, their standards of living—is the foundation on which all political institutions rest. Political freedom, therefore, has neither meaning nor stability unless its economic contents are realised.

This has become almost a trite saying: that political freedom without economic freedom has no meaning. The standards of living of the general masses can only be raised rapidly if there is a national plan for economic development. This will require a widespread technological revolution in industry and agriculture. This is where your importance lies, for, if I may say so, you and others will form the personnel for that coming technological revolution.

While, therefore, all realise the importance which technical training must play in the economic development of India, it is indeed paradoxical, and to say the least, tragic to find that young men who have gone abroad at government expense or at their own expense for higher technical training, are at the moment finding it difficult to get suitable employment when they come back. Does this denote that we have already a surfeit of technical personnel? You will all agree that this is farthest from truth and this strange malady only signifies that while we have sent abroad hundreds of young men for technical training, there has been little planning in this regard. The Government of India has now, therefore, decided not to send any more scholars outside for training which is available in India and again if the government selects scholars for going abroad for training at government expense, the government must ascertain beforehand what facilities for employment these scholars would receive on return. The output of technical personnel must be synchronised in quantity as well as distribution with the rate of economic development which we are going to undertake in various lines.

For a number of reasons which I need not recount at this stage, our economic programme has been somewhat lagging. Nevertheless, we have not been quite idle. We are doing the spade work for the establishment of a number of very vital industries and when these industries are actually established, they will form the solid ground work on which economic development of our country may proceed. For example, we are now getting project reports prepared for a number of industries. One or two new steel works with a capacity of one million tons will be established and preliminary reports in this regard are under preparation. Project reports for the establishment of industries for the manufacture of synthetic oil from coal, heavy electrical plants and also of wireless transmitters and radio valves are also under preparation. We are also going to set up an industry for the manufacture of telephone cables, machine tools, diesel engines, tractors, penicillin, etc. Detailed investigations for the establishment of these projects have been taken in hand actively. These government schemes alone, if we are in a position to implement them, might cost us anywhere between 200 to 300 crore of rupees. You will agree that this is nearly as much as we can take up immediately within the limitations of our present resources.

The fulfilment of the programme of industrial expansion which the Government of India has undertaken in a spirit of practical idealism requires the cooperation of all and not the least the cooperation of friendly foreign countries without whose technical assistance progress is likely to be exceedingly slow. India is, therefore, not approaching this problem in any narrow nationalistic spirit but in the belief that world prosperity like world peace is one and indivisible and that in this effort she would get the willing cooperation on honourable terms of countries more fortunately placed.

When these plans go through say, within three to five years, there will be a great demand for technical personnel, for without very great increase in the supply of technical personnel no economic development plans can be put through. The provision of technical and managerial personnel is one of the fundamental conditions of economic progress even in advanced countries like England where higher technical education has taken on a new emphasis. The system of technical education in Great Britain is being reorganised according to the recommendations of the Percy Committee which expressed the apprehension that the position of Great Britain as the leading industrial nation was being seriously endangered by a failure to secure the fullest possible application of science to industry. The Scientific Manpower Committee which was appointed by the Government of India went into the question and it came to the conclusion that even leaving aside the requirements of government for their contemplated large scale public works and development projects and to meet the immediate requirements of industry alone we have to plan for at least a four-fold increase in the output of all categories of personnel if we are to meet our needs for the next four or five years.

This computation is based on the basis of the figures of capital issues already taken out by private enterprises. You will easily realise that if the new government projects which I have mentioned above have to be carried out what large increase in our technical manpower would be required. Our budget for technical personnel can of course be worked out properly only by a detailed analysis of the actual development programme along different lines which we are going to embark upon in the next three or five years. Nevertheless, we can make a rough assessment of our future requirements of technical personnel. It has been computed that about one hundred high grade technologists would be required for the chemical industry involving a capital outlay of ten crore rupees and it has been suggested that since for the next fifteen years the capital investment of all industries was likely to be in the neighbourhood of Rs 1,500 crore, India must produce at least 15,000 high grade technicians assuming that the requirements of various industries for high grade technologists would generally approximate to that for the chemical industry. The above is, however, a rough and ready method and a better approach to the problem would be to ascertain the requirements of technical personnel in relation to capital investment in respect of each industry employing such personnel. The output of technical personnel must then be related to the total demand among various categories thus computed. We can get an idea of the dimension of our task by illustration of the experience of Russia. At the inception of the first five-year plan, the Soviet industry as a whole had at its disposal a staff of technical personnel numbering 58,000 only. This figure was continuously raised under the successive five-year plans until in 1939 it reached the impressive figure of 9,590,000 out of a total population of 170 million.

From the foregoing, it would be evident that once we undertake the development plans in right earnest, shortage of technical manpower will be a major factor limiting the rate of progress. The provision of technical education in order to train the necessary technical and managerial personnel is one of the fundamental conditions of economic progress. Even the advanced countries of the world with ample facilities for technical education already in existence are making renewed endeavours to enlarge these facilities. The Sarkar Committee, which was appointed to report on the establishment of technical institutions, tartly pointed out that facilities for education in this country are so meagre and insufficient to meet even the existing demand that the establishment of a few technical institutions even before detailed survey is completed can never be regarded as leading to a surfeit of such facilities.

I hope I have spoken enough to impress on you the importance of the provision of an adequate supply of technical personnel for the economic development of the country. For many years to come, our technological institutions will be unable to supply the top-grade personnel and know-how, which would be required to put through the development projects we have on hand. We have perforce to import foreign technical assistance in the initial stages but we are developing a system of appointing Indian understudies with sufficient general training attached to the foreign technical personnel so that these understudies can rapidly train themselves up in a practical manner and take up complete charge of the units. On the recommendation of the Sarkar Committee, the government has decided to establish four higher technical institutions. The government will also help the expansion of facilities in specialised institutions and university departments. Maulana Azad has already given you indications of increased facilities which you will be getting in the years to come.

Your institution, along with other universities and institutions will, I hope, be able to play a great part in the provision of technical education in our country; without which economic progress would be thwarted. I am very grateful that I have been enabled to come in close touch with you all and have the opportunity of knowing something of your expanding field of activities.

Speech delivered at the annual function of the Science and Technology Association of the Delhi Polytechnic on 2 March 1949

22

ROLE OF STATISTICS IN EDUCATION

An eminent statistician has remarked that knowledge of statistics is like knowledge of foreign languages or of algebra, for it may prove of use at any time under any circumstances. The study of statistics had its origin in the compilation of facts and figures for purposes of administration, of the State, and in this sense the subject must have been in existence from the earlier times. The Egyptians, Babylonians, Romans, Chinese and the Persians used to preserve detailed records of the resources of the State. In India, administrative statistics reached a high state of organisation nearly 2,000 years ago. In the classic period of Sanskrit culture, there are numerous references to detailed statistics of various kinds in inscriptions as well as in technical treatise. Due importance was also attached to descriptive statistics in the administration of the State under the Muslim rulers. Reference need only be made to the *Ain-i-Akbari*, the great administrative and statistical survey of India compiled during the reign of Emperor Akbar. In the early days of British administration, each department under the Government of India used to publish statistics relating to subjects under its control until 1871 when the post of Director General of Statistics was created and a central organisation was gradually developed. On the analytical side, modern statistical methods were probably first used in India in an organised form about twenty-five years ago by the distinguished scholar, Sir Gilbert Walker, in connection with his pioneer work on weather correlation and the forecasting of the monsoon rainfall in India. The reorganisation of agricultural research following the Royal Commission on Agriculture gave a great impetus to the study of analytical statistics in this country.

As a method and technique of estimation, statistics is as helpful in natural sciences as in sociological studies. But to the layman it is its utilitarian aspect that appeals most strongly, and I think I shall not be wrong when I say that ability to offer assistance in the solution of the diverse problems of national life has given the chief impetus to the progress of statistical studies, and research in western countries. Statistical methods have already become indispensable in industry in connection with the specification of standards, the testing of raw materials and finished products, economic control of mass production in factories as well as in industrial research. In public health and medicine, modern statistical methods are being increasingly used in all progressive countries. In the sphere of psychology and education, the period of preliminary experiments is over and systematic work on intelligence and achievement tests has been started in many centres. The possibilities of application of analytical methods in connection with vocational selection and guidance are immense and must be properly explored for the solution of the problem of middle class unemployment.

In the domain of economic enquiries, Indian economists and statisticians must find increasing scope for their energy and talents in the years to come. Here we have a vast and virgin field likely to yield rich harvest to pioneer workers. Policies and programmes are being formulated having for their object the economic uplift of the masses. Such programmes, if they are to achieve the objects they have in view must be broad-based on accurate data, such as figures relating to income and wages, cost of living and indebtedness. It is for a syndicate of scholars, of economics and statisticians to take up such problems and evolve the technique necessary for measuring the relative well-being of different class and communities. The problem of comparative tax burdens of various groups is another issue which will loom large in the period of reconstruction that lies ahead. Equally important is the question of compiling on an accurate basis statistics of production in India in relation to agriculture and fisheries, forests and minerals, organised industries and cottage industries. Figures in respect of the average national income in India, based on guesses and conjectures, are notoriously inaccurate and it should be the aim of statisticians to place such facts on a scientific and accurate basis.

I have no desire to add further to the lists of problems affecting national welfare to the solution of which a knowledge of and experience in statistical methods may be successfully applied. Useful work is already being done by officials and non-officials in some parts of British India and of the native states. The Indian Statistical Institute has helped to bring together scholars engaged in the investigation of diverse problems in scattered parts of India and to establish personal contacts among them, the importance of which need hardly be emphasised. The institute has also arranged to impart training to new recruits and to men already employed in work in various provinces. It must not overlook however that the field that yet remains to be traversed is too expensive for the limited resources of the institute or of individual workers. It is the paramount duty of the State to assist them liberally in the work.

The universities in India must also play their part in the task of supplying trained statisticians whose service should be availed of in increasing numbers by the government and other organisations in the solution of the many problems that fall within their jurisdiction. Here in Calcutta under the auspices of the university, a work on analytical statistics was done by Sir Brajendra Nath Seal more than twenty years ago which I believe inspired a small band of workers towards further activity, ultimately leading to the development of the statistical laboratory and the institute. Statistics has also remained included for many years in the curriculum of studies of the MA examination in economics and provisions have been made for its teaching. There is no doubt, however, that this branch of learning has since grown in volume and importance, and there should be no further delay in providing adequately and satisfactorily for the systematic study of the subject and its research at the university.

We are fortunate in having as the president of the first session of the conference a scholar of eminence. Professor Ronald Fisher, the second to adorn the most important Chair in statistics in the whole world, the first occupant having been Karl Raison himself. He has also accepted the invitation of the university to deliver a course of special lectures. Under his able and distinguished guidance in the conference, we feel confident, that we will be able to create conditions of service and set up a standard of work and efficiency which it may worthily hand over to succeeding generations. Let unity, search for truth and devotion to duty mark, its deliberations, providing a common ground for mathematicians, statisticians, economists, administrators and businessmen all inspired with a fervent desire to contribute their share, large or small, towards the formulation and fulfilment of policies which will add and increase happiness and progress of the people of India.

Speech [welcome address] delivered at the first session of Indian Statistical Conference on 7 January 1938

23

THE ROYAL ASIATIC SOCIETY AND ITS CONTRIBUTION

The annual report of the society which has just been placed before you gives a brief survey of its many-sided activities. The task of reorganisation undertaken some years back is being carried on with vigour and efficiency. Preparation of catalogue of our books and our invaluable stock of manuscripts and their preservation and repair are proceeding in a scientific way. Slip catalogue for about 13,000 manuscripts made over to us by the Indian Museum, has been made with the printing of descriptive catalogue of Sanskrit as well as Islamic manuscripts. Our journal is now a regular feature of our activities and important works are appearing in the series of our memoirs. *Bibliotheca Indica* has been revitalised and a number of important books has been added to this series during the last five years. Our sale of publications has rapidly increased, indicating a welcome appreciation on the part of scholars and general readers. The funds thus available are being utilised in further useful undertaking. We have just decided to print the second and third volumes of the *Ain-i-Akbari* revised and edited by our renowned colleague, Sir Jadunath Sarkar. The society is grateful to the Government of India for granting facilities for use of paper without which our publication department would have come to a standstill. The last twelve months witnessed a record increase of our members and they have come from all classes of enlightened people, irrespective of race, creed and community.

The outstanding activity of the society during the last year relates to the proposals made in connection with cultural reconstruction in India. The main topic of my address today will deal with this question, so vitally affecting the country's future welfare and progress. The society does not claim to have said the last word on the subject. Our proposals will, however, form the basis for a fruitful discussion and will serve to stimulate public opinion. The proposals that have emanated from the society have been carefully examined by two ably-constituted committees representing diverse points of view. I deem it, however, my duty to record my appreciation of the pioneer work done in this connection by one of our esteemed colleagues, Mr Justice Edgley, who in spite of his onerous duties as judge has served the cause of Indian history and culture with all the zeal and fervour of a devoted scholar.

When the Royal Asiatic Society of Bengal was founded in the eighties of the eighteenth century, science still formed a part of general culture. The study of man and nature was the avowed object of the scholars and philosophers of those days. The study of man was not yet dissociated from the study of nature. All human achievements whether embodied in traditions and institutions, both civil and religious, or those in the field of nature. But the world has moved far since those days. Science has made such great strides that it has far outgrown its original scheme. It has brought so many comforts to us that however relative their importance may be in the history of human efforts, it has almost dazzled our eyes and thrown cultural studies into the background. This has not been without its baneful effects. Science, almost snatched away from the hands of those selfless philosophers who brought it into existence for the solution of higher problems in nature, has been applied, much to the awe and indignation of its makers, to purpose that have brought disasters to humanity. It has often failed to render that service to us which it could have done within the original scheme. Time has, therefore, come when science should be made to yield its due place to human culture.

Science is essentially international and does not represent the true ideals and aspirations of any particular nation. Only in the field of its application, it is conditioned by national exigencies. If such exigencies are disregarded, if the national needs and requirements are ignored, if the local conditions and capacity for adaptation are overlooked, the application of science produces results that are not beneficial to the nation. The ideals and aspirations of a nation are best represented by its culture. It cannot be denied that in India too, in spite of the variety in languages, religions and physical types, there is a basic national culture. Under the influence of environment, whether geographical, physical or ethnic, we have evolved through millenniums of years' cultural traditions which bind us together into an Indian nation, however different our religious convictions may be. Sinister propaganda may cloud our vision for the moment and keep the integrating elements separate for a time, but if we search our hearts we will at once discover those inclinations which we have inherited from age-long traditions of a common culture. All creations in the field of literature, philosophy, painting, sculpture, architecture and music, irrespective of the zonal, communal or religious affiliations of their creators, move the hearts of all of us alike. They alone stand as the symbol of our unity and nationhood.

When therefore, we are on the threshold of a new age, as it seems, and when there are talks of all-round reconstruction in various spheres of our national life, we must try to realise once more our true cultural ideals and aspirations. All reconstructions, whether scientific, industrial or economic, must go hand in hand with a cultural reconstruction of the nation. That alone can arouse to the highest degree that consciousness in us which is required, especially at this moment, to stand as a united Indian nation in the true sense of the term. Such a reconstruction will inculcate in us love for the country, respect for its history, tradition, literature, arts and monuments and arouse in us a balanced sense of pride for all that was ours and for all that we have inherited from the past. This sense of pride must come from a proper evaluation of our cultural heritage so that it does not become over aggressive. History has shown us in a poignant manner what harm an aggressive nationalism can do to humanity. In our study of the past, we have received from the west an unassailable method, but it must be admitted that this method alone cannot unfold the past in its true perspective. Those who are born in the tradition, who have inherited the culture of the land through ages and have a sense of respect for that heritage are in a better position to apply the method with the greatest amount of success. The study of the past does not mean the dissection of a carcass. The past is not a dead past. It has brought the present into being and those who live in that present are best qualified to discover the subtle links between the past and the present which constitute the very life of a civilisation.

The annual address which was delivered by Sir William Jones on 24 February 1785, the second year of the then newly started Asiatic Society of Bengal, contains these significant words: 'The civil history of their (Asiatic) vast empires, and of India in particular, must be highly interesting to our common country; but we have a still nearer interest in knowing all former modes of ruling these inestimable provinces, on the prosperity of which so much of our national welfare and individual benefit seems to depend. A minute geographical knowledge not only of Bengal and Bihar, but for evident reasons, of all the kingdoms bordering on them, is closely connected with an account of their many revolutions: but the natural productions of these territories especially in the vegetable and mineral systems, are momentous objects of research to an imperial, but which is a character of equal dignity, a commercial people.' The Asiatic Society of Bengal inaugurated in the time of Warren Hastings, the first Governor General of India, was thus the first organisation whose business was not only to collect materials, both literary and archaeological, for the past history of India, but also to amass concrete information about her vast natural resources. The selfless efforts of its organisers and generations of its members, both European and Indian, during a little more than a century and a half of its history have brought together a mass of materials which are so worthily displayed in the pages of the past and present volumes of its journal. The various collections of Indian objects of archaeological, geological, zoological, palaeontological, entomological, anthropological and ethnological character, which were so assiduously made by its previous members, actually served as the substantial nucleus of the Indian Museum, Calcutta, one of the finest museums of the world. The literary efforts of its past alumni inspired to a very great extent not only many outsiders but also several eminent children of the soil like Raja Rajendralal Mitra to engage themselves in the work of throwing considerable light on the then little known history of India's past culture and tradition.

The task of writing a true and connected history of pre-Muslim India has been rendered extremely difficult by the colossal loss caused to ancient Indian monuments due to a policy of destruction pursued by foreign elements who periodically visited India, either for plunder or for gaining political control over her destinies prior to the advent of the British rule. Such monuments constitute the principal source for a systematic reconstruction of our past history and the preservation and proper study of what little is still left to us are of utmost importance in this respect. When we study the history of the previous attempts for the preservation of our cultural inheritance, during the early and middle periods of the British rule in India, we are confronted with the absence of any active interest of the government in this matter. The noble efforts of such individuals as Jones, Colebrooke, Wilson, Princep, Kittoe, Cunningham, Fergusson, Raja Rajendralal Mitra, Bhau Dauji, Bhagawan Lal Indraji, Ramkrishna Gopal Bhandarkar and others in collecting materials for the past history of Indian culture and publishing them were mostly made in their private capacity. The original example of duty which was set to government by this band of enthusiastic workers could not but evoke some sort of response, of however tardy a character, in the former, and some of them, such as Cunningham and others, were given official status and encouraged to pursue their useful activities. But even then the government, especially in the last part of the company's rule, were culpably ignorant of the nature and magnitude of this kind of work on account of their total inability to grasp the real values of things. Lord William Bentinck is regarded as one of the most enlightened Governor Generals of India and yet it was in his time that the Taj Mahal was on the point of being destroyed for the value of its marbles. It was the same ruler of India who sold by auction the marble bath in Shah Jehan's palace at Agra, originally torn up by Lord Hastings for a gift to George IV. After 1857, a solemn proposal was made by the then government to raze to the ground the Jama Masjid at Delhi, one of the noblest ceremonial mosques in the world. As late as 1868, the gateways of the Great Stupa at Sanchi in the Bhopal State were on the point of being destroyed and one of them, the eastern one, was about to be presented to Napoleon III, the Emperor of the French. Be it said to the credit of John Lawrence, one of the members of the government, that this great act of spoliation was successfully prevented through his efforts. Some sculptured pillars of the beautiful Ajmere temple, turned hastily into a mosque during the early Muslim period and now known as Adhai-din ki Jhompra, were pulled down by a zealous officer to construct a triumphal arch for the then Viceroy to pass under. Innumerable sculptural and architectural pieces from Sarnath, belonging to Brahmanical and Buddhist shrines of great antiquity, were carried away by official orders from the site and thrown into the Ganges as ballast when the Dufferin Bridge was being constructed at Benares. Many more such instances of vandalism of greater or lesser magnitude can be cited for which the government of earlier times can be held directly responsible either through errors of commission or omission.

It was, however, in the time of Lord Canning, the first Viceroy, that archaeological work in India won for the first time some sort of permanent State patronage. The Archaeological Survey of Northern India was constituted in 1860 and Cunningham was appointed in 1862 as Archaeological Surveyor and afterwards the first Director General of Archaeology in India. The twenty-three volumes of old archaeological reports that were published by him and some of his able assistants show what good use was made by him and his lieutenants of the limited opportunity with which they were provided. Then followed a long period of partial stagnation and occasional spurt in the governmental activities of preservation and study of the ancient and medieval Indian monuments. It must be said to the credit of Lord Curzon, one of India's most forceful Viceroys and Governor Generals, that he recognised the full value of this work. He very correctly pointed out in his speech before the members of the Asiatic Society of Bengal in 1899 that—'it is in the exploration and study of purely Indian remains, in the probing of archaic mounds, in the exploration of old Indian cities and in the copying and reading of ancient inscriptions, that a good deal of the exploratory work of the archaeologist in India will in future lie…A curtain of dark and romantic mystery hangs over the earlier chapters, of which we are slowly beginning to lift the corners. This also is not less an obligation of government. Epigraphy should not be set behind research any more than research should be set behind conservation. All are ordered parts of any scientific schemes of antiquarian work'.

The reconstituted Archaeological Department of India from the time of

Lord Curzon onwards worked under the able guidance of Sir John Marshall, and it was in the latter's period of official tenure that one of the most outstanding archaeological discoveries of India was made by a Bengali archaeologist of eminence, the late Rakhaldas Banerjee. The discovery of the prehistoric sites in Sind and lower Punjab regions, which after systematic excavation yielded invaluable mementos of the Indus Valley culture, was an event of far-reaching importance, for it changed a great deal of our preconceived notions about the nature and antiquity of Indian culture. Another important result of the activities of the Archaeological Department was to inspire many private individuals and societies with ideas about the systematic collection of materials for the past history and culture of our country. Varendra Research Society, to mention only one among the latter, proves to a remarkable degree what good work of this character could be done by a band of enthusiasts inspired by the deepest love for the cultural achievement of their own land. The University of Calcutta took a leading role in the work of throwing considerable light on early Indian history and culture. The practical side of this work, namely, the collection of archaeological and artistic materials, which was not at first taken up by it, has since been energetically adopted. The Asutosh Museum, at present an indispensable adjunct of the University of Calcutta, has within a very short period of its existence more than justified its creation. Thanks to the devoted zeal of its curator, it can very well be regarded now as one of the few repositories of materials of inestimable value for the study of art and culture of Bengal. We shall watch with interest the recent attempts to revitalise Indian archaeology due mainly to the energetic efforts of India's new Director General of Archaeology.

I do not look at Indology from any narrow angle. To me, Indology means much more than a mere study of India's past language and literature by a limited group of scholars; it is a message born out of healthy mass culture, a message of the people of India to the world. Indian people have lived peacefully side by side with her neighbouring peoples and races for millenniums together. When Indian nationals visited foreign lands, they carried with them not arms, not ammunitions, but messages of peace and goodwill. Cultural intercourse between India, on the one hand, and China, Indo-China, Malaysia and the

South Sea Islands on the other is now a matter of history. People of India were equally catholic in their assimilation of other cultures. The Greeks, the Scythians and the Huns came as enemies, but were ever absorbed within our social fabric. Unity amidst diversity was the greatest achievement of Indian culture and civilisation. The crusaders against Brahmanical Hinduism, Buddha and Parsvanatha, were not branded as heretics but received the same respect as is paid to its own founders. Rishi Charvaka, the champion of materialism, is held in the same high esteem as is offered to Vasistha or Visvamitra, the torch bearers of the orthodox faith. Social equity and justice was the watchword of our life. Every one found his own place in the social and economic life of the land, destined to play his own part and to fulfil his own mission. Every citizen was only the part of a complete whole, a mere limb of a dynamic social organism. There was a thousand-fold diversity no doubt, but this diversity was never compartmental; it blended into a unity in the ultimate purpose—the welfare of mankind irrespective of one's birth, wealth, creed or religion. Education was given the highest place. The learned are respected everywhere, the king only in his own land (*Svadeshe pujyate raja vidvan sarvattra pujyate*). The average standard of education was high enough to produce scholars, and the kings were ever ready to support them, to find their material needs so as to ensure them abundant leisure for following study and research.

Research does not mean a mere excavation of the past; its main task lies in building for the future. Organised study and research requires a study centre, an academy for the cultivation of arts and sciences. Our society has afforded so long a meeting ground of scholarly men, old and young, wholly engaged in the pursuit of knowledge following diverse branches of study in different organisations. But the demands of the age are greater. We should from now begin to think in terms of broad basing our foundation so as to serve the purpose of a full-fledged academy of research, which must have its own whole-time scholars and fellows, dedicated to the cause for which the society stands.

As I said in my last address, the society, though remaining a learned one, must continue to be a well-equipped and functioning centre from where new information and knowledge may be disseminated to the public in various fields of intellectual activity, social and economic, literary and scientific. I am glad to tell you that the society during the past year, has sought to elevate the intellect of the people and to broaden their minds and sharpen their curiosity by means of a series of lectures and discussions on important branches of knowledge, both ancient and modern. It has undertaken to publish a volume, embodying select lectures delivered at the society's discussion meeting, which would serve as a good introduction to Indian life and culture. Another volume embodying results of modern scientific researches is also under preparation. These two volumes will bring home to the people it serves the fruits of investigations of scholars in various fields of intellectual activity.

Let me emphasise that I do not at all minimise the need for a radical reorientation of the economic and industrial policy of India. A country whose educational and economic backwardness is a standing disgrace to human civilisation has got to be placed on her feet again and its people must get the fullest advantage of its inexhaustible raw materials. But let me state at the same time that neither can India attain her full strength and glory nor can she contribute worthily to the cause of stabilising human civilisation, if we ignore the need for a proper cultural reconstruction in India. The proposals made by the society are of a far-reaching character and they deal with such problems as establishment of a national museum, of a school of Indian architecture, of a national cultural trust, of a national academy of arts and letters, of national parks, of a central record office in Bengal, of a travellers' department in India and also the future development of the Archaeological Department. The proposed all-India institution, we have emphasised, must be allowed to function as free and autonomous bodies enjoying full measure of State support but worked and organised by outstanding representatives of diverse cultural and scientific interests and occupations, all working together for revitalising Indian life and civilisation.

The bicentenary of the birth of our founder, Sir William Jones, falls next year. It is my privilege to call upon you to prepare for the celebration of this occasion in a manner befitting the memory of that great Orientalist who paved the way, by establishing this society, towards a common meeting ground of the culture of the east and the west. The west has failed to show mankind the way to peace and happiness; it has led us into the blind alley of death and devastation. The torch in the orient, in India and in China, is still alight, still ready to serve the ailing humanity and to show her the path of truth. The future of the world lies in a just recognition of freedom for all, which must be the principle of peace yet to come. In the words of a thoughtful western writer, the abnormal unhealthy experience of war has only given the countries glimpses of each other fighting, in deep distress, wounded, dying. The peoples have not had the experience yet of living together, respecting and honouring each other as true equals. In the renaissance of the Middle Ages, it was the east that gave to the west. In the modern renaissance of Asia, it was the west that gave to the east. But now each has something to give to the other and from this mutual need and richness there will spring, if the times are free, life for mankind richer and better than anything we have yet known. It has been truly said, today the peoples of the east and west need each other. Nothing must be allowed to keep them apart—neither the greed of merchants nor the ambition of empire-builders and dictators, nor the prejudices of the arrogant. The plain peoples of the arrogant. The plain peoples of the earth must find each other, they must discover that they are alike in their simple and deep desires. East and west—we are rightly reminded—we do long for the same things, for love and home and children; for work whose fruit will feed the family; for peace, for freedom in which to live and think and grow. These are not impossible longings, not dreams that cannot be realised. They are the rights of all mankind. But the plain peoples must work together to achieve them, and give them to each other or they will not have them. And how can they honourably work together, except as friends, true and equal, ceasing to be strangers and forsaking the role of the exploiters and the exploited?

Animated by a passionate longing for breaking the barriers between the east and the west, based upon the fundamental concepts of the mighty civilisation of India, our illustrious founder called upon all true lovers of peace and seekers after truth to open every door of approach, to cultivate every source and seekers after truth to open every door of approach, to cultivate every source of knowledge, to try to find out by every possible means the ways and habits and beliefs and hopes of all peoples, so that with common knowledge and in mutual understanding we may strive together for a good and peaceful world. May his idealism and his far-sighted vision animate the present and future workers of the society so that it may fully contribute to usher in a new era of peace, progress and freedom in India and in other parts of the civilised world!

Speech delivered at the annual meeting of the Royal Asiatic Society of Bengal on 5 February 1945

For Education

THE VISVA-BHARATI BILL DEBATE IN THE INDIAN PARLIAMENT

Dr Syama Prasad Mookerjee expressed his commitment for education in different discourses on diverse fora. It may be witnessed in his speeches in the Indian Parliament during the discussion on the Visva-Bharati Bill in 1951. The following excerpts from these speeches contain his concern for Rabindranath Tagore's vision of Visva-Bharati, autonomy of the university as an institution in its academic matters, and even service conditions of its employees. Also, he argued against vesting of large powers in the Visitor, that is, the President of India, and government interference in the university affairs directly or otherwise.

Dr SP Mookerjee: It would be much simpler to decide the main question at issue. Is it the intention of the government that the university should be permitted to alter the terms and conditions of service of any employee to their prejudice? Usually that is not the case. Take the large number of employees under government after Independence. The general position was accepted that without the consent of any employee the terms and conditions of none of them would be prejudicially altered. Why not accept that principle; that in offering revised terms and conditions of service to any employee; the terms and conditions will not be altered to the prejudice of any employee. A simple amendment like that will meet everybody's case. In fact, knowing as I do the affairs of Visva-Bharati, the salaries and the terms and conditions which are at present open to its employees are not extravagant or as favourable as under government service, so it will be nobody's intention to alter them prejudicially to the interests of the employees, if there is any chance, their prospects would be further improved. So we are more or less having an academic discussion. I suggest that we may leave the clause as it is. It amply protects the interests of the employees. In one particular case, a particular professor gets six months and then goes away, but if you want to make it clear, I suppose you do not want that the university should be entitled to alter the terms and conditions prejudicially to the interest of any employee. I suggest that you may make that clear. (1 May 1951, 7833)

Dr SP Mookerjee: There is one rather important principle—and I am sorry I have not given notice of an amendment in this respect—to which I would like to refer. It relates to clause 6 (b) where the university is given power to maintain colleges and bhavans or halls or recognise colleges and bhavans. But what exactly will be the position of the schools at Santiniketan? This bill obviously covers the cases of colleges which means institutions after the matriculation stage. According to the Secondary Education Bill which has been passed in West Bengal recently, all high schools in West Bengal will come under the control of the Board. Then what happens to the school situated in Santiniketan? I am definitely of the view that this bill will never succeed and Visva-Bharati will never succeed unless you allow Visva-Bharati to maintain its own schools right from the kindergarten stage. There is a new type of secondary education which has been imparted at Santiniketan which in fact, was a special gift of Rabindranath Tagore. That is how Santiniketan's activities started. Unless the child is taken up at the very initial stage, it will be impossible to maintain Visva-Bharati at the proper standard. We cannot do that if we allow the university control only over the colleges. I know the Education Minister's intention and the intention of Parliament and of the whole country. I suggest government might have a small amendment and add 'schools' also so that the position may be clear beyond any doubt whatsoever. (May 1951, 7842-7843)

Dr SP Mookerjee: If you have schools under the Secondary Education Board following different curricula and different syllabi and adopting different types of examinations, then Visva-Bharati will never prosper. You must trust the university to admit students right from the child stage up to the highest stage. Then you can build up one organic whole according to the ideals which pervaded the establishment of this institution. I would, therefore, ask the Education Minister to accept this suggestion of mine. (1 May 1951, 7843)

Dr Deshmukh: I would like to say a few words on this suggestion made by Dr Mookerjee. This change suggested is very necessary and desirable not only from the point of view of existing schools in Santiniketan but also those which the university will recognise and which it would thus be legally entitled to maintain. Schools will include certain other institutions also such as a school of economics and such like things. We know that certain authorities and universities prefer to call them schools. These also will be covered if we have the word 'schools' added on. There is much to be said in favour of this amendment that has been suggested. (1 May 1951, 7845)

Dr SP Mookerjee: The amendment which has been proposed by Dr Deshmukh will clear up certain doubts which were in existence in the minds of members of this House and indeed in the minds of many people outside. Knowing as I did the intention of the Honourable Minister, I had during the last few weeks personally discussed with many people whom I met when they expressed their misgivings as regards the ultimate results which may follow the establishment of a statutory university at Santiniketan. The fear generally expressed was that the university might become just a stereotyped institution of the like that we have in different parts of the country. I know that the Maulana Sahib was anxious from the beginning as in fact he has made it abundantly clear today, that the intention of the government is to maintain intact the great ideals for which the founder stood. For that reason, the clarification of the founder himself is essential. I knew personally how the mind of Rabindranath Tagore worked with regard to government control and government interference regarding Visva-Bharati. As you know, Sir, years ago the institution at Santiniketan was completely independent and I vividly remember the day when he came to meet my father who was then in charge of the affairs of the University of Calcutta and made a suggestion as regards possible cooperation between University of Calcutta and Visva-Bharati, maintaining intact the complete academic freedom of Visva-Bharati. Although the Indian Universities Act did not make such cooperation possible, yet a certain device was made and Visva-Bharati had worked during the last thirty years as an institution where work of a special kind was being accomplished and at the same time its students were being permitted to sit at the examinations of the University of Calcutta. Rabindranath's great fear was that if the university came under official control, its very purpose would become difficult of accomplishment. In fact as he said in one of his great speeches, its soul was likely to be destroyed. Those who are acquainted with his great writings know of that story which he wrote of a bird which was kept in a golden cage. Beautifully served but not allowed to go out of the cage and how money was lavishly spent on the maintenance of the golden cage which was studded with jewels and how fruits not fresh from the nature's garden but artificial foodstuff were brought into the cage so that the bird might develop its own life as the king thought it should. Later on, everyone was anxious about the external features of the cage but the poor bird had died and no one took any notice of it. That is how he described the system of education prevalent in this country. He abhorred nothing more than external restrictions and regimentation. It is for this reason that we have to be extremely careful that the objectives of this university should be very clearly laid down by statute and also a constitution should be given to it which would enable it to function properly and make it impossible for any government to interfere with its internal working. (1 May 1951, 7866-67)

Dr SP Mookerjee: That was what I was going to say. Apart from the mere mention of the Supreme Being, as the Maulana Sahib put it before us just now, is it really necessary that these particular words should remain there?

I would like to address myself on this point. First of all, as has been emphasised by one or two speakers, it is not for us to edit the objectives of the founder. We have no right to do that. If you say that you do not accept the objectives, do not pass the bill, and say government is not prepared to pass the Visva-Bharati Bill on the model that Rabindranath Tagore thought should be its objective or ideal.

Secondly, apart from the theoretical approach to the problem, to my mind, it is vital that these words should be there. Now, look at the clause as it stands minus those words. It refers only to the external activities concerning the study of religions, art, culture, architecture, philosophy, literature of so many great civilisations and an effort to discover a unity amongst them. That will be the external activity of scholars and professors and others who would be prepared to work in this great untrodden field. But, with what mental objective will this work be carried on? Knowing the little that I do of the writings and intentions of Rabindranath Tagore, the great stress which he laid at every stage was not merely on the material pursuit of these great studies but also the spirit in which those studies should be undertaken. It is this spiritual background which it was his dream and ambition to bring into the orbit of the university. That must be the chief characteristic of an institution like the Visva-Bharati. Otherwise, it is meaningless. You can have other universities where similar formal studies will be made, studies of comparative religion, of comparative art, comparative literature, comparative architecture and so on. But the new element in the study of these, where Hindus, Muslims, Christians, Sikh, Jains, and people drawn to Santiniketan from all parts of the civilised world would meet and discuss amongst themselves the great principles underlying their own studies, will be the spirit in which these studies, will be undertaken and that is one of the very important objectives of this university. Therefore, I would most humbly request the Education Minister that he should make no effort to edit the objectives.

As I read the amendment of Dr Deshmukh, I find he simply says the objectives as were declared by Rabindranath Tagore be embodied in the Schedule—we are not doing anything more and anything less. Therefore, if you try to edit or omit a portion which in my humble opinion is a vital portion, I believe it will be doing an act of sacrilege. I know Maulana Sahib's intention as he has made it abundantly clear in respect of a number of amendments where he did not take up any formal attitude at all. Quite rightly and as becoming of a scholar and thinker of his eminence, he was prepared to come forward and say that in respect of all these matters it was his desire that the university should reflect the ideals and thought of Rabindranath Tagore. For this reason, I very strongly urge that the objectives should be left exactly as they were pronounced by the founder without any alteration whatsoever.

As I said that the condition of success of a university at Santiniketan will not only be the acceptance of the objectives for which the university stood, but also the giving of a constitution which will enable it to function properly. Here I am not without misgivings. When I look at the structure of the constitution, frankly speaking, I do not like the large powers of control which have been vested in the Visitor, who is this Visitor? The President of the Indian Republic. Will he act on his own responsibility? Obviously not. He will have to act on the advice of the Education Minister and his advisers. This means that you bring this institution practically into the arena of party and political controversy. I am not suggesting that the government should have no control whatsoever. So far as the general financial administration of any institution goes, obviously, when the State grants funds for the purpose of working it, it will be its duty to ensure that the money given to the institution is properly spent and spent for the purposes for which the grant was made. Even with regard to academic policy, it may be the responsibility of the government periodically to have examined the working of statutory institutions in order to find out whether the purposes for which such an institution had been established were being properly carried out, a responsibility which could only be undertaken by persons who are competent enough to sit in impartial judgment over the activities of such an institution. That happens in England which very zealously guards the freedom of its universities, where Royal Commissions sit from time to time in order to find out how the working of the institutions is going on and how far they advance the national interests. But you have proposed to clothe the Visitor with powers to approve the statutes and also with the overall power to supersede any ordinances which will lay down conditions for study and research, etc, vesting of such complete arbitrary powers including the vetoing of ordinances is not desirable and not consistent with the spirit of the scheme itself. I shall not go into details. When those clauses come up for discussion, I hope we will have a further opportunity of discussion and we may make suitable changes with the help and under the guidance of the Education Minister himself. Here is a case where there is complete agreement on all sides inside the House and also in the country generally. This great experiment that Rabindranath Tagore made unaided, unhelped, and for which no support came from his countrymen in the days of its beginning is today receiving statutory recognition at the hands of our government and at the hands of our Parliament. I believe that is a great advance, for which the Education Minister will legitimately feel proud. But I would humbly request you not to do anything which may not only destroy, but even impair the efficiency of this institution or make the attainment of the objectives for which the founder stood difficult. A few days ago, it was given to me and you were also there to see the Sri Aurobindo Asram at Pondicherry, call it an international university, where work of a different kind is being done. A great experiment is being made, not according to the stereotyped work with which we are familiar. There will be nothing but good to the country and to the civilised world if such institutions are given statutory recognition and State patronage, and given the fullest freedom to carry on their activities in a manner which will not only redound to their credit, which will not only advance the great objectives which their illustrious founders have had, but also do credit to the entire civilised humanity.

And lastly, as Rabindranath Tagore always used to say, freedom must be the very breath and life of this institution. We should do nothing to destroy that freedom or do anything to regiment the working of this institution. I am fully aware that even though you may pass this bill, and you lay down with clarity the conditions for keeping its constitution free and unfettered, everything will ultimately depend on how far Visva-Bharati succeeds in collecting within its doors the right type of men and women to carry out the work of the institution. Theirs will be a great responsibility. And if Visva-Bharati attracts the men and women of the right type—and they are not easily available—they by their concerted and untied efforts and harmonious endeavours can succeed in making this bill actually effective. It is only then that our purpose will be served. That is a responsibility which we are throwing on Visva-Bharati; and I have not the least doubt in my mind that with the cooperation of all, although it is situated in one corner of India, with the cooperation of all people from all parts of India and the great thinkers and savants from the different parts of the world, we will be able to make this institution worthy of its name. (1 May 1951, 7868-7871)

Dr SP Mookerjee: ...The next point is about the possibility of government interference. Now we have been able to amend the original provisions to a considerable extent. I do not mind what exactly the provisions of the law are; it all depends on the spirit in which a particular enactment is worked. How the intentions of all, whether belonging to government or outside, is that the fullest possible freedom should be given to those who are in charge of the affairs of this university to carry on their activities consistent with the objectives of the founder. I would therefore, especially request the Education Minister not to interfere with the detailed working of this institution. That also is a very important consideration. Freedom is the essential condition on which such an institution can grow. Let us not make mistake about one point. This was a new experiment which Rabindranath Tagore made in the field of education. His efforts were greatly doubted by his contemporaries within the country. But when recognition came from savants and people who knew about new experiments in education outside India, then many people in India started being attracted to this institution. Now let us not try to develop education on one and a single pattern. We have some universities also which are being modelled on different lines. Here is a new experiment consistent with our genius and aspirations, which can be very fruitfully pursued and which luckily today has found the seal of approval from the hands of the government of the day. I think if we proceed on sound lines we will be able to show results which will not only do credit to this country but which will help in solving many intricate problems which face human civilisation today. (3 May 1951, 8010)

One other thing I would like to mention before I conclude. While framing the statutes one has to take care to see that all those rigid conditions which are attached to the appointment of professors and others and also to erection of buildings and other formalities should not be included in the working of Visva-Bharati. It is not necessary that every professor should draw a salary of Rs 1,000 or Rs 1,200. People who are drawn to Visva-Bharati are very eminent men who have practically devoted their life to that institution and are satisfied with a subsistence allowance. If any attempt is made by the central government to have standardised scales of pay for the staff because members of the staff of other universities are not satisfied with less that I think will be a mistaken idea. I am not suggesting that they should be starved. Everyone who works there must be given conditions of service which will enable them to live properly. But it is not necessary that we should standardise their salaries. Similarly, with regard to buildings we do not want large buildings there. We have spent lakhs and lakhs on palatial buildings elsewhere. Those who have visited Visva-Bharati know how many classes are held in the open garden. When I was delivering my address at the time of the last convocation in the absence of Shri Jawaharlal Nehru, it was a delightful and inspiring atmosphere. It was one of the many innovations of the poet, under the inspiration of his great father. Let us not try to interfere with such liberties that such an institution has been enjoying. These are the special features of Visva-Bharati. Although they may be external features and characteristics, yet they are very valuable and they are indicative of its peculiar attitude towards many problems which face that university. We must be able to preserve them intact and develop them in the future. (3 May 1951, 8011)

Dr SP Mookerjee (West Bengal): I do not wish to say much on the general question of policy of giving large powers of inspection to the Visitor, who happens to be either the head of a State or the head of the Indian Union. We will have to work for ensuring conditions so that the university may function in an atmosphere of freedom. Of course, the government is responsible not only for finding funds, but also for cursing that the universities get a machinery which will enable them to perform the functions which are allotted to them by the statute. Here the powers which are given in the President as Visitor are extremely wide in character. The powers given here include not only the right to inspect or order inspection regarding administrative and financial matters, but regarding academic questions also. I would like to suggest for the consideration of the Honourable Minister a compromise which I think should meet the exigencies of the situation. Obviously, when grants are made to a university it should be somebody's business to see that so far as administration and financial management of the university go, there is nothing that can be complained against. If the Visitor feels that occasionally enquiries should be made or if complaints are made against such administration justifying an enquiry, let us have a provision to that effect. But to have a provision of this type enabling the Visitor to direct inspection regarding every academic matter which may come within the purview of a university, and then also to be the final deciding authority as regards the implementation of any recommendation which may be made by such a committee of enquiry, I think, is extremely harmful for the proper development of such a university as we are contemplating. It practically means that the entire academic policy of the university under the law may be subject to directives which may be issued by the Visitor. Of course the Honourable Minister may say that these are intended for really emergent occasions. If such an emergent occasion should arise when a university, such as the Visva-Bharati is found to neglect the academic responsibilities which are entrusted to it, then the university, which is a creature of statute, may be dealt with in so many other ways. You can stop the grant; you can amend the law; you can influence the decision of the university through pressure of public opinion. I would, therefore, suggest this to the Honourable Minister; I am not suggesting any format amendment. Because I am leaving the matter in the hands of the Education Minister; if he is prepared to accept this idea, then his advisers and draftsmen may prepare a proper draft amendment of this clause so as to keep the powers of inspection in the hands of the Visitor in regard to administrative and financial matters, but with regard to academic matters, let the Visitor have the power to bring to the notice of the university any matter concerning its academic activities and to make any suggestions for their improvement if such suggestions are really called for. Obviously. If we follow such a procedure, then any university worth its name especially one of the character that we are contemplating will not do anything which may be against the real academic need of the character that we are contemplating will not do anything which may go against the real academic need of the country or of this special institution. I would beg of the Honourable Minister not to endow the Visitor with such wide powers so that on any and every matter concerning the university he may direct an enquiry and also force the results of such an enquiry and his decisions thereon upon the university. So far as I have been able to find, Sir such a drastic procedure is not in existence anywhere. The universities in England enjoy a special autonomy and they are extremely reluctant to part with such autonomy even though they are in receipt of large funds from the government. As you know, the University Grants Commission is working in the UK consisting of distinguished educationists and other administrators, and by cooperation and understanding with the universities, they are able to influence the working of the universities in a way which is fully consistent with national interests. Also the right vests in the Parliament of England to appoint a Royal Commission from time to time if such an occasion arises for enquiring into the affairs or activities of particular universities. Of course, we are working under a different pattern. I hope gradually our universities will be completely free from any sort of control or interference from government. I am not saying this because government interference is bad as such; but we are visualising the development of our country on democratic lines and naturally the powers of government will vest in parties which may be ruling over the destinies of the country for the time being. It is of the utmost importance that our universities should function as really independent organisations where the teachers and the workers will be entitled to express their viewpoints on matters which concern their academic activities and also on matters of national importance completely free from fear or from expectation of favour. That is also the policy which the Honourable Minister has in view. The compromise which I am suggesting. I think, will meet both the points of view. If the Honourable Minister is agreeable, then, instead of continuing the discussions now on this clause, he may instruct his advisers to prepare a draft half an hour later. Meanwhile, we may continue with the other amendments. (2 May 1951, 7941-7943)

Dr SP Mookerjee: In the opinion of some of us, the Visitor should not be given large powers to cancel any ordinances or direct the university to accept whatever he decides. Here, the powers of the Visitor will be limited to two items; first if the Visitor considers that there is any matter which is inconsistent with the Act, then his decision shall be final and he can cancel any ordinance and that cancellation shall be binding. The second is, under sub clause (7) if there is a difference of opinion between the Executive Council and the Academic Council regarding the justification of a particular ordinance, then that matter will have to be finally decided by someone and that may be left to the Visitor to decide as proposed in the bill. These are the purposes for which I am suggesting these amendments, which the Honourable Minister has seen and his advisers also have looked at from the drafting point of view. They may be accepted. (2 May 1951, 7976).

Dr SP Mookerjee: My friend Professor Shah said that the draft as proposed is not entirely acceptable to him. Nor is it to me, but this is the amendment which government is prepared to accept in order to accommodate the various points of view which were expressed on the floor of the House. If honourable members would refer to clause 10 as it stands, they will find powers are given to the Visitor to direct an inquiry to be made or inspection to be made into all affairs of the university and such affairs may relate to its building, library, equipment, any institution maintained by the university, examinations, teaching and other work conducted or done by the university. Once that inquiry is ordered, then the university will also be entitled to be represented thereat. Later on, the Visitor may address the vice chancellor with reference to the result of such inspection and enquiry and call for the comments of the university. After receiving the comments, the Visitor may, according to the draft as it is before us now, direct that certain changes should be made or that certain steps should be taken by the university and such directions shall be entirely binding on the university. Some of us had felt that this clause should not be there at all and that the President should not be given such wide powers of inspection at all. It is felt by others that even if the powers are given, they should not relate to academic matters at least which means that the enquiry must be confined to administrative or financial matters alone. This amendment which is acceptable to the government provides that while the Visitor will have the right to direct an enquiry to be made into all matters administrative, financial or academic without any restriction being put upon his discretion, the final directives which may be issued by him to be binding on the university will relate not to academic matters but only to financial and administrative matters. In other words, if any proposals are made relating to academic questions, those proposals will be sent to the university and the university will be asked to consider them. How far they can be implemented will be a matter for the university to decide. To that extent, we have made a positive gain. The Visitor will not have the power to give any final directions to the university regarding academic matters. If the powers of the Visitor could be removed altogether even in respect of the enquiry to be made, it would be perhaps acceptable to Professor Shah and others, but the government feels that the right to order an inspection need not be curbed but the final decision to implement conclusions in respect of academic matters may be lost to the university. This may not be a cent per cent compromise. (2 May 1951, 7986-7987).

THE BENGAL SECONDARY EDUCATION BILL DEBATE

Syama Prasad Mookerjee, even after relinquishing his office as the vice chancellor of the University of Calcutta, remained committed to his concern for education. His interventions in the Bengal Secondary Education Bill Debate 1940 constitute a historical document, as he argued in a sustained and logical manner for autonomy of educational institutions. He deprecated encroachment by regulatory offices on educational institutions and denounced discrimination in them on the lines of caste, creed or community. He took on individuals and offices who, according to him, tried to vitiate the educational atmosphere for their political ends. His ultimate sentence in the debate summed up his concerns, '...education may be saved and strengthened for paving the way to communal harmony and understanding in this province and for national solidarity at this critical juncture in the darkest hour of the history of our Motherland.' Editors

Syama Prasad Mookerjee: Sir, the amendment which has been moved by Mr Manmatha Nath Roy raises some very important issues to which I desire to draw the attention of the House. In the first place, Sir, an attempt is made to replace the word 'approved' by the word 'recognised'. If you look at the body of the bill, you will find that there are three different terms used in connection which desire to obtain recognition from the Board. In the second place, there is a provision that every school must be approved school, shall also be registered. In the third place, there is a provision that an approved and registered school only will be entitled to the privileges of recognition. Now, Sir, let me ask the government what possibly can be the reason for attempting to device this complex machinery for granting recognition to schools which may desire to come under the board. What is the present position not only in this province but in other places? If an institution desires to be recognised, it applies for recognition and it submits itself to the conditions which are prescribed by rules or regulations of the authority concerned. Now, what can possibly be the reason that a school must be separately approved before it can be entitled to the privileges of recognition? It is not my purpose here to divulge the discussions which we had with representatives of the government during the last fortnight but no satisfactory explanation was forthcoming. At one time, it was sought to be suggested that approval was necessary for different kinds of schools. If that is the explanation, then why use the word 'approval' at all? You may prescribe different sets of regulations or rules which will control the conditions of recognition for different types of schools. We are anxious to simplify the administration of secondary education, we do not want to put additional obstacles in the path of schools which may otherwise be poor and which may not be in a position to fulfil those conditions. What we suggest here is a simple procedure. Use the word 'recognised' for all kinds of schools, admitting that there may be occasions to have different formulae of recognition which will be prescribed by rules or regulations. Indeed, Sir if you turn for a moment to section 20, sub-clause (2), you will find that it is laid down that a secondary school which is not approved and registered by the Executive Council shall not be eligible for any grant-in-aid. A student of a secondary school which is not so approved and registered shall not be entitled to any scholarship awarded by the provincial government or the Board and a penal clause is added according to the report of the select committee that a secondary school not so approved and registered shall not be eligible for recognition by the Executive Council for presentation of candidates for examinations including the matriculation examination of the University of Calcutta. We look upon provisions like these with distrust and with disfavour, academically they are unnecessary. Administratively, they will prove to be a cause of undue harassment. That is with regard to the two terms used 'approved' and which are unheard of and which are not to be found in any of the provisions governing secondary education either in this province or elsewhere.

Then, Sir, with regard to the other point, why should the provincial government approve or recognise schools? I understand a situation may arise that before the Act comes into operation there must be some authority to approve schools. I understand that necessity arises because otherwise elections cannot be conducted in a proper manner—elections that will include approved schools. Our definition is simple and straightforward. What are the schools today in existence? Schools recognised by the University of Calcutta. Schools recognised by the Board of Secondary and Intermediate Education, Dacca. We also suggest that if there be any other class of schools which the government considers should be included in the approved list. I do not think there can be any objection to include such an additional category. But let us know clearly and specifically what we are about. What we want to lay down is that until the Act comes into operation, until the Board or the Executive Council functions for the purpose of granting recognition as we would like it to be called, all schools which at the commencement of the Act are recognised by the University of Calcutta or by the Board of Secondary and Intermediate Education in Dacca should be deemed to be recognised schools. That means that regulations prepared by the Board have been framed; recognition will take its own course. These are the two important questions which arise out of this amendment; it has nothing to do with communalism; it is a question of pure academic importance; it is a matter on which every side of the House should support. We shall all demand of the government that we want a simplification of the machinery for the control of secondary education in this province. We do not want additional obstacles to be put in the way of schools which are already in existence or which want to start their new career. Frame your rules and regulations and ask all the schools to come under the purview of these rules; or frame different sets of regulations for different types of schools which will come under the purview of the Board, but for Heaven's sake do not start by paying above importance to the administrative side of the machinery of the Board; do not start by having approval, registration and recognition before a school can have the elementary liberty of sending up candidates to the university examinations or examinations conducted by the Board. I hope the Chief Minister will see his way to accept this amendment which is very reasonable and which, if accepted, will be consistent with the best ideals of educational administration.

Sir, I beg to move that for sub-clause (9) of clause 2, including the proviso the following be substituted, namely: '(9) 'Secondary Education' means education other than primary or post-matriculation examination and includes: (i) General Education, namely: (a) Secular Education open to all communities, (b) Education which combines instruction in general subjects with instructions in subjects appertaining to Islamic culture and religion. (c) Education which combines instruction in general subjects with instructions in subjects appertaining to Hindu culture and religion, (d) Education entirely in subjects appertaining to Islamic culture and religion, and (e) Education entirely in subjects appertaining to Hindu culture and religion, and (ii) Special Education, namely: (a) Technical Education, (b) Agricultural Education, (c) Industrial Education, (d) Commercial Education, and (e) Other types of vocational and special education as the Board may determine.'

Sir, yesterday the House discussed another suggested amendment regarding the definition of secondary education. The definition as given in the bill I consider is extremely defective in character. In fact, Sir, this is no definition at all so far as secondary education is concerned.

The bill says that secondary education is education other than primary education or post-matriculation and the provision lays down that the provincial government may, by notification declare any form of education to be or not to be secondary education, and secondary school is an institution in which secondary education of such undefined character is imparted.

Sir, I believe it will be acceptable to all sides of this House that secondary education, the advancement of which is said to be the main purpose of the bill should be defined with as much precision as possible. I admit that it may not be possible to have a definition which will be entirely exhaustive in character, but at the same time not only does the government owe it to itself, not only does the legislature owe it to itself, but the public at large has the right to know what is the kind of education or what are the kinds of education which are going to be controlled and supervised and developed under the new Board.

Now, Sir, if you trace the history of the development of secondary education in this province, you will admit that one of the gravest defects which confronts us—and it is not any particular community that is confronted with this question, it is a question that confronts all communities—Hindus, Muslims and Christians residing in this province—is that the present system of secondary education has been predominantly literary in character. That has been criticised by the Sadler Commission and that has produced certain results in the social and economic life of our province which seriously affect the integrity and welfare of all communities residing in Bengal. It is not my purpose here to trace in detail the reason why secondary education came to be predominantly literary in character. Briefly speaking, the reason historically is that from the very beginning there was a demand that through these institutions a particular type of Bengali would be created who would be suited for various kinds of work, mainly administrative in nature for the purpose of keeping intact the wheels of a bureaucratic machinery. That is how English education developed in this country nearly a hundred years ago, but today we find that the result has been chronic unemployment; we find that our boys who pass the matriculation practically have no opening. They go to join the ordinary intermediate classes. From there, they do not know where to turn to. They go and join the ordinary degree colleges and then they go and overcrowd the university. There are now some openings in the lines of engineering, in the lines of medicine and in some other technical lines, but they are of so slight and insignificant character that the general trend of educational progress has been seriously affected in the province as a whole. Therefore, we consider it essential that if the purpose of the bill is not merely to control schools, most of whom have flourished in this province out of their own effort, if the purpose of the bill is to effect real improvement in the educational system of the province, then all sides of the House must clearly demand it from the government that they enunciate their policy here, and now that secondary education will not merely remain confined to general education of a literary type as now, but will definitely be directed to various channels in the lines indicated—technical, agricultural, industrial and commercial. This I consider, Sir, to be a vital recommendation which the Opposition is making and which the Coalition Party ought to accept without any hesitation if the interests of education are really at its heart.

Now, Sir, what are the objections, why such education cannot form part of secondary education today? We have been told that one of the objections is that there are insuperable practical difficulties in convincing certain departments of the government to transfer control over these sections of education to the department of education. I am told that technical education and industrial education are controlled by certain other ministers of the government and it will take months, it will take years before those ministers can be convinced of a very elementary proposition which has got to be fulfilled if educational progress is really our goal. I cannot understand the logic or the sincerity of this objection, if you can by one stroke of the pen claim to bring under the control of the Board nearly 1,500 schools who owe their existence to private munificence and charity, who have never come to government with a beggar's bowl in their hands, if you can do that with one stroke of the pen, what is there for the legislature to be prevented from demanding from the government that it must agree to transfer special education like technical, agricultural, industrial and commercial to the control of the new Board of Secondary Education.

There are two aspects of the matter which we ought to bear in mind. There may be special types of schools which exclusively concern themselves with such special education, technical, agricultural, industrial and commercial, as we find to be in existence in some parts of the country, and particularly in all free countries outside India; or there may be education that will be given a definite technical or vocational bias in the existing institutions, thereby preparing the students for practical life in a better fashion than what they are capable of being today. This is one aspect of our proposal which I do not think has any communal tinge whatsoever, but is closely, very closely related to the future welfare of all communities in this province. Unless this new Secondary Education Board is going to be a sham, it must bring under its control with the least possible delay these types of special education for which a new policy will have to be devised and its administration placed under the control of the Board. This is one aspect of the matter.

The second is a more comprehensive definition of general education. This matter was debated yesterday from another angle of vision. There are many amongst us who hold that general education should be of a secular kind altogether. Many of us also hold this opinion that this new Board which is going to be created should concern itself only with secular education. That proposition was placed before the House yesterday, and the proposition was rejected. In other words, it is the viewpoint which the government shares with a majority of this House, which was explained by the Chief Minister yesterday that, so far as Muslim interests were concerned, there is a strong feeling amongst them that there must be included within the system of general education such elements of Islamic religion and traditions which they consider to be vital for the completion of the education of their children. I shall make my position clear in respect of this matter. It is true that there has been this opinion strongly felt and expressed in this country for the last hundred years that general education should have nothing to do with religious education. But I believe, Sir, seeing things not only as they are existing in our country, but seeing things as they are developing in countries outside India, that it will be a fatal mistake if we divorce education from our highest religious ideals altogether. I believe Sir, that it is possible to shape our education policy in such a way not that we shall train our students in a particular religious dogma, or in the observance of particular religious rites, but our education may be so shaped and modeled as would be fundamentally based on those eternal truths which lie embedded in the religion of Islam or in the religion of Hindus. There will be no conflict whatsoever, for it is true that if religion has resulted in feuds, it is not that religion has been at fault; the fault has been with men who mistook the scope and ideals of religion and tried to divert religion to purposes for which religion was not really meant. It is just like the place of science in the life of the people. Today, science is being utilised, science is being prostituted for the purpose of bringing devastation to humanity. Will anyone dare say for that reason that science is bad, that science has to be neglected and relegated to the background in educational institutions and in the human society? On the other hand, the reply really would be that science was not intended, was not meant for the destruction of human beings but it is man himself who has brought it down to that level. Similarly, if religious ideals and principles can be correctly related with our educational system so as not to turn out boys and girls from our institutions who would become narrow-minded bigots but will cultivate the true religious spirit and will also understand and respect religious points of view of others, then I believe that a day will come which will be good for the Hindus and the Muslims residing in Bengal and in India as a whole. The proposal which we make, therefore, if summarised, comes to this: let there be different types of general education. Let one type of general education be entirely secular and open to all communities, which will have no connection whatsoever with any cultural or religious traditions of a particular community. That will be followed by education which will also be partly secular. In other words, in imparting such education you will have English, vernacular, science, mathematics, rudiments of history and geography, Hindu or Islamic culture, the bias being so connected with the tradition and culture of the Islamic community or of the Hindu community that no community will have anything to fear of the other. Then you have lastly the (d) and (e) types of traditional training which was imparted in the old type madrasas and old tols which have existed in this country from time immemorial.

The proposal which we are formulating contemplates that there will be final examinations at the end of these particular types of education. That is a point which I would like to make absolutely clear. If you look at the amendment which I have the honour of moving, general education which will include partly secular education open to all communities, will have at the end of each course a final examination on the passing of which it will be possible for candidates to go up for higher studies in the university or elsewhere.

Similarly, with regard to (b) education which will be partly secular and which will be connected with Islamic tradition, it will also have a final examination at the end permitting successful candidates to go and join the university or pursue their higher studies just as they may wish. So with regard to (c). So far as (d) and (e) are concerned, there will be separate examinations which, of course, will be based on orthodox training. Not necessarily permitting them to join the university courses as they stand but permitting them to receive higher training in such educational institutions as may be provided.

That, in a nutshell, is the scheme which I have the honour of presenting to the House on behalf of the Opposition. Without divulging any secret, I may say this, that it represents an agreement between the government and the Opposition, as the discussions have been going on during the last fortnight. It has been agreed that if we approach the education problem from this point of view it will not make the Muslims suspicious, it will not make the Hindus suspicious and that it will leave the door open for secular education where Hindus, Muslims and Christians may flock together without any reserve. It will leave the door open to those Muslims who desire to receive their education based on their faith and on their culture. It will give a similar right and privilege to the Hindus of the province and lastly, it will leave the door open also for the Hindus and Muslims to receive their training according to strict orthodox lines as has been the case during the last one century or more in this province.

The only difference between the agreement which has been reached between the government and the Opposition, although the point of view was pressed by us, is with regard to the time limit during which such special education like technical education, agricultural education, industrial education should be given effect to. It has been impressed upon us that the government should be given a time limit within which such education should be transferred to the Board of course, theoretically, and even from practical standpoint, we do not consider that there are insuperable difficulties in persuading some of our estimable ministers to transfer the control of technical, agricultural, industrial and commercial education to the charge of the new Board of Secondary Education, but if there are insuperable difficulties, it should not prove difficult for the Opposition and the government to come to an agreement that a reasonable time limit should be imposed within which the government will hand over the control of such types of special education to the Board.

Sir, before I take my seat I would only say this that here we are considering a problem from an absolutely detached point of view; we are considering the future development of secondary education in this province, not particularly for the purpose of dominating the interest of one particular group or community. We are visualising a system of education, which will give the fullest liberty to the Muslims of Bengal to develop their education according to lines which they consider to be right and proper and similarly, it will give equal right to the Hindus to develop their education in a manner consistent with their best traditions and ideals. I believe, Sir, that it is only on this basis of equality that Hindus and Muslims respecting the points of view of each other can sit together with their minds open absolutely to permit each other to develop the educational system in a manner consistent with their best tradition which will lead to the highest development of the province as a whole. It is only then that it will be possible for the Board or any other constituted authority to frame a national system of education suited to the best ideals of our beloved Motherland.

Sir, I rise to give my wholehearted support to the motion for circulation of the Bengal Secondary Education Bill for eliciting public opinion thereon.

For four days, Sir, we have discussed in this Assembly with great earnestness and vehemence, problems of education which await solution for the benefit of the children of the soil. During the last three years, the present ministry has been responsible for introducing various controversial legislative measures and performing administrative acts, but I believe, Sir, it will be true to assert that there has not been any measure so vital as this to the largest interests of the people of this province. Sir, I am opposed to the main principles underlying the present bill, and I regard it not as a measure intended for educational advancement but as a definitely reactionary step which requires the strongest possible resistance both inside and outside the legislative chamber.

Sir, opposition to this measure is widespread and not confined to a limited few. Opposition is the natural outcome of fundamental differences in outlook, and any government which has a grain of responsibility left in it will carefully and impartially take stock of the grounds for opposition and not force it only with its strength of majority of votes inside the legislative chamber.

Secondary education Sir, is perhaps the most important of all the educational stages in a country, for, on the one hand it links education up to the highest stages—it leads to a university life which can be developed to the best expectations of the nation. On the other hand, secondary education gives the nation a band of trained men and women in diverse spheres of useful activity, and again, Sir, it is through secondary education that a country can be blessed with a large number of efficient teachers so essential for any progressive scheme of elementary education.

Sir, I regard to say that the speech which the Honourable Chief Minister delivered or was made to deliver on the opening day of the discussion of this bill—some portions of his speech at any rate—bore the marks of the bureaucratic standpoint so familiar in this country not many years ago, which was then also expressed eloquently but ignobly by a certain class of self-constituted western administrators who came to join Imperial Services for preaching the doctrine of perpetual trusteeship and viewed educational expansion as a dangerous feature.

We have heard Sir, unworthy aspersions made on the University of Calcutta. There is no system of education anywhere in the world which is perfect. None is aware more than myself of the shortcomings and deficiencies of my university. But bearing in mind the circumstances which brought it into existence, the motives that controlled its administration for the first half of a century, the meager assistance the university and schools and colleges received from the State and the constitution it was made to work under, Sir, one cannot but feel grateful for the rich contributions it has made towards the development of our national life.

Sir, one speaker has said that the university has been an agency of British imperialism. A greater libel could not have been uttered. The speaker stands self-contradicted, for he himself and thousands of other students and products of the university itself have bravely striven to rid India of foreign domination.

If the allegation is made that the university has not directly concerned itself with any political movement, I shall plead guilty to the charge. For, whatever may be our politics outside the university, has been instrumental in the hands of a foreign bureaucracy, I shall say, Sir, that it is an accusation which is as unworthy as it is baseless. Trace the events which stirred the minds of the people of this province during past political agitations. Attempts were made on many occasions to apply the laws of repression against men and institutions, and Sir, who will deny that within the limited sphere of universities' powers, the University of Calcutta, more than any other similar institution in India, has kept its door open to all persons and institutions irrespective of political or other considerations? It is indeed remarkable that a university which was established by State Act has fought against State control and interference in a manner which may worthily stand comparison with famous universities in any free country in any part of the civilised world. (Cries of "Hear! Hear!" from Congress benches.) Freedom first, freedom second and freedom always—this noble expression was uttered by a son of the university at the university Senate with 80 per cent of its members nominated by the Governor of Bengal and voiced by Hindus, Muslims and Europeans alike.

Sir, another critic asserted that the university has grievously neglected Muslim interests—a charge, Sir, which cannot for a moment stand the test of scrutiny. Though served predominantly by Hindus, equal opportunities for education were liberally given to all communities. The backwardness of a community cannot be cured by unjust and unfair aspersions made on the more progressive community or by placing artificial restrictions on the further advancement of the latter. As an incontrovertible evidence of the university's apathy towards Muslim interests, one of my friends to the left yesterday solemnly read out, followed by applause from Coalition benches, certain extracts from a Bengali book containing alleged anti-Muslim sentiments. The condemnation was apparently complete but the only slight hitch in the way of our accepting the condemnation arises from the fact that this very book, though only once a recommended book in the university list seven years ago but omitted from it since then, has been a prescribed book sanctioned by the Textbook Committee of the government of Bengal in 1937, in 1919 and in 1940. Any stick is good enough, provided it can strike the University of Calcutta; whether the attack is based on truth or reason is a matter of secondary importance!

Sir, the question of Muslim representatives on the university Senate was referred by the Honourable Chief Minister who regretted that the registered graduates never elected a Muslim fellow. There is no doubt that it is a matter of the deepest regret, but I ask Mr Fazlul Haq in all humility how many Muslim graduates have cared to enroll themselves as registered graduates of their alma mater and showed their readiness to pay a magnificent sum of Rs 10 per year to the coffers of the university? We had two Muslim-registered graduates in 1914, four in 1924, nil in 1940. Comment is needless, for even my friend Mr Shahabuddin says, 'obviously comment is needless'. Does this much advance the insistent claims of my friends to the left for an effective voice in all public bodies merely because they are numerically larger in population? What about the endowments? The university has received nearly one crore of rupees mostly during the last 34 years—a period when according to the government it started on its course of deterioration and, Sir, of this one crore rupees a sum of Rs 24,000 came from our Muslim countrymen, about Rs 9 lakh came from the Christians and the rest came from the Hindus. If you want to control the university because you are the majority community in this province, I would say, treat the university as liberally as the Hindus have treated their alma mater. Let me repeat that in spite of Hindu liberality, the university has served all the communities alike and has steadily advanced the cause which it has made its own.

Sir, the ideas on which the university has grown during the last forty years are compatible with the highest notions of Indian nationalism. The revival of a great seat of learning where Indian culture and civilisation would receive their due homage from Indian scholars, of a seat of learning where the highest scientific training would be imparted with the help of Indians, where east and west would meet on a footing of perfect equality and an Indian would be taught to feel proud of his national achievement without hesitating to imbibe the best element of western knowledge and skill that has been the ideal which has inspired the work of persons connected with the University of Calcutta. There have been inherent weaknesses which prevented the university from a fuller participation in the national life of the country. But let us not forget that it has not been the fault of the university, but it is inexorably connected with the fate that belongs to every subject nation which has yet to attain its political freedom and make its universities and educational institutions fountains of free knowledge and free thought. The University of Calcutta has brought light and education to millions of our people. But for its bold and vigorous policy they would have remained steeped in ignorance today. Further, it has demonstrated the ability of Indians—this is an aspect of its activities which I especially like my Muslim friends to understand and appreciate—it has demonstrated the ability of Indian scholars to participate in the highest work of teaching and research and to carry on original investigations in diverse branches of knowledge, in letters and science, which have to a certain extent helped to raise the intellectual status of India. My mind goes back to 1940 when the deliberations on the Indian Universities Bill were going on and there, Sir, the ex-Director of Public Instruction of Bengal, himself a Fellow of the Royal Society, made an astounding statement that Indians as a whole were incapable of doing original research work. That challenge was accepted—first by the University of Calcutta among all the seats of learning in India, and it certainly rebounds to the credit of us as Bengalis and as Indians that our sons have been found to be equal to others coming from western countries, where facilities for education are given far more generously than what can be expected in a poor province like Bengal.

The Chief Minister in his opening speech suggested as if the university's power in respect of high schools commenced only after the passing of the Indian University Act of 1904. As a matter of fact, this power it has enjoyed almost since the establishment of the university in 1857. It is, therefore, essential to bear in mind that the bill seeks to reverse a system that has been in operation for nearly eighty-five years and educational interests imperatively demand that the new system would be a clear and unequivocal improvement upon the existing state of things consistent with the need and aspirations of the people.

Let me now come to the period of the Sadler Commission. Today, after twenty-two years the Sadler Commission is being quoted with the same devotional loyalty as scriptures are quoted by a class of persons. (Cries of Hear! Hear!) Let me state at once that this bill vitiates the fundamental recommendations of the Sadler Commission regarding the Board of Secondary Education. The Sadler Commission made elaborate recommendations for the reconstruction of most comprehensive character. It never approved of any piecemeal legislation, nor did it ever imagine that its proposal would be twisted and mutilated so as to enlarge the importance of control of and transfer of power to governmental authority. We have heard much about the defects of the present educational system, about the standard of education. Who is there who will be wholly satisfied with our educational system today? Who is there in any country whose people are wholly pleased with the education they receive and are not clamoring daily for further improvement and for further expansion? In our country, secondary education has spread mainly through non-official support and patronage, and however much you may attack the university today, 90 per cent of the Indian members of this House sitting here would have remained without education unless the university had boldly followed a scheme of expansion of educational facilities and encouraged the opening of schools in the remotest corners of the province of Bengal. Numbers might have swelled at the cost of efficiency, but let me ask; would efficiency have suffered in the way in which it had suffered, had successive governments considered it their duty to spend more on education?

It is often said that the university did nothing but derive fees from the matriculation examination. That is far from the truth. What about the spirit underlying the new matriculation regulations? What is the history of the new matriculation examination which propounded a new educational theory now accepted practically throughout India? Sir, I would not deal here with the various attempts that were made by the university to give proper place to our mother tongue in the syllabus of studies of the university, but who will deny that one of the reasons why education has suffered in this country has been that English, a foreign tongue, has been the medium of our instruction from the lowest stage of education? That was discovered to be one of the chief defects in the Sadler Commission's report. The Sadler Commission submitted its report about 1919 and in 1921 that much-abused University of Calcutta called a conference of headmasters in Bengal and Assam and brought in the managers of schools throughout the two provinces and sat to discuss how the educational system, so far as the secondary stage was concerned, could be reorganised. Important recommendations were formulated based practically on the report of the Sadler Commission, but perhaps if the university erred, it erred on the side that it went even a few steps more than what the Sadler Commission was prepared to go. Subject to obvious exceptions, vernacular was made the compulsory medium of instruction and examination. There was provision for physical education, manual work, science, history and geography. What happened then? The syndicate considered the recommendations, the faculties met, the Senate met; weeks and months passed and its recommendations containing the considered viewpoint of the university and practically all the interested educational institutions in the two provinces were forwarded to the then government of Bengal. Then what happened? The government sat tight over the matter for two years. And you now talk of your anxiety to reform the educational system of Bengal! And two years later, the reply went from the then Ministry of Education presided over by no less a person than the Honourable Mr AK Fazlul Haq. And Sir, what was the reply that the government, though sympathetic at heart, was unable to accept the proposals for educational reform propounded by the university? One of the reasons advanced by the then government was that the university had gone even beyond the recommendations of the Sadler Commission because it sought to make the mother tongue of the people the compulsory medium of instruction in schools. Then, Sir, you know and you know much better than anybody else how nearly eleven years passed before the regulations could be approved by the government of Bengal, during the period when the Honourable Mr Azizul Haque was the Minister for Education. The fundamental principles that the university had proposed as early as 1922 were accepted by the progressive government of Bengal in 1935. Not till 1940 could the first examination be held under the new regulations. If, Sir, the province has lost nearly twenty years before these very important changes in the national system of education could be introduced, surely the blame does not rest with the university, but with other people, some of whom are today clamoring for control as if control is the be-all and end-all of the educational existence.

Now, Sir, the university during the last four years has vigorously pursued the scheme for the training of teachers of secondary institutions and nearly 50,000 men and women have gone through the portals of the university.

I know, Sir, that with the limited resources that we have, we have not been able to do as much as we would like to do. But here again I ask—what was the responsible government doing and how was its responsibility discharged? Was it not incumbent upon the government to provide for extensive schemes for the training of teachers and has not the Sadler Commission recommended that without training of teachers it is impossible to do anything for the advancement of secondary education? What again about the salaries of teachers? Has any step been taken for the purpose of giving increased pay to these poorly paid teachers who really form the backbone of educational administration today? Sir, I consider it a libel if anyone asserts that our education has suffered because our teachers have neglected their work. I have mixed with them, particularly I have seen the enthusiasm with which they have taken advantage of the opportunities given by the university during the last five years, and it is a matter of astonishment how these poorly paid teachers, who do not in some cases even earn Rs 30 per month, come all the way to Calcutta at their own expense and try to profit by the instructions which the university had imparted for their benefit and for the benefit of their schools.

Sir, much has been said about dual control. I know what dual control is and how dual control has injured the cause of education. But here again I cannot but refer to the attempts made by the university to obtain better coordination between the work of the university and the Education Department of the government, I believe. Sir, it was in 1934—six or seven years ago—that Mr Bottomley, Director of Public Instruction, and myself, sat together for weeks and months and tried to formulate a comprehensive set of rules which might be accepted both by the Department and the university and applied to all educational institutions—aided or unaided. We agreed to change the spirit of the rules; we agreed to establish better relationship between the university and the Department. The syndicate accepted the rules, and the rules were forwarded to the government six years ago but, Sir, it will surprise the House to know that during the last six years on final orders have yet been issued from the government of Bengal with regard to these rules (Cries of 'Shame!' from the Congress benches) and you talk of educational reform! I hear one of my friends on the other side asking me to wait for the reply. Sir, the reply will never come and if the reply comes for State reasons, under the circumstances it is useless to blame the university. The university has done what it could possibly do within its limited sphere for the purpose of advancement of secondary education. Sir, real improvement is impossible unless you are prepared to spend lakhs and lakhs of rupees for the improvement of educational institutions where education is now being imparted.

Sir, much has been said that the university at various stages opposed the formation of a Secondary Education Board. Sir, I can claim to have some knowledge of the detailed provisions of the measures which had been brought forward from time to time since 1923 and also the circumstances of their origin and the manner in which they were resisted by the university. Let me say this without fear of any contradiction that the university has all along felt the need for a properly constituted and fully equipped Board of Secondary Education enjoying both power and responsibility, and the fact that previous bills had been opposed was mainly due to the consideration that these schemes were designed not in furtherance of education but I say and say deliberately, to arrest the progress of education. (Cries of 'Hear! hear!' from the Congress benches.) Even today Sir, let me say without the least hesitation that I for one would be willing to extend the establishment of a Board of Secondary Education in this province, provided it is consistent with the fullest demands of education and is not designed as a political or repressive measure. It will not be possible for me to dwell at length on the provisions of the various bills that were formulated from time to time, but I know it, Sir, as a matter of fact that one of the bills affecting the University of Calcutta travelled all the way from Bengal to London and there that bill was placed before no less a person than Sir Michael Sadler. In the bill, Sir, let us not forget, that the authors attempted—and such an attempt is now being made by the present authors—the bill attempted to reform education in the province in the name of the Sadler Commission's report. But, Sir, the object was nothing more and nothing less than to provide for full governmental control over education. The memorandum submitted by Sir Michael Sadler on that bill went to the then Secretary of State and also came to the then Viceroy of India and ultimately resulted in the abandonment of that bill. In that memorandum, there were seething criticisms of the provisions of the bill which Sir Michael Sadler declared as utterly unacceptable, disclosing an inordinate anxiety for obtaining State control such as even the Czarist Russia would have hesitated to provide in the worst days of imperial autocracy. And you talk of your anxiety to provide for educational reform! My charge against the present government of Bengal is that the bill which they have dared bring forward before the legislature under the cloak of educational reform is not based on the report of the Sadler Commission, is totally inconsistent with its fundamental recommendations and must be rejected without hesitation by all lovers of true progress as something mischievous, as something poisonous.

Where does the bill differ from the recommendations of the Sadler Commission? The fundamental defect of the bill is that it tightens the grip of official control over secondary education and places it entirely at the mercy of the government. However much the Honourable Chief Minister may attempt to delude the public of Bengal, thanks to the clever manipulation of facts indulged in by his adviser or advisers, who by the way have justified their special pays, special allowances and special duty allowances by sacrificing whatever educational idealism there might have remained in him or them to the exigencies of party politics and communalism; however much the Honourable Chief Minister may attempt to mislead the people, the facts must stand as facts and truth must stand out as truth. 'Rightly or wrongly' said the Commission, 'the proposal to transfer the responsibility from the university to the Department of Public Instruction has become associated in the public mind with designs unfavourable to the wider diffusion of educational opportunity. Our evidence shows that this suspicion is strong in some parts of India, but it is nowhere more deep-rooted than in Bengal. In Bengal such a transference would jeopardise the good understanding between the government and the educated classes upon which the prospects of effective reform mainly depend.' Let me ask, Sir, were these observations borne in mind when the Executive Council of the Board of Secondary Education was constituted mainly of officers of the Department of Public Instruction? No reply. The Sadler Commission made it abundantly clear that the Board must be autonomous in so far as its administration was concerned, and it must be free from official influence and interference. All these are not my words, Sir, I am taking them verbatim from the report of the Sadler Commission. The ultimate responsibility of the State was recognised, and a remedy suggested for the discharge of this responsibility. In one sentence, the relationship was summed up. 'The Board should be in such a relation to the government and the legislative council as will secure to it the necessary grant from public funds and will lay open its work to general review along with that of other parts.' Mark the words 'general review along with that of other parts' of the educational administration of the State. There were two directions only, in which government influence was contemplated to be exercised. Apart from the fact that some representatives were to be appointed by the government not to pamper political or communal interests, on the ground of their special knowledge of education and experience, the majority of the Board would be non-officials and in no way under direct governmental control.

Let me pause here for a moment and ask if this fundamental requirement has been fulfilled in the constitution of this Board. It is no use ignoring facts. Who will deny today that a Board of fifty members of which at least nineteen will be Muslims, who will be keeping full pace with the policy of the present ministry and seven nominated Hindus (by the way, are Hindus so backward that they must come through the door of nomination?) who will act as nominated members of the ministry and a few other ex-officio members, who will dare assert that the Board will not have a comfortable majority of those who will be bound to remain under the control of the ministry and fail to exercise independent judgment? (A voice: 'Sometimes.') One of my friends says pertinently "sometimes". Not always! I know, Sir, conscience is biting hard. But even a Board so constituted will not have the responsibility of unfettered administration. This is where another charm comes in. The real works of the Board is to be entrusted to an Executive Council which was not contemplated by the Sadler Commission and its composition is worthy of close scrutiny. It will consist of fourteen members of whom six are directly under the government control and in fact steeped in the mysteries of Secretariat administration. Of the remaining, 8.6 are to be nominated by the Board of fifty constituted in a manner which will make it subservient to the government.

It is this Executive Council which will really function as the most powerful body on whose decisions the fates of thousands of schools and lakhs of children will depend. One of the fundamental features of the recommendations of the Sadler Commission was that the Board should not include inspecting officers barring the headman, namely, the Director of Public Instruction; one of the reasons for this obviously is that these very officers are to submit reports which have to be impartially judged and scrutinised by the Board itself. According to the new dispensation, it is these inspecting officers—remnants of the office of the Director of Public Instruction—who will have the predominant voice in the administration of secondary education of this province, and yet we are told that the present government of Bengal are shedding tears of crocodiles of the Sadler Commission and are greatly desirous of posing as great champions of education in this province.

Let me ask you, what will be the relationship between the Board and the government? The commission made it abundantly clear that the Board should enjoy freedom—this again is the language of the Commission—to act upon its own responsibility in framing and enforcing the regulations for diverse purposes. But its ultimate responsibility to the government of the country was recognised in a clear and emphatic manner. The Commission said that with regard to financial matters, the Board would submit its estimates to the government and the latter would have the opportunity of withholding its assent from any proposals which did not meet with the approval of government language of the Commission again. Let me pause here, Sir, and ask what is the nature and extent of control which has been envisaged by government under this bill. Not only the Budget is to be passed by the government, but not even a single penny can be spent by the Board even though it may have money of its own without previous governmental sanction. Even the inclusion of an item of expenditure in the Budget will not be deemed to be sanctioned by the government in some circumstances. The Board will virtually be a part and parcel of the Secretariat. What about the regulations of the Board? The regulations were left to be determined by the Board itself—mark the words of the Commission. 'The regulations of the Board will be published and would therefore come within the cognisance of the government and of the legislative council and be open to criticism from either body'—mark the words, where is the provision that every regulation has to be submitted to the government for previous approval as is mentioned in the draft bill before the Assembly? Such criticisms, the Commission proceeded to say, would naturally carry great weight with the Board, but it was left there. Let me pause here and ask, what are the provisions in the bill? The regulations will be subjected in each case to the previous approval of the provincial government, and all matters falling within the purview of the Board are to be conducted under the direction of the government. Conditions of grants-in-aid, conditions of recognition of schools, appointment of staff, fixation of fees, examination results, admission of students, supervision and the administration of schools, these are some of the vital matters which will fall within the scope of the regulations, and they are not only to be determined by the Board which will itself be subservient to the government, but such determination will again be subject to the previous approval of the government. And yet, Sir, Brutus is an honourable man, and yet, Sir, the Honourable Chief Minister expects us to believe that he is piously intending to follow the report of the Sadler Commission. I have said just now that there are only two directions in which government was given power to interfere with the work of the Board. One, as I have said, is with regard to the passing of financial estimates and the other relates to a more vital matter. But let the House note the language in which this vital power was given to government. The commission said: 'The likelihood of the Board coming in conflict with government upon grave questions of public importance was remote.' Remember, Sir, that there was no truth, no suggestion whatsoever that the government was going to interfere with regard to the internal administration of the Board or to dictate to it the principles on which the great task of educational reconstruction would be undertaken. It has been said, Sir, that the regulations of the Calcutta University are subject to the approval of government. But if any freedom has been denied to the university to frame its own regulations unhampered by governmental dictation, is that now to be quoted as a precedent that deserves to be perpetuate and the future Board of Secondary Education, the reformed Board of Secondary Education, is to be tied on that ground to the chariot wheels of government and its independence destroyed to the detriment of the country's welfare?

The Commission said: 'If the Board came into conflict with government upon grave questions of public importance, the government should have the power of overruling the Board,' and it proceeds to state that 'such action would follow a procedure which would at once mark the gravity of the situation and bring the question at issue before the public and its representatives.' The words of the Commission run as follows: 'We recommend that the government should have the power after due enquiry to require as an extreme measure the resignation of the Board, but if this step is ever taken it should be necessary for the government immediately to lay before the legislative council for its consideration and discussion the papers showing fully the matters in which government and the Board were in disagreement and the reasons which have led the government to require the Board's resignation.'

In the bill, the Board has been constituted on lines which make it a tool in the hands of the government and is wholly against the letter and spirit of the report of the Sadler Commission; bodies and institutions, like teachers, managers and graduates have been practically ignored or altogether suppressed. The Executive Council is to be composed in a manner which places the official point of view in the forefront and provides the Board with a dangerous instrument for the suppression of non-official educational institution. The Board cannot interfere with the decisions of the Executive Council unless three-fifths of the members of the entire Board agree to such a step being taken. The regulations dealing with fundamental questions are to be passed by the Board after obtaining the previous sanction of the provincial government. Rules are to be made by the government directly without any consultation with the Board at all. Over and above this, the government retains to itself the right to inspect the officers of the Board and of any secondary school in the province, to suspend the proceedings of the Board, of the Executive Council and of any committee under it; and, lastly, the government retains the power to remove the members of the Board and to reconstitute it without even providing for any statutory safeguard before such drastic action is taken. Sir, it is a travesty of truth to say that the present bill follows the recommendations of the Sadler Commission. The one object of the bill is to officialise education and that has been done with full vengeance in utter disregard of the educational traditions of this province and forgetful of the warnings of the Sadler Commission itself.

Sir, let me now continue to describe how the bill is at variance with the other important recommendations of the Sadler Commission. One aspect is the question of finance. True, the Commission stated that the existing system cannot be patched up. The Honourable Chief Minister was tutored to quote this particular passage while criticising some of my remarks about finance made outside this Assembly, but there was no reference to the few remarks that followed this passage in the report. True, Sir, that the present system cannot be patched up, but then the Commission proceeded to say: 'What is needed is far-reaching reorganisation and such a reorganisation is impossible except on two conditions. It must have behind it a strong movement of public opinion and it must be accompanied by greatly increased expenditure form public funds.' For secondary education alone, it pointed out that an annual extra expenditure of 1 crore and 50 lakh of rupees would be necessary to make, what the Commission describes, our schools 'thoroughly efficient'. Of course, the Commission recognised that such a huge sum would not be available immediately; but two years ago the present government has received a report from a special officer indicating the amount of financial assistance required for reform of secondary education, and it will be of interest to members of the House to know that the extra amount suggested in that report, framed only two years ago, was at least 43 lakh of rupees extra which was spread out for a period of seven or eight years. The Chief Minister in criticising an extract from one of my speeches expressed his profound surprise that I had ascribed the present defects of education mainly to want of financial assistance. But it still remains to be seen what educational reconstruction is possible by mere transfer of power from one body to another or by dividing it among three or four bodies or by concentrating powers in the government alone. I say, Sir, with a full sense of responsibility that the contributions made by the government—I am not referring to the present government here in particular, but to the government of this country in general—towards education had been niggardly. They compare ridiculously with what other countries have done. Year before last, the Board of Education in England spent as grants-in-aid 65 crore of rupees for the improvement of education in Great Britain. (A voice from the Coalition benches: 'What about their Budget?') Never mind, but what about the proportion of expenditure spent on education as compared with other nation-building departments get much less than what is absorbed by, say, such departments as exist for the maintenance of law and order, defence and general administration.

Now, Sir, there is another vital matter in respect of which the bill departs fundamentally from the recommendations of the Sadler Commission, and that is the relationship between the new Board and the university. The bill provides that the matriculation examination will remain under the control of Calcutta University. Now, Sir, the Sadler Commission desired to provide for united control in the sphere of secondary education, and one of their chief recommendations was that the examination must be left in the hands of the Board. If it is said now that there were adequate reasons why the matriculation examination should be left in the hands of the university, obviously it is necessary that the relationship between the university and the Board should be determined on academic grounds, on a basis different from that followed by the Sadler Commission. The Sadler Commission looked at the matter from one point of view, and if it is now agreed to depart from that point of view, it is essential that the relationship between the Board and the university should be different from what is mentioned in the bill. Sir, it passed my comprehension that a university will be called upon to hold an examination with whose syllabus and courses of study it will have little concern. I do not ignore that on the Matriculation Syllabus Committee, the Universities of Calcutta and Dacca have been given representation. But it should not be ignored that the final responsibility for determining the conditions to be fulfilled by schools and candidates in respect of the examination will rest with the Board. The Board will act in accordance with the regulations framed with the previous concurrence of the government of Bengal. It is against all canons of sound educational efficiency and administration to empower one body to frame the curriculum and ask another body to hold the examination (Interjections from the Coalition benches.) I am glad, Sir, that my friends have started agreeing with me on some points.

In England, Sir, the relation of the universities to the secondary schools has been briefly noted in one of the authoritative books, *Universities in Great Britain* by Professor Ernest Barker of Cambridge. I shall just read out a few sentences from it. We hear much about powers being given to the university; the university should not be allowed to interfere with the matriculation and so on. Now, this is what is stated in the book: 'The universities in various ways affect to a great degree the character and curriculum of all secondary education. They furnish the teachers; and both by their matriculation examination and by technical examinations they conduct for the scholarship which they award, they influence the courses. Nor is this all. The universities are examining bodies for all these schools. They conduct the examinations for certificates; they prescribe the curriculum on which these certificates are awarded. These certificates are in the nature of passport into a career for those—and they are the great majority—who do not proceed to the university. In controlling this system of passports, the university plays a considerable part in the general scheme of national education.' Now, Sir, I ask the Honourable Chief Minister to mention one country in any part of the civilised world where the examination is conducted by a university and the curriculum and the courses of study are prescribed by a body other than the university.

Sir, the bill discloses an actively hostile attitude on the part of the framers of the bill towards the Calcutta University. After all, Sir, secondary education must be closely linked with the university stage and if the educational interests are not to suffer, there must be a broader recognition of the responsibility of the university to shape and guide the cause of education in the best interests of the nation.

Sir, much abuse has been heaped on the university on the ground that it derives a large income from examination fees and from the sale of university publications. Sir, it is astounding to find that the law is going to prohibit not only that the university should not prescribe textbooks—because that is a power which will be transferred to another body—but that the university will not even publish books which may be used in any secondary schools. I believe, Sir, this is an entirely novel doctrine, a new type of educational idealism which has been propounded by the present government of Bengal.

Sir, the bill departs in another respect from one important recommendation of the commission—government schools will remain under the control of the government; we will find that one of the essential conditions mentioned in the report was that the Department of Public Instruction should have nothing to do with the control of government schools. But there is no mention of deprovincialisation. Resolutions have been passed by this House, suggestions have been made before the government, but there is no mention that government schools are going to be deprovincialisd. Nor is it suggested that such schools will be administered by the Board. That is the regard which is paid to the Sadler Commission's report.

I come now, Sir, to the communal character of the Board. (Noise from the Coalition benches.) I am glad I have now been able to satisfy my friends because I knew they were becoming impatient.

Sir, the Honourable Chief Minister has observed that the university did not oppose communal representation before 1937. That is true. I admit, Sir, that is so. That the university had been anxious to see the Board containing a certain number of representatives from different communities was sufficient evidence of its desire to see that the Board maintained a representative character without losing its academic predominance. But the university was compelled to alter its viewpoint when it discovered that academic considerations gradually tended to recede to the background and there is a clamorous demand for the progressive realisation of Communal Raj in Education, not on the Board alone but on all bodies connected therewith and indeed in the educational administration of the province. If the Sadler Commission reserved three seats for securing what it regarded as effective Muslim representation, the government gave 14 per cent to Muslims in the 1926 bill, 16 per cent in the 1928 bill, 17 per cent in the first bill sent to the university in 1937 before the advent of the present popular government and 41 per cent in the second bill of 1937. It was at this stage that the Senate rejected the principle of communal representation as it clearly tended to outweigh all considerations of academic reform and efficiency. Now, Sir, that report of the Committee was signed among others by Sir PC Ray, Mr Wordsworth—today three years later, of Castor Oil fame (Loud laughter)—and two Muslim educationists, one of whom is himself a government servant. That was the unanimous report submitted by the University Committee.

Sir, the bill has introduced the communal principles in a most pernicious manner touching elaborately even the constitution of bodies which will select publications and textbooks and frame the syllabus and the curriculum.

Sir, there are two other details which I shall briefly touch upon—one is the proposal for the establishment of district committees. Sir, in the 1937 bill, this district committee was mentioned in greater detail in that in the document and it was mentioned that the chairman of the district committee was to be nominated by government. Sir, we have seen the manner in which powers have been exercised by district magistrates with regard to the administration of secondary schools about which I shall say something presently. And I do consider that if district committees are going to be constituted on that basis, the officialisation of the schools will be completely achieved.

Sir, the other matter relates to the clause providing for the automatic withdrawal of recognition of schools after two years. That is a drastic provision and may be utilised in a manner—I say 'may', and none can say 'must be' utilised—which will seriously injure a large number of schools. Sir, the Honourable Chief Minister referring to my criticism on this clause was coached up the other day to observe that the university in one of its own bills—I ask you to note 'own bill'—made a similar provision and the government has simply followed the university. What an anxiety to abide by the wishes of the University of Calcutta! But, Sir, I say it is wholly inaccurate to suggest that this was a bill of the university's own. In 1928, a government bill was sent to the university and in the definition clause—not a penal clause as included in the present bill—a similar suggestion was embodied, and it is true that at that time, 12 years ago, the university had not perhaps the ground nor the occasion to question the possible danger of such a clause. The Sheffield scheme of cutting the number of schools into one-third of its present number by a quick and sharp governmental razor has yet to come. That 400 or 500 schools will satisfy the cause of secondary education in this province was propounded by the special officer of the government of Bengal. (Mr Fazlur Rahman: It is untrue; it was never accepted.) Mr Rahman in the largeness of his vision makes no distinction between truth and untruth. But I never said that it was accepted. I say that the Sheffield scheme did come and it made us nervous about similar provisions connected with the Secondary Education Bill. But, Sir, my charge against the Chief Minister is that he has suppressed facts and that he has attempted to mislead the House as regards the university's views on this provision. (Question!) Question as much as you like, but you will be only questioning the truth. He said nothing of the fact that he was referring to 1928. I am not blaming him; he was tutored. He is not expected to hunt all the record of the university and the government to find out where the truth lay. I shall ask him to consider the facts himself before they are presented to the legislature and to the public of Bengal. It was very cleverly suppressed that this very question was examined again in 1937, when another bill went to the university containing a similar provision. And these were the words of the University Committee in its special report: 'such a provision naturally raises doubts in the minds of the people as to the motives which have inspired the formulation of this measure'. Could anything be more condemnatory of the clause which was included in the bill? This report which characterised the bill as a reactionary measure was signed by Sir PC Ray, Mr Wordsworth, Dr BC Roy, Mr Justice CC Biswas, Dr Q Khoda and Professor Siddiqi, and this was accepted without a single dissenting voice at the meeting of the Senate. And who were present at the meeting? The Director of Public Instruction himself and the special officer who had not a word to say in support of the provisions of the bill or in opposition to the university's observations. I think I have said enough to satisfy any unprejudiced critic that looked upon (this) as a purely educational measure. This bill will not be acceptable to the people of this province.

I shall now point out why we are so much opposed to the transfer of control to the present government. I have demonstrated that the amount of control transferred to the government is far more excessive and radical than was contemplated in the report of the Sadler Commission. A claim for such increased control is based on the theory that we have now a popular government. I am entirely opposed to this measure in the best interest of the country for the sake of Hindus, Muslims and all. Education should not be officialised in this country nor should the educational institutions be built up on a basis of rigid regimentation of rules and regulations emanating from government sources.

Let me say, Sir, without hesitation that even the control exercised by the university has in some respects standardised our work in schools in a manner which is not consistent with the best interests of education. But my objection to officialisation is not confined merely to any abstract principles that government should not have a dominating voice in the matter of education, but it has a direct and definite bearing on the manner in which the administration of the province has been carried on by the present government of Bengal. The present constitution does not give us a government of Bengal. The present constitution does not give us a government that represents the will of the people as such. So long as communal representation remains, government is influenced by communal and not national considerations. In this province, we have tasted the bitter fruits of officialisation during the last three years; officialisation has meant in Bengal a type of party politics and communalism, which is vitally against the educational progress of the province as a whole. So long as the policy of the government is not changed, I am not prepared to support any measure of so-called educational reforms which makes the voice of the present government paramount and vital in the sphere of education. Examine the history of the activities of the present government in the sphere of education and you will find that not only has it not made any contribution towards the educational uplift of the people as a whole, but has acted in a manner which has specially prejudiced the claims of the Hindus of this province. You may ask me why is it that I am apprehensive of the disastrous effects of the officialisation? How can I forget that in this province today out of 1,500 high schools, barring a few, all owe their existence to Hindu support and influence, although in most of these institutions education was open to members of all communities? In high schools, out of 3,50,000 pupils, nearly 75 per cent come from the Hindu community, about Rs 1,15,00,000 are being annually spent on high schools and out of this amount only Rs 15 lakh is paid by government and out of Rs 1 crore about Rs 80 lakh is paid by the Hindus and the rest by the other communities. Now, Sir, even if you take the government institutions you will see that only 30 per cent of the pupils reading in government institutions come from the Muslim community. If you take Middle English Schools, you will find that nearly 68 per cent of the pupils are Hindus.

(A voice: 'That is not correct.') That is the government statement. If that is not correct, I am not to be blamed. If you take the contributions made by the Hindus and Muslims for the maintenance of Middle English Schools, you will find that nearly 60 per cent of the fees are paid by the Hindus, 20 per cent by the Muslims, 10 per cent by the government and 10 per cent by local bodies. We have heard these days a lot about the claims of the Muslims as a majority community, but I wish it to be remembered when plans of reforms of secondary education are initiated that the bulk of the people to be immediately affected are Hindus and that the bulk of the contribution to be made will come from the Hindus. I am referring to the recurring fees paid by the Hindus, but if we take into account the capital expenditure on school buildings and other equipment you will find that more than a crore of rupees has been contributed by the Hindus for this purpose. The same thing is happening in the university. If we take the prizes and scholarships awarded on the result of the matriculation examination, we find that Rs 1,75,000 have been endowed to the university which maintains 86 scholarships, medals and prizes, and out of this sum Rs 1,300 has come from the Muslims. All these 86 scholarships, barring only four, are open to all the communities which shows the liberal outlook of the Hindu donors who were inspired by only one ideal and one alone: the encouragement of education irrespective of caste, creed or community.

Why am I so nervous and apprehensive of the official control being exercised by the present government of Bengal in the field of education? Because in the field of education, communal considerations and party polities have marked the administration in a manner which perhaps has no parallel in any other part of India during the last three years. In many cases, in the matter of appointment of teachers, in the matter of approval of the managing committees, in the matter of the appointment of inspecting staff, in the matter of recommendation for recognition, extra-academic considerations, [and] hostilities to Hindus have weighed with the present government and with some of its offices in a manner highly inimical to the progress of education in the province as a whole. Sir, I charge the present government with having polluted the administration by pursuing a sordid policy based on party politics and communalism. I hope you will permit me to refer to instances where the Education Department has proceeded on lines hardly consistent with the academic welfare of the schools. In one school in Mymensingh (I took the facts at random), the authorities were informed that unless a Muslim headmaster was appointed, the grant-in-aid would be withdrawn and subsequently the university was intimated by the school authorities to carry out the instruction of the Inspector. In another school, a similar demand was made in respect of a teacher and the matter had been officially referred by the university to the Director of Public Instruction for report. In another school in Basal, the headmaster was served with a notice of dismissal so as to carry out the instructions of the Inspector for the appointment of a Muslim. I can understand the anxiety for appointing a qualified Muslim whenever a vacancy occurs but during the last three years there had been a systemic tendency to get rid of existing Hindu incumbents for the purpose of replacing them by Muslims. (Cries of 'Shame! Shame!' from the Opposition benches). In Barisal, one was threatened with personal violence, making over the charge of his schools to the sub-divisional officers, who was the president of the school committee. In one school, the students began to clamour for 'Muslim' demands and it was strange to find that the students were permitted to send in their application directly to the District Magistrate and not through the headmaster or any other authority, and the District Magistrate ordered the Muslim sub-divisional officer to visit the school, and he in the presence of the students took the school authorities to task for neglecting Muslim interests. Even the Inspector did not know that such a charge was brought against the school and the school authorities had no information whatsoever on the subject.

Under the Government Education Code managing committees of aided schools are subject to the approval of the District Magistrate. Now Sir, the manner in which this power has been transferred to the District Magistrate makes us suggest that the time has come when the Education Department may easily be abolished and if that performance is possible, my friends Mr Fazlul Haq and Sir Nizamuddin may combine into one holy unity, the Education Department being placed under the Department of Police and the Criminal Investigation Department. A member of a committee at Narayanganj was disliked by the Distract Magistrate and the District Magistrate straight on cancelled the election not on communal ground but on political grounds without reference to the Director of Public Instruction, without reference to the university and without reference to anybody! Now, Sir, the university intervened in that case and what happened? That member was allowed to continue. Really there was no just reason for removing that member of the managing committee. We find that the officers have interfered with the election of all the members and the entire election set aside because there was no Muslim. There university suggested that one Muslim could easily be co-opted if necessary. If a particular teacher is not liked, why should the District Magistrate exercise this function without any reference to the Inspector, without reference to the Director of Public Instruction or without any reference to the university? Climax came the other day when a demand was made by the District Magistrate to remove an elected member in Midnapore, although the school was not receiving any aid whatsoever from the government. This is the manner of educational reform to which government stands committed and more control is going to be transferred to that government! I am sure that my Muslim friends will admit that although now the power is being applied mainly against the Hindus, the time will come when the table will be turned, and many Muslims—(A voice: 'You want to take that power to yourself.') I am not suggesting that the power will come into my hands. But even the present government will exercise the power against Muslims who may not say 'Ditto' to its views and orders. I can give you instances where even Muslim members had to be removed where their politics was not liked by the district officer concerned. These are dangerous symptoms which make us extremely nervous about the transfer of control to the hands of government in the sphere of education.

Sir, I was referring to the interference of the district magistrates with the managing committees of secondary schools. Sir, when I said district magistrates, I included within that category also officers representing the Military Intelligence Department. Sir, we hear now that the education system of the province is uncontrolled but let me ask the House, Sir, that if 600 of the high schools in the province are today under a system of surveillance by the police, the Military Intelligence Department and the district officers, what more control does the present government of Bengal want over the affairs of secondary institutions? Sir, in matters of grant, favouritism has been openly shown. Older institutions which deserved assistance have been kept out of the list or in the alternative conditions are attached to grants which it was impossible for them to accept consistent with educational needs and traditions. Sir, in one case in Barisal there were two schools—one started by Hindus and the other by Muslims. Sir, there was a suggestion that the two schools should be amalgamated. The Chief Minister himself was interested in one of the schools and the university ultimately decided to grant recognition to the Muslim school as well, although it had not carried out the requirements which were fixed by the university. In the letter which the Chief Minister wrote, the original of which is before me, and the letter which the Director of Public Instruction wrote to the university, it was agreed that both the schools, the Hindu and the Muslim schools, would be placed on an equal footing especially in respect of support from the State. In February, the order of the university was passed and within one month a sum of Rs 700 was paid by the government to the Muslim school. Then the authorities of the Hindu schools came to the university and enquired: what was the reason for the differentiation? A letter was then sent to the Director of Public Instruction protesting against the breach of faith, and the reply was characteristic—we were told that the grant was made from the discretionary grant of the Honourable Chief Minister; well, where does this money come from? The money comes from public funds (A voice: 'Or from the discretion of the Chief Minister?') or from amounts discretely or indiscreetly placed at the disposal of the Chief Minister? The Director suggested that if the Hindu school also similarly applied to the Chief Minister, through the Director of Public Instruction, a grant would be made to that school as well; Sir, that was two years ago—in August 1938—and the grant has yet to be made in August 1940. In the meantime, a recurring grant has been sanctioned for both the institutions, but that additional sum of Rs 700 which was paid to the Muslim school in violation of the undertaking given by the Chief Minister and the Director of Public Instruction gives us only an illustration of the deliberate differentiation made between one school and another on communal grounds.

Now, Sir, let me mention here a more glaring case which was brought to my notice some time ago. A girls' school open to all communities in Rajshahi with about 200 pupils was sanctioned a grant—a magnificent sum of Rs 4 per month while on the contrary a recently started junior madrasa confined only to Muslim girls with about 150 girls on the rolls was sanctioned a sum of Rs 150 per month. I am not grudging the amount which is spent for the advancement of Muslim education or for the education of any community that may be backward, but my charge is that deliberate distinctions are being made on communal considerations by the present government, and I am not prepared to transfer the control of education of the 3 lakh of Hindu children in the high schools and nearly 2 lakh in the middle schools to the care of the present ministry. In one school, the grant was threatened to be stopped by the sub-divisional officer as the school did not subscribe the *Azad*. A subsidy of Rs 30,000 to the paper was not sufficient, but the services of the sub-divisional officer must need be utilised for a wider circulation of the paper that supports ministerial policy. In another, a teacher had to lose his job because he was opposed to the present ministry. It is not communal at this time. That teacher had the temerity to oppose the policy of the ministry and he was served with a notice to quit.

Now as regard textbooks, the less said the better. Allegations have been openly made as regards the most unsatisfactory nature of the work of the Textbook Committee. Opinions may honestly differ on the suitability of particular textbooks, but when special communities for the selection of textbooks are deliberately constituted on communal and non-academic considerations, let me ask, what remains about the future improvement of the educational system? There are Muslims who, although they possess higher qualifications, have not been taken in but poorly qualified persons have been taken in who would meekly go and serve the authorities—the powers that be. Sir, mutilation of the Bengali language, distortion of historical facts and a flagrant disregard of academic standpoints are the characteristic features of the work of the Textbook Committee in Bengal the post of secretary of which is reserved for a Muslim, why Sir? What is the need for reserving the post of secretary of a Textbook Committee for the whole province for a member of a particular community? Why not give it to the best man, best qualified man available? Why show communalism even in this particular sphere, which will not be for the benefit of any party whatsoever?

Sir, as regards the inspection staff, nearly 75 per cent of the appointments have gone to Muslims during the last three years. It is a most interesting study to see how the figures in 1937 before the advent of the present ministry have practically been reversed, not on the basis of 50:50, but have practically been reversed to the advantage of the Muslim community, particularly in the selection of inspectors. Of course, I do not mind if qualified Muslim inspectors are appointed, but what I do say is that you irreparably injure the cause of education when these appointment are controlled in such a manner that you encourage an atmosphere of communalism. I have got a list here of some qualified Muslims in the Education Department—who were superseded and whose cases were not taken into account for obvious reasons—not because of communalism, but because they failed to pander to the needs of party politics.

No, Sir, if this be the state of administration of the Education Department in respect of secondary education, what has been our experience with regard to the administration of primary education? There, Sir, I find—I am not going into details—that although the education fees is demanded from the Hindus in almost all the districts, the manner in which the administration of primary education is going on is something that requires very serious consideration. In the constitution of District School Boards such as in districts like Noakhali or Mymensingh or Bogra, Hindus are not taken on such boards. (A voice: 'Why not?') It is not for me to say why not. In the Noakhali District Board, no Hindu has been elected. In the district of Mymensingh, no Hindu has been elected (A voice: 'Hindus have been elected.') I am glad, Sir, that in my lengthy speech at least one mistake has been found. I understand that one Hindu has been elected. (A voice: 'Two Hindus have been elected.') In the election of the Barisal School Board, I heard only three days ago that no Hindu had been elected shall I be contradicted? There is no reply. But that is not the only point. The point is not merely that no Hindu has been elected. But how have the nominations been distributed? (A voice: 'What about Howrah?') I am coming to Howrah. Don't be impatient. It is nearer home. With regard to nominations to District School Boards where Hindus have not been elected, almost all the persons that have been nominated are Muslims. In Noakhali, all the nominated members have gone to the Muslim community. (Cries of 'Question' form the Coalition benches.) I am not referring to the ex-officio members. What is the use of your questioning truth every time? With regard to districts where the Muslims are in a majority, the plea is that as these are districts where the Muslims are in a preponderating majority, obviously the nominations should go the Muslim community. But when you come to Howrah where no Muslim has been elected, all the nominated seats go to Muslims because that is a district where the Hindus are in a majority and the Muslims are in a minority and the protection of minority interests is one of the privileges of the present ministry of Bengal! Sir, that is how the administration of the District School Boards has been going on under the control of the present Minister of Education. Sir, teachers have been appointed not on the ground of merit. Here again communal percentage has been raised in reference to the population in a particular district. In a particular district where 70 per cent of the population is Muslims, 70 per cent of the teachers in primary schools must be Muslims, irrespective of qualifications; but in West Bengal, where the Muslims are in a minority, the doctrine of fifty-fifty must come in. There you must have equal distribution. I have said enough to show that it is impossible for us all Hindus to agree to the transfer of control of education to an organisation which is subservient to the present government unless and until by deeds and not by mere words, we are satisfied that educational problems will be looked upon from the educational standpoint. (A voice: 'What about the Calcutta University?') You may abolish the Calcutta University and add a fresh chapter to your record of destruction. What I have said is sufficient to demonstrate that the bill as framed by the government will not serve the cause of education: on the other hand, it will retard the progress to education and specially imperil the future of Hindu advancement.

Mr Wordsworth on behalf of the European Group stated yesterday that the Secondary Education Board must be constituted as the government party wanted it, and that communalism had to be swallowed, not as the best solution of the present problem but as something inevitable, though distasteful.

He compared communalism with castor oil? I wish he had compared it with arsenic. His analogy hardly does any credit to his power of reasoning. Castor oil is distasteful, but it is taken not for any mischief, not for the fun of it but for the betterment of human constitution, it is something that you cannot retain but eliminate within a short space of time. If communalism is swallowed or if this bill itself is swallowed, will it lead to the solution of the present educational problems? Will it ease communal tension? Will it reduce communalism in any measure whatsoever? The European Group asked us to submit to something that is inevitable. If that policy of surrender to the inevitable, irrespective of right or wrong, had animated the British people in Great Britain today, then England would have laid herself prostate at the feet of Hitler long ago. It is only in this country that the doctrine of inevitableness is preached with an air of superiority. Accept British rule and remain a subject race under British tutelage, for that is inevitable. Accept communal award, for that is inevitable. Sir, today the advice comes from the European Group that although the so-called Education Bill may destroy the very foundation of our cultural heritage, it must be accepted as inevitable. Sir, the suggestion comes from the European party because it knows that the education of European and Anglo-Indian children is protected under the statute. They know that although they may come to be associated with the Board for the purpose of matriculation examination, if the occasion arises they have other available means for safeguarding the educational interests of their children reading in India. Only last week, the syndicate of the Calcutta University considered an application from all the European schools in the city asking for a permanent exemption from the operation of the regulation regarding the medium of instruction. We gave them exemption for a period. But they were apprehensive as regards their future and they asked for permanent protection and the University of Calcutta, the much-abused and much-maligned University of Calcutta, gave that protection to the European and Anglo-Indian residents without the least hesitation only seven days ago. Let me ask Mr Wordsworth and his friends, would they tolerate as representatives of their group such interference in their schools as is now witnessed in our educational institutions under the present administration? What would the European schools do if the government pressed upon the managers of these schools to appoint teachers on the basis of communal percentage? Many European schools today admit a certain percentage of Indian students. Suppose a demand is made that a certain percentage of teachers must be taken from the Hindu community and a certain percentage from the Muslim community, although they may not be the best candidates available, what would they do? Would the managers of schools like to have their names scrutinised by district officers or investigating officers and excluded on the ground of party politics? Would they permit the inspector to come and dictate the acceptance of special textbook on the ground of communal authorship? Would they allow interference in matters of detail such as is being done by inspectors in respect of aided institutions in Bengal today? It is easy for Mr Wordsworth and my friends to my right, but it is painful for me when I see their attitude. I know it is easy for them to say, 'We support the principle although we know that it is bad and unsound,' when they know that the children of their community will be protected from its pernicious effects. One illustration I shall give to show the manner in which communal differences have developed and created a situation in education circles today, which requires the most urgent consideration. It is about a school in the sub-division of Chandpur in Comilla. Some time ago, the services of two teachers were dispensed with—one a Hindu and another a Muslim. There were Muslim members on the managing committee and all agreed that the services of these two teachers should be terminated and if possible, a Muslim science graduate taken. And that was done, although the school was an unaided school under predominantly Hindu management. Then the trouble started. The boys started the trouble under the influence of other Muslims in the locality that a demand must be made that the headmaster, a Hindu teacher, must leave the school. Do you know what is happening there today? Inside the school, the boys are mocking the headmaster when he comes to his classroom and openly demanding that they do not want to read under a Hindu headmaster and that they want a Muslim headmaster! The sub-inspector, not of schools, but of police has come to the scene and he is assisting in the perpetuation of this sort of disturbance. The Muslim sub-divisional officer has come to the scene and he is asking why the demand of the Muslim students should not be met. Three days ago, the Muslim magistrate went to the scene. Well, this is the state of affairs which is going on. I ask, Sir, my friends, is it not simply playing with fire? If today, Sir, this state of things spread in all the educational institutions of the province and the Hindu students, of which there are lakhs and lakhs, make the demand that they will not read under Muslim headmasters and teachers although otherwise they may be very well qualified, if this sort of retaliation starts, then there will be nothing but confusion and chaos in the whole province. This one illustration will give you an idea of the kind of atmosphere that pervades thy province today.

Sir, I often ask myself what is the remedy of the present situation. It was not without any amount of pain that I decided not to serve on the Select Committee. By serving on the Select Committee, if I knew that it was really going to lead to educational expansion, it would have been one of my privileges and duties to do so. But, Sir, we did not want to serve on the Select Committee, because we knew that the principles, the fundamental principles of the bill were such that they must be altered, if it is going to be an educational measure at all; and when there was no chance of that being done, it was useless to serve on the Select Committee. I shall not refer in detail to the remarks made against me personally in the Chief Minister's speech. One observation of his is not without a touch of humour. My opposition to the bill made by Mr Fazlul Haq doubts the balanced sense of my judgment. Sobriety of judgment and adherence to any principles are qualities of which none in India will accuse Mr Fazlul Haq and it is but natural for him to look at others through the prison of his own mind! Let me, Sir, say it without any hesitation that this bill is fundamentally unacceptable to us, and even if it is adopted by the House as a result of governmental majority, we are not going to accept it outside the legislature. We shall consider it a sacred and imperative duty on our part to resist its operation in every possible manner. The Honourable Chief Minister and his supporters think that the Opposition to this bill is inspired by a handful of persons who are acting from some selfish motives. It is but natural for men who themselves are actuated by the basest motives in passing legislative and administrative measures calculated deliberately to cripple the rightful interests of others, that they should always be anxious to impute motives for the actions of other people differing from them. But if members of the Cabinet and their supporters have eyes to see, they will have noticed that the bill has evoked a protest, the like of which has not been witnessed recently, and fortunately for the sake of the justice of the cause, in spite of political and other differences, all sections of Hindus have combined to oppose the operation of this bill.

Let it not be forgotten that nearly 75 per cent of the children reading in secondary schools belong to the Hindu community and it will be our endeavour to see that the vast majority of these children should have nothing to do with any educational institution that will work under the domination of this Board.

There are three courses open to the government. One is to listen to the voice of reason and abandon this measure and try to formulate a bill in consultation with educational interests, not necessarily confined to universities; looking upon problems of education solely from the point of view of education, from the point of view of those millions of children irrespective of caste, creed, or community, on whose proper and efficient upbringing the future welfare of the province will largely depend.

The second alternative will arise only if the government, which represents the Muslims, really considers that communal consideration and party politics, which means communal politics of a particular brand, must play their part in the formulation of a scheme of educational reconstruction. In that case, I should say that we Hindus should be given the liberty to develop our education in a manner that we would consider best suited to our needs. I make this proposal after a good deal of deliberation and as the one possible solution of the present impasse; if for some years Hindus and Muslims living in Bengal can thus separately proceed with the task of their educational reconstruction in an atmosphere devoid of bitterness and conflict, it is more than likely that sooner than we expect they may both agree to evolve a national system of education consistent with the needs of the province. (Mr Abdul Wahab Khan: 'We shall have a Pakistan here') No Pakistan here! We shall remain here in Bengal. Let the finances be distributed in accordance with the number of pupils reading at various stages and let the professional institutions be maintained on a non-communal basis. Such separate provisions have existed in several countries faced with minority problems. Muslims urge in season and out of season that although for ninety years they have received education during the British rule mainly in institutions founded and maintained by Hindu money, that the Hindus have been responsible for destroying their culture and retarding the growth of their education. If that is their true estimate and apprehension, it is better that they should take control of their own education for some years to come. Even if they so desired, let them have their Muslim university at Dacca. A distinguished professor, respected for his scholarly attainments and worldly wisdom, working at the university had noticed on day the word 'Dacca' with a disfigured 'D' and somebody who, perhaps, had already peeked into the future with the vision of a seer had replaced 'D' by 'M'. That was nearly 15 years ago and let Mr Fazlul Haq and his supporters earn the achievement of giving that university a name which tradition has already earned for it in practice. We, however, demand it as a matter of right that fullest facilities for educational expansion must be accorded to us unhampered by considerations of party politics and communalism. Before I leave this topic, I shall refer to the baneful effects of party politics in the sphere of educational administration in Australia, which has openly favoured official control of education as the Bengal ministry is today attempting to do. The words are taken from the *Education Year Book:*

> The present system links education far too closely with political events and uncertainties. It does not protect the schools sufficiently against the possibility of ignorance or bias on the part of the government of the day. Ministerial policy in education is practically determined by the private views on education which happened to be held by members of the Cabinet, and chiefly by the members of the government who is given the portfolio of Education, the educational system lending itself in the most dangerous way to the machinations of an unscrupulous or partisan government.

Words which the present ministry should carefully ponder over before it is too late to mend.

The third alternative is for the government to pursue this bill and to force all classes of people to accept its provisions. As I have said before, so let me repeat here again that we shall never accept this bill and shall paralyse its operation if it is forced upon us. Education has been to us a vital and sacred thing in the building up of our national life, and we cannot allow the death knell of our culture and progress to be sounded by a band of reactionaries, who have been impelled by a short-sighted policy to formulate their scheme of educational deformation, utterly unacceptable to all progressive sections of the people. It may be that resistance to this bill may bring us into conflict with the authorities and it might lead to situations which will involve much suffering and sacrifice; I say this not in a spirit of threat but with a deep sense of responsibility that to us the bill raises issues of a fundamental character. They admit of no compromise and we are ready for fighting this new menace. Its acceptance especially means to us the end of education of the Hindus and a cry must go forth to every Hindu child reading in the educational institutions, to every Hindu guardian and to all others interested in the welfare of our people that if any self respect is left in them, that if they are not to reduce themselves to a state of subservience in the field of culture as they have been reduced in the economic and political spheres, they must be prepared to face this organised campaign of oppression at any cost whatsoever. Let it not be forgotten that this bill affects Hindus more than it does anybody else and what right has any government to force on us a measure concerning the future of our education which we regard as utterly unacceptable? This government has forfeited our confidence and we are not prepared to place our educational destinies in their hands. Take the referendum of any Hindu constituency, if you dare do so. If in this hour of crisis when civilisations are crashing and noble cities and institutions are being ruthlessly destroyed, when millions of human lives and billions of pounds are being sacrificed, if at this crisis Bengal is to be thrown into chaos and confusion, let history record that the challenge came from a group of persons, who, acting in the name of communal electorates were out to crush the rightful claims of a minority, a minority that become the eyesore of the British government, because it was the first that had sounded the clarion call of political freedom. War for justice, war for the liberation of mankind, war for the enthronement of right and reason—wonderful platitudes these are, but they are reduced to the standard of inevitable castor oil when the Hindus of the province are to be crushed. But let me say this, that a minority though we are, it yet retains sufficient patriotism, courage and influence to stand boldly for the vindication of its just rights and it will consider no cause nobler and greater than the preservation of culture and education for which it would be prepared to face the most dire consequences, to sacrifice life and all before accepting as inevitable something that it detests as unclean and unworthy, something that must be thrown into the limbo of oblivion, not for the sake of the minority alone, but for the highest interests of the province which through joys and sorrow we have loved and revered as a perennial object of devoted worship and loyal service. (Loud and prolonged cheers from the Congress benches and cries of 'Hindu Ministers resign'. A voice from the Coalition benches: 'A pious wish!').

Sir, I rise to support the motion for recommittal of the bill to the Select Committee. Sir, in the history of this province, there have been legislative measures which have called forth strong criticism from the public at large, but I believe, Sir, that within recent years, as Mr Wordsworth pointed out a few minutes ago, no measure has aroused such bitter and such widespread controversy as the Secondary Education Bill. The opposition has been for its own sake merely. The opposition has not even been due to the fact that there have been important elements in public life of this province which have been opposed to the general policy of administration pursued by the government during the last four years. The critics included persons not only belonging to different political parties and organisations but also men and institutions who had nothing to do with politics whatsoever but who thought it their sacred duty to oppose the fundamental principles underlying the Secondary Education Bill. May I ask, Sir, the government and its supporters to pause for a moment and to consider to ask themselves, why did men belonging to such differing points of view agree to condemn this measure? They have done so not because they thought that it was a pleasure to oppose a bill which was supposed to be a bill to secure the educational advancement of the province, but they did so because they considered it to be their duty to oppose a measure which was calculated to retard the progress of education, and if accepted unchallenged, would sound the death knell of education itself.

Conscious as I am of the great contributions which education has made in this province during the last one hundred years, I shall be free to confess that there are important directions in which educational reform has to be affected before education could serve the real needs of the people as a whole. I shall also freely confess, Sir, that of all the different stages of education, secondary education is from some points of views the most important. The adoption of a correct standard at this stage can only make any national system of elementary education real and effective and also furnish an appropriate basis for that noble super structure of higher education which would reflect the genius and aspirations of the people at large. It is because I feel genuinely and I ask my friends who do not see eye to eye with us to believe me when I say so, it is because I genuinely feel that secondary education today requires urgent and imperative reforms that I have considered it my duty to scrutinise the scheme for its reorganisation and to ask myself whether the proposals really aim at better provisions for educational facilities of the children of Bengal, irrespective of creed or community, or whether in the garb of educational reform, it is proposed to sacrifice the basic ideals of education and to curtail its expansion. If we want better education, as undoubtedly we do, we want more education also.

Education must also be saved from the destructive influences of party politics and I do not care what the particular brand of that party politics is. Today, more than ever, we stand in urgent need for devising a system of education which will not be governed by a regimentation of rules and regulations drawing inspiration from the political views of a particular group or caucus. The correct relationship between the State and education has always been a matter of debate, but it is of supreme importance that while allowing the State general powers of supervision, the educational policy must be allowed to divert to channels leading to consequences detrimental to the welfare of the people. We must allow education to be shaped by men who are actuated by educational ideals and not swayed by political creeds or dogma. We must permit our educational institutions full freedom and scope to develop their activities according to their best light and judgment. This freedom will not be lost, but will create that greater freedom on which our country's destiny must ultimately be based. If party politics or an aggressive totalitarian State policy be allowed to influence education, it will produce most baneful effect on the development of our national life. We in this province, Sir, have very special reasons to entertain our distrust of wide powers of interference being given to the government constituted under the present law. So long as communal award and separate electorates continue, we see no prospect of the establishment of a really representative government which will command the confidence of the different sections of the people. In particular, the administration of the province for the last four years under the control of the present ministry has left us with bitter experiences. It has filled the minds of a very large section of the people with very grave misgivings and uncertainty about the future protection of the legitimate rights and interests of nearly one-half of the population of this province. We are firmly opposed to political influences in the sphere of education. We dislike official domination as it is detrimental to sound educational progress. In Bengal, political and official domination is closely linked up with communal squabbles which, if unchecked, will sound the death knell of true education.

Let me now, Sir, briefly place before you the reason why we do not wish that the government should proceed with the bill as has been introduced into the House. The definition of 'secondary education' as is given in the bill disclose a lamentable want of the sense of realities of the framers and supporters. It leaves the matter to be determined by the provincial government in such a manner as it may consider fit and proper from time to time. One of our greatest defects has been the predominance of the literary type of education which renders many of our youths almost unfit for practical vocations. Our greatest need today is to divert educational, agricultural and commercial educational education. What we ask is this: should not the government undertake to include this important aspect in the bill and authorise the Board to proceed with a scheme of expansion without any delay whatsoever? We do not want the matter to be left to chance or to the whims of a particular government, present or future. We want the legislature to lay down the policy here and now.

Again, the bill apparently seeks to include within its scope certain special institutions closely related to Islamic culture and tradition. The scope of general education or special education open to a community must be clearly determined by us, so that both the Board and the people at large may know the extent of the activities entrusted to the Board. We want our secondary education to develop purely on secular lines. There may be many both amongst Hindus and Muslims who may like to see a sound general education generously provided for their children which at the same time will be properly correlated to their own cultural and religious ideals. There may be others who may be desirous of seeing the development of education based strictly on orthodox principles. To my mind, such different systems of education with an ultimate standard, which may be approximately equalised, should remain in charge of separate authorities, each being assured of just and ample protection and patronage at the hands of the State. If, however, the Board is to include within its scope specialised education for one community, the claims of others as well must be equally recognised. The bill, as amended, leaves this very important question vague and undecided. Without funds, no reform is possible. In fact, money, want of resources, has been our chief stumbling block in the past. The bill, as revised, provides for an additional grant of Rs 25 lakh in five years. This is better than what was originally provided for in the bill. Who will deny that even this amount is ridiculously low? A sum equal to at least 50 per cent of the existing expenditure on secondary education should be the minimum State grant, and according to this well-accepted principle, when I say well-accepted I mean not only in provinces outside Bengal, but also in countries outside India—they should give us at least Rs 85 lakh in place of the proposed Rs 50 lakh in the course of next five years. Will the government make the provision before they claim to exercise control and supervision through the Board? The Board, as contemplated, will be a part and parcel of the Bengal Secretariat. The powers given to it do not endow the Board with the autonomy which it must possess if it is going to serve the cause of education whether of Hindus or of Muslims or of any other communities. All its regulations will require the previous approval of the government. It will not be given even the liberty to frame its own rules. It must be done by an overgenerous and overzealous government. Its Executive Council which will be its principal body is so balanced and adjusted as to reflect principally the viewpoint of the officials and persons nominated by the government. The same criticism applies to the constitution of the Board. Its budget and its powers under the financial provisions are so securely limited that it is almost reduced to a third rate department of the Bengal Secretariat. Not satisfied with constituting the Board in a manner so as to keep it under the heels of government, not satisfied with controlling its finances, the government retains to themselves the right to rescind and cancel the resolution of the Board or of its committees, to remove the members, to dismiss the members and to do other acts which render the formation of a separate board entirely useless and nugatory; to my mind only two simple clauses can serve the purpose of the present bill. First, let it be laid down that the government of Bengal, so long as the present ministry is in power, may deal with any secondary school in Bengal in any manner that they deem fit and pass such orders as they may consider expedient in their own interests.

Secondly, let it be laid down that the government of Bengal be empowered so long as the present ministry is in power to deal with the University of Calcutta in any manner that it may in its 'unwisdom' consider to be just and proper. You may ask me why I refer to the University of Calcutta. It has been said that the university has opposed the bill, particularly the persons connected with the university have criticised the bill, as the university was going to be deprived of a power which it has enjoyed for the last eighty years. Let me say this without fear of any contradiction that the university has never opposed the idea of the establishment of a properly constituted Board of Secondary Education with power and resources to serve the cause of education in this province. If the university has in the past opposed particular measures, it is not because it disliked the principle of the establishment of the Board but believed genuinely that the proposals under consideration were not intended for educational advancement but for either mischievous restriction of education or for providing machinery which would further deteriorate its cause. The bill as revised has a peculiar way of approach in respect of matters vitally affecting the University of Calcutta. I can understand a Board of Secondary Education that will hold its own final examination or examinations, recognise schools for the purpose and control the conditions of admission to such examination. But who has ever heard that the Board will not only lay down conditions for admission to its own examinations but also to the matriculation examination of the university? I believe it is a sacred right of every self-respecting university throughout the world to determine its own admission tests. The report of the Select Committee goes a step further and to crown the humiliation of the University of Calcutta, which is one of the objects of the present bill, suggests that the university will not be entitled to hold its own admission tests but shall be bound to accept the examination of the Board for the purpose. To my mind, the normal and rational course to be followed if educational reform is the main object of the framers is to permit the Board to lay down its own courses of study, to recognise its own school and to hold its own examinations. One paramount condition should be that all matters connected with the examination, syllabus and textbooks should be entrusted to an authority or more constituted under the statute on academic consideration which will command the confidence of all parties and will be a guarantee for the maintenance of the proper standard of such examinations. The bill may also lay down that the content and standard of this examination should be such as will enable the students to be admitted to any university. It will then be for the Board and the Calcutta University and other universities in India to come to an agreement that the University of Calcutta will normally accept the examination as equivalent to its own admission tests. After all, if matters are looked upon from the educational standpoint—it will be a tragedy if it is otherwise—there is no reason whatsoever why the university and the Board should come into any unnecessary conflict leading to consequences which will be disastrous to the best interests of the children of this province. While the report of the select committee indicates the anxiety of the government and its supporters to take away from the university its right to hold its matriculation examination, there is no mention anywhere of any proposal on the part of government to compensate the university for the loss of its income. The activities of the university depend on the income from fees, endowments and State grant. The State grant covers about 15 per cent of the total expenditure of the university. The failure of the government to provide for a State grant by way of compensation of loss of university revenue can only be interpreted as its desire to see that its activities may be crippled by giving the university a blow from which it can hardly recover.

Let me now refer to the features of the bill which are connected with communal consideration. It is one thing for the government to provide the bill that the Board should represent different interests both from the academic standpoint and also from the point of view of education of different communities. But one has only to glance at the detailed provisions of the bill, the composition of the Board, the Executive Council and the various committees to discover how deep has the canker of communalism entered into the body of the bill. It is officialisation and communalism of the Bengal brand that gives us a bitter mixture of gas and poison which even the special castor oil of Messrs Wordsworth and Co. will not be able to counteract.

Not satisfied with providing for distribution of seats among elected and nominated non-officials, even the officials are divided into separate communal zones if official X is a Hindu, official Y must be a Muslim. If official A is a Hindus male, official B must be a Muslim female. Let me ask if both communities are not prepared to call upon the officials to act as true servants of the people as a whole and not of one community in particular, will it be possible for any government to run the administration of the province in a manner that will inspire the confidence of the public at large? We have taken strong objection to the appointment of the president being made by the government directly. Particularly in view of the very wide executive powers which the president will enjoy, we consider it necessary that this appointment should be made solely on the consideration of education expansion and efficiency. The reported stories associated with many appointments directly in the hands of government have been too many. Lately, there might have been occasions when the hands of the government have been either gently forced by strange and unknown considerations or rudely influenced by pressure from party opinion. Our alternative suggestions in this respect include; first, the election of the president by the Board itself; secondly, appointment by government out of a panel of names to be proposed by the Board; and thirdly, appointment by government on the recommendation of a specially composed committee which may include persons such as the Minister of Education, the chairman of the Public Service Commission, two vice chancellors of the Calcutta and Dacca Universities and an impartial expert adviser such as the

Education Commissioner with the Government of India. We believe if the last alternative is accepted, it will ensure the appointment of a worthy person as the president of the Board who will not only command the confidence of the government but also the confidence of all sections of the public at large. We insist upon making a statutory provision to this effect, so that the selection of the president may not be thrown into the melting pot of any personal or political group jobbery.

Another serious defect in the bill is that for an unknown period which may extend to even fifteen years, the Board will be deprived of the services of its own inspectorate. You will recall that one of the serious defects from which the present system of secondary education suffers is that the university has no inspecting staff of its own and it passes my comprehension how in any bill which seems to improve the present condition of affairs there should not be a strict and stringent provision that the Board will from the very beginning have at its disposal the services of a competent inspectorate staff.

I think I have given sufficient indication of the retrograde nature of the bill. We met the government and certain nominees of the Coalition Party during the last few weeks at successive sittings of a conference. I do not purpose to disclose our discussions during the present debate but let me record, Sir, my appreciation of the very free and frank manner in which the different viewpoints were placed before the conference and its sub-committee. I have always felt that the situation in Bengal, especially in respect of its communal atmosphere, will not improve unless both parties are prepared to face the differences in a spirit of mutual understanding and toleration. Sweet words will not remove barriers or secure smooth sailing. There is deep-rooted mutual distrust. There is strong mutual suspicion. Either the gulf of differences will be widened and bitterness will be piled upon bitterness resulting in consequences not helpful to either party or to the province as a whole or while agreeing to differ on other matters which have yet to be explored it is possible for us to take up education as a separate issue and find out if any honourable settlement can yet be reached on this question.

I genuinely believe that it is only on education, rightly planned and executed, that Bengal's great future will depend, and that Bengal must include all parties and communities who stand for the welfare of the great province, Hindus, Muslims, Buddhists, Christians, Europeans and Anglo-Indians, all uniting together for the educational uplift of the sons and daughters of Bengal. It is from this point of view—that for the last fortnight we had incessantly worked and were genuinely anxious to bring about a solution acceptable to all. There can be no settlement between yes and no. An honourable settlement means the embodiment of the largest measure of agreement without sacrificing any principles and cherished ideals. I believe a Hindu may well remain a loyal Hindu, a Muslim a faithful Muslim and a Christian a true Christian, and yet all be patriotic Bengalis and Indians. Our education may be so devised as to rouse the legitimate pride and respect in all of us for our own culture and tradition, at the same time, we may all learn the value of tolerance and understanding and submit ourselves to the ennobling influences of a common citizenship, which would call forth some sacrifice from each of us, not for the purpose of weakening any element, but for the purpose of strengthening the foundation, solid and true, of that great Indian nationhood, which has been the dream of every patriotic son and daughter of India. Our discussions brought us, Hindus and Muslims, nearer together than many of us had perhaps anticipated. They broke down on certain points which both sides regarded as fundamental but in my humble opinion not yet insoluble. I shall ask the government and its supporters to hold their hands and not to proceed with the present bill. Nothing will be more welcome to the Honourable Chief Minister and to the general public in this province than an agreed measure of educational reform. We the elders may fight our battles in other spheres of differences but if both of us are anxious that our children should receive better education than what we have ourselves received, why should we not put our heads together and be determined to come to an honourable agreement acceptable to both parties? The agreements already reached make far-reaching changes in the bill necessary. Other important points still remain to be explored. The House cannot possibly consider this bill in its present form and be asked to accept important amendments piecemeal which we and other members of the Assembly have not yet seen. The entire structure of the bill must be reframed and only then can the House and public determine how far it goes to meet the viewpoints of its critics. On this ground alone I would appeal to the Honourable Chief Minister to agree to refer back the bill to the Select Committee for further consideration. Let there be no misgiving on one fundamental point. The bill, as it stands and as it has been introduced into the House, is utterly unacceptable to us. It is not aimed to serve education and it specially injures the interests of the Hindus who have been responsible for the building up of hundreds and thousands of schools in this province where all communities have received their education. By one stroke of the pen, it is proposed to withdraw recognition automatically from all high schools after two years, and the onus will be thrown on them to satisfy the Board in respect of their claim for continued existence. These schools, may I remind the House, have all been granted recognition under law and mostly on reports of government inspectors themselves. This alone shows the spirit of callousness which has characterised the policy underlying the present bill.

The Chief Minister the other day issued an appeal asking all parties and organisations to unite and eloquently said that in this hour of national peril, when civilisation itself was challenged, all controversies must be hushed. That was the expression which he used in the appeal. The test of the sincerity of his appeal will arise today. Here is a measure of controversy which, for valid and cogent reasons, is disliked by a large section of the people who feel that their vital interests are about to be jeopardised. They are willing to offer the hand of cooperation. Negotiations have brought the contending parties nearer each other than ever before. Is it a case of declaration of war like the attack on Iran, a case of ultimatum that if within a certain date we do not fall in line with the powers that be, the measure will be forced on the province by reason of the voting strength of the party supporting the ministry? If that is the attitude of the government, if that is the attitude of the party supporting the government, the Chief Minister's appeal was not worth the paper on which it was written. But I hope and trust, Sir, that the good work which we, who have fought with each other so long, have done during the last fortnight will not be destroyed by a section of the members of this Assembly, and while there is yet time, education may be saved and strengthened for paving the way to communal harmony and understanding in this province and for national solidarity at this critical juncture in the darkest hour of the history of our Motherland.

PRESIDENTIAL SPEECH AT THE FIFTH ALL INDIA CONGRESS OF THE ARYA SAMAJ

...Yours is not an annual conference that meets to take regular stock of your plans and activities but with the consent of the constituent members of the Arya Samaj, spread throughout India, you are summoned together on special occasions to deal with any emergent situation and formulate your common attitude towards some questions of paramount importance affecting the welfare of Indians and especially the rights of the Hindus. This conference has a great significance in as much as it meets in one of the most critical periods of Indian history. A devastating war is sapping the very foundation of human civilisation just as much the internal conditions of India have been thrown into a state of confusion affecting the political and economic, social and religious rights of the people.

I welcome this opportunity of paying my tribute of admiration to the Arya Samaj for the great work done by it towards the rebuilding of the national life of India. Despite the onslaughts on Indian culture and civilisation throughout the chequered history of our beloved Motherland, despite her political subjugation extending over centuries, sages, seers and savants have appeared from time to time on the Indian scene and by their marvellous powers of thought and action have checked retrograde tendencies and infused new life and vigour into the Indian mind. Thus, we have a long line of great and good men, heroes in thought and deed, Hindu, Buddhist and Jain; princes, patrons and prophets; great siddhas, bhaktas, God-intoxicated saints and devotees; great acharyas with their profound learning who by dint of their intellect attempted to establish a *dharmarajya*; sants, sadhus and *vairagi*s who flourished after the Turki conquest of India welcoming the Sufi mystics and saints of Islam who revealed the message of renunciation, service and devotion consistent with the mighty spirit of Indian civilisation. The impact of relationship between the west and the east brought into existence a remarkable era of Indian renaissance. The nineteenth century gave us great leaders of thought who sought to revolutionise the Indian mind in almost every sphere of activity, religious, cultural, social and political. With the advent of British rule in India and the introduction of western education, there was, however, a real danger of Indian life and outlook undergoing a steady process of denationalisation. There was an equal danger of an over-emphasis on orthodox conservatism and a blind adherence to forms and rites of religious observances, thus checking a correct and vigorous growth of our national life and character.

At this supreme crisis in the history of Indian progress, some great men, of whom Maharshi Dayananda Saraswati was one of the foremost, appeared on the scene and gave a remarkable lead to their country. Dayananda Saraswati's mental and spiritual outlook was orthodox but his was not a blind faith in empty ritual observances or a meaningless adherence to forms and superstitions often masquerading in the name of religious truths. He appeared before the public in India with the Vedas in his hands and gave a new message to bewildered people torn between many sects and loyalties and offered to all an equal place in the social structure of the society, built according to the holiest Indian traditions. It is indeed a matter of congratulations that the members of the Arya Samaj who are the spiritual descendents of the great Maharshi have not kept the light confined within the dark recesses of a sectarian temple. By an astonishing abundance of books, of journals and tracts in almost all the languages in India, they have sought to share with their fellowmen the teaching which they have found to be of vital importance to themselves. The galaxy of martyrs, patriots and workers who have steadfastly proceeded along the line laid down by their great master not only for social and spiritual but also for cultural and political uplift of India have indeed lived dedicated lives.

The greatest service of the Arya Samaj is that it has roused among the people a profound sense of individual and national self-respect, a virility of mind and a love of the country's culture and civilisation, destroying the poisonous sense of inferiority complex which turns man into a coward. Thus, we find the Arya Samaj rousing the people to activity not by mere lectures and discourses on our past heritage and present duties but by strengthening those essential spheres of human life on which depends our future stability. Education consistent with Indian ideals and traditions and also with modern requirements, has received most commendable attention at the hands of the Arya Samaj. Removal of untouchability, so essential to the consolidation of the Hindu race, has been another sphere of work which stands to the credit of the Arya Samaj. To unite Hindus, to instil in them both physical and spiritual strength, to raise their social status, to infuse in them an undying reverence for truth and religion, to call upon them to defend and to fight for their rights, constitute the vigorous planning of the Arya Samaj. In the sphere of religion, it has thrown the door wide open and by raising its catholic appeal it has not only effectively prevented onslaughts on Hindu religion by others but has also dared to receive back into the Hindu fold those who were lured into other faiths and religions.

The Arya Samaj has never actively participated in politics as an organisation. But many of its members have been veteran soldiers in the cause of our country's liberty. Its illustrious founder in his monumental work, the *Satyartha Prakash*, dealing as he did, with all phases of individual and national life with special reference to India, recorded in the clearest possible language his views on the political condition of the country. Thus he observed:

> At the present moment, let alone governing countries, the Aryans, through indolence, negligence and mutual discord do not possess a free, independent, uninterrupted and fearless rule even crushed under the heels of the foreigners.

> When a country falls upon evil days, the natives have to bear untold misery and suffering. Say what you will, the indigenous native rule is by far the best. A foreign government, perfectly free from religious prejudices, impartial towards all—the natives and the foreigners—kind, beneficent and just to the natives like their parents though it may be, can never render the people perfectly happy.

Could there have been a clearer and bolder analysis of our political bondage? Truly did the great French savant Romain Rolland say that Maharshi Dayananda transfused into the languid body of India his own formidable energy, his certainty, his lion's blood. He reminded the secular passivity of a people, too prone to bow to fate, that the soul is free, and that action is regenerator of destiny. 'Here was a soldier of Light, a warrior in God's world, a sculptor of men and institutions, a bold and rugged victor of the difficulties which Matter presents to Spirit, the whole, summing itself up,' said Sri Aurobindo, 'in a powerful impression of Spiritual Practicality.' The *Satyartha Prakash* which he left as an imperishable legacy to his countrymen and to the world at large, was an embodiment of the genius of the Master. Here we see him as a creative artist and also a critic, as a destroyer and also as a builder. Unfalterable was his faith in the eternal doctrines of truth, equality and liberty promulgated by the Vedas and he carried on relentless attacks against all forms of ignorance, bigotry and superstition. He had to face opposition from influential sections of his countrymen who could not at first keep pace with his progressive ideas, but he never deviated from what he believed to be the right path. With transparent sincerity of purpose and undaunted courage of conviction he declared: the truth consists in expounding the truth as truth, and error as error; the exposition of error in the place of truth and of truth in place of error does not constitute the unfolding of truth. The *Satyartha Prakash*, his magnum opus, gives us a picture of the reconstructed society which a free India can build for herself on the priceless traditions of her own culture and civilisation, harmoniously adjusted to modern conditions and environments.

Today a demand has come from the Muslim League that *Satyartha Prakash* must be suppressed as some of its passages offend a section of Mussalmans. It will be for you to consider what effective steps you will take for preventing such an act of arrogant and mischievous intolerance. Indeed, this agitation may itself serve to popularise more and more the great words of truth, courage and wisdom with which this famous book abounds, which have already brought strength and solace to millions, thus serving further to carry into effect the great ideal of liberation of the Indian mind for which the master lived and died. Knowing as I do the solidarity of the followers of Arya Samaj, I make bold to say that any sordid attempt to interfere with our religious rights will be set at naught by their courageous and united resistance, no matter what the consequences may be. I would still go further and say that such an attack will be accepted as a challenge by the entire Hindu race and indeed by all lovers of freedom of thought and of opinion, no matter what their religious persuasion may be. Let us not forget, however, the main reason which have emboldened the Muslim League to make such a preposterous demand. It is due on the one hand to disunity in our ranks, to a sense of indifference to our sacred literature; and on the other to the pampering policy of our rulers favouring one section of the people for perpetuating Indian slavery. Today, the greatest problem before India is the realisation of her political freedom. Without this freedom, it is impossible to give effect to any wide scheme of social and economic reconstruction based on our fundamental rights and traditions. I do not for a moment minimise the need for social consolidation amongst all classes and sections of Hindus which can only be achieved by arduous and systematic work among the masses so that their standard of living and outlook may be raised and all artificial barriers broken down. I would go further and assert that such unity among Hindus must be accompanied, wherever possible, by a just and honourable understanding among all communities inhabiting this country. There must, however, be certain fundamental conditions which must be fulfilled before a real and lasting understanding can be achieved. Today, it has been proved beyond the shadow of doubt that whatever may be the theories propounded by the British rulers, they are not prepared to transfer real power to the Indian people and thus lose their brightest possession. It suits their purpose to encourage the growth of disruptive tendencies amongst different sections of the Indian people, to give importance to all vested interests, specially bolstered up, and to carry on at the same time a ruthless policy of repression, stifling legitimate opposition to the continuance of their arbitrary rule. India's unity and indivisibility must be a vital factor in the new constitution. None knows better than the protagonists of the Pakistan scheme that it is wholly inconsistent with logic and practicability. The League is not prepared to allow the Hindus who form about three-fourths of India's population to determine the constitution of India. It is not even prepared that Hindus and Mussalmans throughout India should jointly settle India's constitution, for in both cases, it asserts that it involves the tyrannical rule of a majority over a minority. It claims at the same time that Muslims in provinces where they are a majority will by themselves decide the fate of crores of Hindus who live as a minority and apparently can claim no right to self-determination. In that case, it will not be 'tyrannical rule of majority over a minority' but an exercise of what is called the fundamental right of Muslims for a separate homeland. Politically, economically and culturally India is and must remain a single unit. It is satisfactory that Lord Wavell unequivocally recognises this, though he has no constructive plan to end the present deadlock. Anyone who seeks to disturb India's unity or to foment disruption is guilty of the highest act of treachery and must be resisted at any cost. Muslim League, left to itself, cannot divide India against the united opposition of the majority of her patriotic children nor can Britain with her sword vivisect India, and guarantee peaceful possession to the disruptionists. But British policy today is encouraging Pakistan regime in action in provinces where Hindus are in a minority and their rights and interests are systematically sacrificed at the altar of sordid communal opportunism. To test the bonafides of the Muslim League as regards its anxiety for the welfare of the Indian people or even the Mussalmans, we have repeatedly offered proposals for closing our ranks, postponing all controversial points regarding the future constitution until after the war and of putting forward a united demand for immediate transfer of power especially for a vigorous and systematic preparation of a national defence of India and utilisation of India's vast resources for her economic regeneration. That door of negotiation is still open though there is little chance of any such understanding being arrived at in view of the unconcealed manner in which all reactionary elements are encouraged by our rulers to put forth their unpatriotic and selfish demands. Today, the remedy lies in creating a national opposition throughout India which will include all parties and sections who are agreed on the fundamental demands of Indian liberty. Let us not try to run after, or cajole parties and persons who care not for Indian progress and freedom but act as subservient tools in the hands of their masters for perpetuating slavery of their country. There are other groups and sections, small and negligible by themselves, but strong and powerful, if they combine, who may well constitute an all-India national opposition laying down the fundamental conditions of our struggle for liberty. It will be the duty of such a body to lay stress on the maximum points of agreement regarding national reconstruction, demand immediate settlement, plead for toleration and better understanding amongst one another and fearlessly resist every encroachment on our civic, economic and political rights. Today, our country suffers from an apparent frustration. It is not the rule of law that functions in India today. Taking the fullest advantage of the war situation, the barbaric impulses of a foreign bureaucracy have forged their varied processes of both swift and slow strangulation of the national will. But can any country be governed for long by sheer force and against the will of her people? Famine and pestilence have removed in less than six months more than two to three millions of men who perished for want of food, medicine and shelter under the very nose of a civilised government. A similar catastrophe may overtake my province in 1944 if the present bankrupt, corrupt and communal ministry [of the Muslim League] is allowed to continue its administration during the coming months. Any other country would have blazed into an open rebellion if such shocking mal-administration had taken place. There is not the least doubt that never in the history of British India was there greater discontent amongst people as is witnessed at the present time. Let me not end, however, with a note of pessimism. We have yet to unite many a disruptive tendency amongst Hindus themselves. We have to fight against a steady growth of fanatical zeal following the demand for India's vivisection and last, but not the least, we have to guard against the onslaughts of the ruling race itself which aims constantly at crippling of Hindu strength and nationalist elements in the public life of the country. The task before us is beset with difficulties and disappointments. Has history, however, at all recorded the achievement of freedom by a subject-race which merely adorns itself in the role of an abject beggar or surrenders on vital questions of principles for a temporary and doubtful gain? Indian history gives us ample evidence that though there were giants amongst men in very generation who could easily be compared to the greatest men in any country or clime, the masses of the Indian people were not always swayed by a very strong and vigorous impulse for protecting their political liberty at any price. The great work that lies before political and other parties in India today, imbued with healthy ideas of national solidarity, is to spread far and wide this love of unity and liberty, this faith in India's inherent right to govern herself, this determination that unless freedom is achieved, life is not worth living at all. Our goal will be reached not by a mere appeal to the emotions of the people or by merely criticising our enemies but by carrying on an active programme of social and economic uplift and making religion a true unifying force for the uplift of human civilisation. This alone will give us that solid base on which an enduring structure of Indian liberty can be safely built. Let us, therefore, carry forward our work in a spirit of dauntlessness, gathering strength from the firm belief that in a world still dominated by power, possession and prestige, it will be given to India, consistent with her mighty past, to help evolve a higher and nobler civilisation not only for the regeneration of an oppressed race but also as a definite step in advance towards that coordination of the mind, matter and spirit without which neither permanent peace can be established nor freedom stabilised in any part of the civilised world.

Bande Mataram!

Delhi, 20, 21, 22 February 1944

VOICE OF WOMEN

The voice of women is the voice of pity and is the voice of human compassion. So far as women are concerned, their sensitiveness is not a mere rhetorical phrase. It is an inborn quality with them. It is essential that in this institution such glorious traits of womanhood must be maintained and it is another point on which the institution deserves our congratulation. I hope that education of women would not be such as would inculcate in them a tendency to imitate men in all their worst features. If only the noble qualities of women are preserved they would not encourage men in their brutal and callous activities. The traits of womanhood are patience, forbearance, no retaliation and no reprisal, and if women are able to cling to these natural virtues with which they are endowed, they would be able to wean away men from their brutal and inhuman activities and to restore civilisation on paths of safety.

I visited the Bani Bhawan. I was greatly impressed with the working of the institution. It is one of those few organisations where a lofty ideal has not remained confined in speeches and pamphlets, but has actually been carried into practice. There is not the least doubt that the work which is being done here is of national importance. If the great problem of village reconstruction in Bengal has to be satisfactorily solved, we shall require the unselfish and devoted labours of hundreds of teachers and workers, such as are trained in this institution.

The presidential address entitled, 'Voice of Women' was delivered on the Foundation Day of Nari Siksha Samti on 8 August 1946. It is extracted from Lady Abala Bose, *Kolkata: Nari Siksha Samiti, [Bengali Era] 1411.*

Dr Mookerjee was a life member of the Samiti which was founded by Abala Bose, wife of Acharya Jagadish Chandra Bose in 1919. Dr Mookerjee was its president from 1947–48 until his death in 1953.

THE TASK OF REAWAKENING THE SOUL OF INDIA

[The Samavartana Utsava was held on 25 December morning at Amrakunja. Separate enclosures for different categories of visitors under the overhanging branches of the historic mango grove, and at one end, facing the auditorium, a raised dais beautifully upholstered, with its foreground decorated with alpona *designs—this was how the stage was set for the enactment of the most important ceremony of the year.*

Among the personages who had been expected to grace the occasion with their presence, Shri Jawaharlal Nehru, our president could not come on account of unforeseen official engagement and Acharya Narendra Deo was unfortunately prevented by indisposition from attending the function. Dr Shyamaprasad Mukherjee, (sic) our vice president, presided over the function and delivered the convocation address.

The conferment of diplomas and certificates was performed by means of ceremony at once picturesquely beautiful and impressive. The adhyakshas *of the different academic departments invited their students who had qualified for the diploma to appear, one by one, before the president and accept at his hands the gift of the Saptaparni, the seven-foiled leaf of the Chhatim tree. So the students came and each received along with the blessings of his* adhyaksha *and his diploma and the*

Saptaparni graciously presented by president of the function. Pandit Kshitimohan Sen recited Vedic verses. A catechism in Sanskrit verses clearly setting forth the high duties of snataka *[graduate] of the Visva-Bharati towards himself, his alma mater and his country was recited in unison by the* snatakas *and their teachers. The two most important items in the proceedings were the convocation address delivered in Bengali by Dr Shyamaprasad Mukherjee (sic) and the Annual Report of the Visva-Bharati placed before the assembly by the Karma-Sachiva, Rathindranath Tagore. The function ended with Santi-Vachana and the Santiniketan song.]*

Dr Mookerjee began his address by referring to the farsighted wisdom, vision and patriotism of Poet Tagore in founding for the first time in modern India a seat of learning that could be truly called international.

Education, according to Tagore's plan, must be a matter of joy and not a burden, both for the teacher and the pupil; it could only prosper in the right atmosphere which he helped in creating. He finally believed in combining best Indian traditions with the wholesome gifts of the West.

Tagore, Dr Mookerjee said, was dissatisfied with the system of education prevailing in India under British rule. He realised that a mere tinkering with the problem would not achieve the results he wished for. He started by establishing a school amidst natural rural surroundings, the main object of which was not any regimented imparting of instruction on the western pattern, but the full and harmonious development of the scholar's body, mind and character, based on radically revised curricula and methods of teaching. He laid emphasis on the use of one's mother tongue at every stage. The subjects taught were comprehensive, dealing with arts and letters, science and agriculture. Thus year after year boys and girls who went out to the world after receiving their training at Santiniketan bore upon them the impress of the Poet's idealism and practical realism.

From the very beginning, continued Dr Mookerjee, the Poet expressed his keen desire to establish a university at Santiniketan where special emphasis would be laid for the study and research of various aspects of eastern culture and civilisation. India, for centuries past, had been the meeting ground of diverse thought movements in Asia. Just as in the olden days, both men and ideas, representing the highest patterns of Indian genius used to penetrate into various parts of Asia, so also scholars from other lands travelled to great seats of learning in India, seeking for new light and experience. Tagore's dream was the creation of a seat of learning in India where scholars, irrespective of race, creed or colour, would assemble from all parts of the world and actuated by a truly scientific spirit, not only resurrect old wisdom now forgotten, but also create new knowledge. He entertained an abiding faith in a spirit of harmony in human culture. There are, no doubt, different forms and patterns obtaining in various parts of the civilised world, each country contributing its share, large or small, through its chequered career of ups and downs. But behind all this, there are abundant signs of uniformity of thought and outlook dealing with the fundamental problems of human advancement.

Tagore claimed that the ultimate peace of the world could be discovered not through ugly competitions between one nation and another, not through political and economic strife, not through domination and exploitation, but by emphasising upon points of common contact and purpose, representing the mighty efforts of generations of seers and savants of each nation towards the fulfilment of human destiny and the advancement of human civilisation. Art, architecture, philosophy, languages, literature, religion—all could be and should be studied from a comparative standpoint so as to discover that great unity in diversity which might ultimately form the basis of a lasting international understandings at once peaceful and harmonious. It is but natural that if a university in India has to keep so high a purpose in view in the sphere of international relations, it must be able to lay a firm foundation in respect of studies connected with Indian culture and civilisation. Until and unless Visva-Bharati is in position to represent the highest traditions of Indian scholarship in all their varied aspects and maintain teachers and scholars, museums and libraries worthy of the cause, it cannot possibly attract workers from countries outside India.

An institution which was represented by a personality of the type of Tagore naturally suffers from serious handicaps after his demise. Yet, it must be said to the credit of the authorities of Visva-Bharati that the lamp that the Poet had lit has been kept burning. The Poet was a born revolutionary and he naturally claimed for himself the right to make experiments in all spheres with which he was connected. He dreaded nothing more than rigidity of rules and regulations which often chilled the very life of an educational institution and made its working wooden and artificial.

According to him, freedom was the life-breath of education. Lest this precious right should be curtailed and his institution become a cheap copybook of some other type whose value and utility he himself doubted, he was at first unwilling to have any connection with any statutory Indian universities or with the government of the day. At a later stage, however, both he and Visva-Bharati came into a closer contact with Calcutta University, whereby, his freedom of action remained undisturbed and at the same time his institutions became entitled to certain academic and administrative advantages.

It has been long felt that the period of experimentation is over and Visva-Bharati has amply demonstrated its usefulness as a living institution. Indeed the greatest memorial to Tagore will be the development of Visva-Bharati on the lines that he had foreshadowed during his lifetime.

Universities in India were founded under British rule in accordance with certain settled actions of educational policy. Visva-Bharati, however, represents a type of its own, which is different from any other Indian university. There is no reason why India should not maintain different types of universities located in various sites, each fulfilling its purpose and serving the cause of progress. While coordination of the activities of Indian universities is desirable in avoiding unnecessary duplications, yet there should be no attempt to mould all on a similar pattern or to ignore the claims of special institutions. For these reasons, Visva-Bharati has approached the Government of India requesting it to give it due statutory recognition.

The Radhakrishnan Commission has ably supported this proposal. We have every hope that very soon the all-India status of Visva-Bharati will be recognised by the Indian Parliament and sufficient funds will be placed at its disposal for carrying out its main objectives. We have zealously to guard against the possibility of the university turning into a mere machine or a lifeless administrative body, overloaded with laws and bye-laws, forgetting or minimising the free and invigorating conditions of its existence. Let not all energy and attention be devoted to the making of a golden cage, the bird inside it dying of want of free air and light.

Indian education is today passing through a crisis. The system initiated by our British rulers about 100 years ago fulfilled its purpose long ago. Through the efforts of great Indian educationists, changes of a fundamental character have been made from time to time though a thorough overhaul has yet to be made. Education wisely planned and rightly executed will ultimately be the principal factor on which the future peace, progress and happiness of the Indian people will rest. Primary, secondary and university education—all stages demand a balanced attention from the State and the public. Expansion and not curtailment must be our motto; preservation of equality must be our constant aim. Cultural and scientific, technical and agricultural, all represent various aspects of educational development, none of which the nation can afford to neglect.

Education is one sphere of activity on which the State can never be accused of overspending. If our planning is sound and administration correct, the more we spend, the more solid will be the results leading to national prosperity and solidarity. While the claims of the masses for educational facilities, which have been denied to them for more than nearly two centuries, can no longer be ignored, yet the State and private benefactors must keep fully alive special institutions like Visva-Bharati which have a great mission to perform in building up a free India.

May the task of rediscovering the Indian mind, fully conversant with our rich heritage and adequately equipped with science and technology, be undertaken by our universities in a spirit of dauntless courage and devotion. In the great task of the reawakening of the soul of India, may Visva-Bharati play its worthy part and thus function as a noble memorial of its illustrious founder.

I can do no better than to conclude by hoping and praying in the language of the Poet himself that 'this institution may be a perpetual creation by the cooperative enthusiasm of teachers and students, growing with the growth of their soul, a world in itself, self-sustaining, independent, rich with ever-renewing life, radiating life across space and time, attracting and maintaining round it a planetary system of dependent bodies. Its aim should lie in imparting life-breath to the complete man, who is intellectual as well as economic, bound by social bounds, but aspiring towards spiritual freedom and final perfection.

Speech delivered at Visva-Bharati Convocation, Santiniketan, 25 December 1950. This report of the address appeared in Visva-Bharati News, January 1951

FOUNDATION DAY ADDRESS, CALCUTTA UNIVERSITY

This assembly is in one sense of greater significance than the annual convocation. Its scope is much wider, for here we stand face to face with thousands of university students and have not to restrict ourselves to graduates alone. Palatial buildings, halls and museums do not by themselves represent the university. The life and the spirit of the university are determined by its alumni whom you so worthily represent. The enthusiasm and keenness which this celebration inspired last year are still vivid in the minds of us all. The men and women who stood where you stand today set an example of devotion and discipline which, in the larger interests of the university and the nation, must not be allowed to disappear with the closing of this annual ceremony. It is imperative that organisation and discipline should characterise your activities throughout the year, so that you may permanently stamp the seal of vigour and vitality upon the corporate life of the university and the college.

The record of work done during the year for development of physical education and the deepening of an esprit de corps is indeed encouraging. The efficiency and morale of the University Training Corps have considerably improved and fill us with hopes for its future. The Rowing Club which will soon have its own home is making steady progress and has justified its existence. I do not ignore that there is yet ample scope for improvement, expansion and coordination. The provision for the better training of our students, especially of the best amongst them, calls for our immediate attention.

The university stands not merely as a cloistered assembly of learning or as a busy centre of examination; it also aims at developing the health and character of its alumni and at moulding personalities capable of the largest good to the province and the nation. This latter purpose of the university I desire to emphasise before you today. If I speak to you about certain habits of mind and action which I earnestly wish you to imbibe, I do so because of my deep-rooted conviction that the future of this province rests with you, the rising generation of its men and women. Regard it not as a common platitude of no serious significance. The period through which we are passing is momentous. You are charged today as being the products of a system of education which makes you good for nothing, which saps your vitality and renders you unfit for sustained and useful works.

Let me ask you, are you going to accept this challenge without protest? Are you willing to let things drift as they are doing today and perpetuate an era of humiliation and hardship? It is for you to be inspired by a practical idealism, to shake off the sense of inferiority from which you suffer and to stand up as men, upright and fearless, determined to achieve what is right and what is just. Let us cultivate the habit of hard and honest work, the habit of enjoying life, and learn to value the dignity of labour. A spirit of invincibility must animate your actions. You must belong to the army of the unconquerable whom difficulties do not daunt nor failures discourage, to whom all things are possible, and the impossible, the most alluring and attractive of all. I long for the day when a spirit of adventure will animate the youths of my province. I know the spirit has been awakened but if it is to live it must be carefully fostered. Why should not Bengal be the first in India to send out a batch of explorers to conquer Mount Everest or some other region still unknown and untrodden? Why should not young men scatter themselves far and wide, actively participating in social service and engaging themselves in pursuits and occupations which lie outside the beaten track?

Let us cultivate the habit of open-mindedness, the habit of unprejudiced facing of all facts that come within our vision. Respect for superiors and appreciation of other people's point of view are among the essential factors for the sound growth of society. Forget not that gentleness of behaviour and politeness are compatible with true strength and independence of character; never sacrifice truth nor surrender your conviction to the care of other men or institutions. In whatever sphere we may work, however great our trials and tribulations, let us respect the inner spirit of men and ever maintain its freedom as our priceless treasure.

One of the essential qualities which you must develop is a well-balanced sense of discipline. The rule of discipline connotes sacrifice, I am aware, may be taken advantage of by short-sighted interested person, thus retarding the growth of full and independent manhood. Bearing this danger in mind—a danger which may assume a colossal character as it may well crush some of the most vital elements in the life of a race—let us recognise that habits of discipline, obedience to rule and corporate action are imperative for the stability of a nation. You must learn to make sacrifices cheerfully and must welcome them, when they are made for the advancements of the truest interests of the country. There must be nothing mean, nothing narrow and nothing unclean about the ideal which will call forth your best efforts. It must be an all-embracing one, noble, inspiring and permanent—the ideal of service and of freedom.

I have spoken on the need for widening your activities and for raising the standard of your work and achievements. I have dwelt on the necessity for training a race of young men and women amongst whom will be found not merely leaders of thought and action in diverse branches of our public life but also an unlimited supply of workers and warriors—all capable, earnest and God-fearing—who will manfully combat ignorance and superstition and strive for the supremacy of truth, right and reason. There is, however, one condition which must be fulfilled if we are ever to attain our goal. *Unity is strength* is an old and well-tried maxim which is of paramount significance at the present hour. While you will strive for individual success, you must never forget that no great and permanent achievement in any field of national activity is ever possible unless we learn to sink our differences and stand united in thought and in action.

Let me, however, remind you that even your university, great as it is, bows its heads in eternal reverence and devotion to the mighty spirit of our Motherland to which you also owe the deepest and the most abiding allegiance. Do we not discover this inspiring undercurrent of unity while we serve our respective institutions? May we not keep this invigorating ideal before us in all walks of life and shape our policy and action accordingly? May we not remember that our ideal is harmony and not discord, freedom and not slavery, not warring factions, castes and communities, each distrustful of the other, but a united Bengal—nay, a united India—marching resolutely towards the goal of self-realisation? May we not regard ourselves as her sons and daughters—Hindus, Muslims, Buddhists and Christians—all loyal to our flags, but all equally determined to find for our great country an honourable place in the Commonwealth of Nations, to restore it to its position of glory and freedom—a country which will not merely be reckoned as a political and industrial power, but also as one which in the light of its culture and civilisation will contribute to the moral and intellectual stability of the world at large? My fervent prayer is that there may rise among you, and among those you represent, men and women inspired by this lofty idealism, who will consider no toil too exacting, no preparation too arduous, and no service too high or too humble for securing the well-being of our beloved Motherland.

Foundation Day address delivered at the Calcutta University on 24 January 1936

CONVOCATION ADDRESS, CALCUTTA UNIVERSITY

Last year, at the suggestion of the chancellor, we decided to make this departure in our programme. We approached the Poet (Gurudev Rabindranath Tagore) with our invitation but circumstances prevented him from complying with our request. As the university wanted to have him and none else to deliver the first address, we repeated our invitation this year. Patience has brought its reward and we genuinely rejoice to have the Poet in our midst today. To the university he does not come as a stranger. We feel proud to count him as one of our honorary graduates, who has all along taken deep interest in the development of study and research in Bengali at this university and who was himself for some time associated with this department.

His presence at the convocation at a time when we are about to launch upon a vigorous policy of making our mother tongue the basis of instruction and examination is not without significance. The new regulations for the matriculation examination are now being introduced in our schools and we confidently expect that they will mark the beginning of a new epoch of cultural development. We can never remain satisfied with making the language of the province the medium of instruction in high schools. That constitutes only one of the means which the university must adopt in order to instil a new life and vigour into its educational system. The university has recently decided to invite the cooperation of well-known writers in bringing out a series of books in Bengali dealing with various subjects, in arts, science, politics, history, sociology, economics and religion, written in a manner which will make useful knowledge accessible to all. This scheme is fraught with great possibilities not merely for the growth of Bengali literature but also for raising the standard of intellectual equipment of the province as a whole, affecting the outlook and activities of every Bengali anxious to make his contribution towards the solidarity of national resources.

I do not propose in my address today to deal exhaustively with the varied activities of the university during the past year. I should, however, assure the members of the convocation and the sympathetic public that, notwithstanding difficulties and obstacles, we have tried to keep the flag of progress flying. Our teachers and advanced students have nobly carried on their duty of making contribution to the advancement of knowledge and progress of ideas in diverse branches of arts and science. Although English was never prescribed as the necessary language for a thesis, we have today awarded for the first time the degree of doctor of philosophy to a successful candidate who wrote his thesis in Bengali and for this he deserves our special congratulation. We have steadily encouraged higher study and research by young and brilliant workers whose single-minded pursuit of learning deserves the highest commendation.

We have adhered to the practice of sending our selected teachers and scholars to foreign seats of learning and they worthily represented us in various countries in Europe, in the United States of America, in South America and in the Far East. In the selection of their subjects for study and investigation, we have paid attention to the needs of various branches of arts and science and have laid due emphasis on technical and industrial training. One of our scholars, himself suffering from blindness from the beginning of his educational career, has been sent to America where he is being specially instructed in the methods for the education of the blind. We have invited distinguished scholars and visitors to come to this university and deliver courses of lectures for the benefit to our teachers and students, one of whom is Sir William Holdsworth, the eminent English writer of legal history, who has agreed to visit Calcutta next cold weather. Here I may recall that our invitation to the Indian Science Congress to hold its joint session with the British Association in Calcutta in January 1938, has been accepted and we expect that our city will be the temporary home of eminent men of science gathered from all parts of the world and also of fellow-workers from other parts of India.

We have continued the task of publishing valuable books and treatises on various subjects like history and politics, languages and literature, religion and philosophy, law, mathematics, anthropology and fine arts, mainly contributed by our teachers and advanced students. In addition to the journals of the Department of Letters and Science we have been helping in the publication of as many as six journals of scientific societies whose activities are not confined either to this city or province, thereby aiming at the dissemination of knowledge affecting the intellectual status of India as a whole. The syllabuses and curricula in several subjects in the Faculties of Art, Science, Medicine and Engineering have been revised thus raising their standards and extending their scope and utility.

There is so much work to be done in the ever-expanding sphere of education that it may well occupy the lifelong labours of generations of sincere and unselfish men and women belonging to all classes and communities. We want men and workers; we want freedom to initiate new and far-reaching policies of expansion and improvement. Above all, let me reiterate that no reform of an extensive character will ever be attained unless both the State and public spirited citizens offer their generous assistance to the university and to its colleges and schools.

Fellow graduates, you are about to enter the arena of life at one of the most critical periods of the history of our province. While you will demand from the university and the educational institutions the right type of training and instruction which will make you men of character, full of vital impulses and ready to take an active and honourable part in all spheres of life, the university cannot obviously undertake the responsibility of finding a suitable career for each and every one of you. I do not claim that the instruction and training that we are imparting today are entirely of the right type or that the response which the students give is always adequate and satisfactory. But you must have noticed that we are steadily attempting to reorganise our system so that it may better serve the changing needs of the country and respond to the living problems of life. So far as lies in our power, we will continue to work in that direction, notwithstanding obstacles and opposition.

But the great problem of the hour is not merely to provide the right kind of training, not merely to save the educational system from being turned into a soulless machine, but to rouse public opinion and to focus the attention of all on the supreme necessity of finding new avenues of occupation and fresh vocations and careers for the hundreds and thousands of youths who are being produced by our universities. We resolutely oppose the policy of restricting education urged on the ground that suitable opportunities for work cannot be found for all university-trained men. We do so, not for any abstract principle or for any sentimental reason. We do so, because we firmly believe that if our country is to be raised to an independent status, enjoying liberty and self-respect, it can be done primarily through the agency of unselfish and patriotic youth, men and women who shine in deeds and not in words, who in their thousands will be called upon to dedicate their lives to the task of social and educational, economic and agricultural, industrial and political uplift of the millions of their brethren whose voice today is choked under the deadening influence of poverty and disease, of strife and dissension, of ignorance and superstition.

Who, I ask, can ever undertake this gigantic task of national reconstruction, which will signify the emergence of our Motherland from the shackles of oppression and servility, but a race of Indian youths, proud of their culture and traditions, armed with western skill and knowledge, fearless and straightforward, determined to work and stand united under a common banner of progress and service. The men are here and more will come if we want them. There stand the mighty problems of reconstruction, apparently baffling solution. The stupendous task cannot be directly organised by any seat of learning, whose duty will be mainly to provide society with men and women trained according to correct systems and ideals. In the corporate interest of the nation, it will be the paramount duty of the State and of men and organisations capable of influencing our destinies, not to permit as much idealism, enthusiasm and trained skill to be wasted or turned into unproductive and undesirable channels, but to take them up with boldness and sympathy and to employ them in diverse fields of activity, calculated to bring in their train an era of peace, progress and prosperity. Such a project of expansion and constructive work requires for its fulfilment of drastic revision of many of the existing policies of the State and other organisations; it will involve a vast expenditure of money; it will require ceaseless and persistent efforts, combined with courage, honesty and sincerity of purpose, which must never fail in the face of difficulties and opposition. I fervently hope and trust that it may be given to men and women educated at this university to help to formulate such a far-reaching scheme of national reconstruction, capable of gradual accomplishment, to educate public opinion on its great potentialities, to organise the active support and cooperation of all sections and parties in the community and to place it before the nation as an irresistible demand—a demand which requires fulfilment not for the mere purpose of finding work and occupation for those who are entitled to them, but for the larger interests of the province, for its healthy development and progress and for freeing it from the bondage of perpetual dependence and domination.

Convocation address delivered at the Calcutta University on 17 February 1937

CONVOCATION ADDRESS, CALCUTTA UNIVERSITY

Last year the address to graduates was delivered in an unforgettable manner by Rabindranath Tagore. This year we have amidst us Rev CF Andrews whose great sympathy with Indians and whose selfless devotion to all just and humane cause have won for him the respect and affection of men of all classes and creeds.

Before I make a rapid survey of some of our chief activities during the year, may I pay my tribute of respect to the memory of some distinguished persons whose death we have had to mourn since the last convocation. Diverse were fields of work of Sir Jagadish Chandra Bose, Dr Sarat Chandra Chatterjee, Dr Heramba Chandra Mitra, Dr Kashi Prasad Jayaswal, Dr Syamadas Mookerjee, Dr Indubhushan Brahmachari and Rev Fr FX Crohan. But each of them was actuated by the same spirit of devotion to duty and service to the cause of India's uplift. Each contributed in his own way to her intellectual progress, believing firmly in the vigour and vitality of the youth of the land; and to their making, they nobly and cheerfully dedicated their lives.

We have continued the policy of sending selected scholars abroad and the subjects for investigation included education of the blind, banking and currency organisation, standardisation of drugs, aromatic chemicals, plant physiology and physical chemistry. We have not been forgetful of the need for organising courses of lectures by distinguished scholars, Indian and Europeans. During the year we had amongst us Sir William Holdsworth speaking on English law, Professor Fisher on mathematical statistics, Professor Myers on industrial psychology and vocational guidance, Professor Radhakrishnan on comparative religion, Mahamahopadhyay Pramathanath Tarkabhushan on Vaisnavism, Dr Syud Hassan and Dr Sudhindranath Ghosh of Geneva on European and far-eastern problems, Dr Evart on Austrian culture, Sir Daniel Hamilton on India and the empire, Dr Dudley Stamp on modern geography, Dr FW Thomas on the literature of India and greater India.

Apart from the mere routine duties done, many of our teachers in the university and in the colleges have applied themselves to original work and inspired young scholars to follow in their lines, which have won for them recognition from various parts of India and abroad. Some of them have undertaken special topics for investigation at the instance of other bodies, official and non-official, and are thus making a definite effort to give a wider public the benefit of their study and research. We are anxious that the departments of science as also those of economics and commerce should be brought into closer contact with practical problems of industry and trade affecting the interests of the province at large; and we are exploring the means for securing such cooperation.

The scheme of expansion of women's education under the Viharilal Mitra Trust is now being prepared by an able Bengali lady graduate who was deputed to visit educational centres in India and draw up a report. The university, I expect, will soon be in a position to formulate the lines of future activity in this field and carry out a programme of reform which will be of benefit to Bengal, both socially and educationally.

The art museum which was opened last March is steadily growing into a useful institution. The collections amount to 1,228, and include valuable gifts from friends in and outside Bengal. Our aim is to lay special stress upon the forgotten treasures of Bengal, and exploration of different regions in the province for collection of specimens has already been planned. With the permission of the Government of India and acting in close cooperation with the Archaeological Department, we are just organising an excavation of the historic site of Bangarh in Dinajpur, directly undertaken by our staff and students.

Our main endeavour is to find out openings in such branches of trade and industry as do not at present attract qualified Bengali youths trained at the university. I do earnestly plead for support from all chambers of commerce and other bodies who are in a position to assist us.

A proposal now under consideration relates to the institution of a special course of training in agriculture and cottage industries. I hope this may help to turn the attention of our youths to practical pursuits and open a new source of productive energy which will be of benefit to themselves and to the province as a whole.

Much as I admire the keenness of a few select athletes and sportsmen, I would once again emphasise the imperative need for improving the health, vigour and vitality of all students and for turning the enthusiasm of thousands of mere student-spectators into active participation in games and physical exercises.

Stagnation is one of the dangers which threaten a public institution such as ours, overburdened with numerous problems of administration, not all of which are easy of solution. The rapid survey which I have placed before you will, I hope, convince you that we have not been oblivious of this danger. However important and fundamental the changes which we have recently introduced in various parts of our university organism, the time has now definitely come when we have to probe deeper into our education system as a whole and strive strenuously for improvement. Public opinion in this province will not for a moment tolerate any proposals which under the cloak of reform may aim at restriction of facilities. We want more education, and better education, and any reformer who can satisfy us in this respect will find enthusiastic support from all. While on the one hand we have to guard against the dominance of vested interests, we must also recognise that existing institutions which have worked for the advancement of education under tremendous difficulties cannot be deleted by a stroke of the pen. True statesmanship must discover a satisfactory way of readjusting and utilising all existing resources, both in manpower and materials, and evolve a new system of education capable of complete fulfilment before long.

University education originated in this country not in the desire for the conservation and betterment of our traditional culture, our arts, crafts and industries, but mainly for imputing to us western ideas through the medium of a foreign tongue. It has had, no doubt, its beneficent results. It has produced a large number of scholars and helped in the creation of a new literature and the development of science. Professions like law, medicine and engineering, have rapidly grown a part of this programme and absorbed some of the best Indian talents. But in the main, it has merely ensured a regular supply of indigenous machinery for the smooth working of a powerful bureaucracy. It did not aim at educating the people at large. The masses remained untouched. No attempt was made to correlate the different stages of education—the primary, the secondary and the university—so as to build them up into a harmonious whole. Too often these stages have been regarded as separate, watertight compartments, and we hear of projects for improving one at the expense of another. We hear today of restriction of university education, of reducing its sphere of influence, of making examinations its chief function and thrusting it into the background for the sake of encouraging primary education. Nothing could be more disastrous than such a short-sighted policy.

We, on the other hand, want to see established a sound policy of national education, which will ensure a steady advance from the lowest stage to the highest. We want to see primary education developing widely and laying the foundations of literacy, of right conduct, of healthy activity and of a breadth of outlook which will render possible the growth of a national consciousness. We want to see secondary education spreading far and wide, satisfying the requirements of a sound and liberal education and leading its recipients to diverse fields of intellectual, useful and productive activity. Then, in the last stage we want to see university education as a natural continuation of such a varied type of secondary education, providing for higher and advanced work, not only in the liberal and professional studies but also in science and technology, in commerce and agriculture. We want to see the syllabuses and course of studies so remodelled, systems of training and examination so reorganised that the young learner may grow up not as a mechanised recorder of information and theories, not as a dry specialist, but as one whose latent power is well roused, whose critical judgement is strengthened and whose capacity for wide thinking and application of knowledge to problems of life is developed to the fullest extent. We want to see such an education being imparted, without neglecting a study of the English language. We want to see the amplest provisions made for the supply of teachers ready to dedicate their lives to the cause of upbringing of the youth of the country, comprising both leaders and followers, healthy in body and intellect, disciplined and open-minded, generous and upright, fearless and patriotic. We want to see such a wide and beneficent policy of education, receiving unstinted aid from the State and from the public, and freed from the baneful influence of party politics and communal wrangles. We want to see the adoption of a State policy which will make possible a wide absorption of educated youths, now and in future, in the work of rebuilding Bengal in all its phases, social, economic and political.

Through education, more than through anything else, we can attain these cherished hopes and aspirations; and let us stand united to serve its sacred cause. I hope and pray that in the years to come it may be given to us all in whose hands rest responsible powers, to leave aside disputes and differences, to put our shoulder to the wheel of progress and to help in inaugurating an era of constructive work which will make our great province a happier place to live in and will give it a position of supremacy in matters concerning India as a whole. I hope and pray that in this task of reconstruction touching upon every phase of our national life, the University of Calcutta may play its part with courage, wisdom and foresight, and inspire in the hearts of thousands of her sons and daughters an abiding sense of loyalty and affection which will sustain her in her days of trial and of triumph and lead her on from strength to strength towards the fulfilment of her destiny.

Convocation address delivered at the Calcutta University on 5 March 1938

ROYAL ASIATIC SOCIETY

We have amongst us two distinguished guests whose presence we greatly value. Prof Hill has brought with him a special message of good wishes from the Royal Society of London. The mission that has brought him to India is closely associated with the work which this ancient society has accomplished for generations past. I sincerely trust that his visit will be followed by a well-coordinated and effective policy of collaboration between men of science in India and the State resulting in rapid scientific progress and economic and industrial development of this great country. We have also amidst us today a distinguished representative from China, Dr Li Fang Kuei, who has come to Calcutta with messages of greetings from the Academia Sinica and the Sino-Indian Society to our society, thus forging another link of fraternity between two ancient civilisations which have lived from time immemorial as friendly neighbours, each influencing the other with the fruits of its imperishable genius.

The society completes this year the 160th year of its existence. Its illustrious founder, Sir William Jones, was actuated by a passionate zeal for the advancement of knowledge and he saw, with the vision of a seer, the manifold opportunities for original investigation and research open to scholarly men, especially those from the west who came to serve their careers in India whether in the sphere of official administration or of commercial enterprise. He placed before his contemporaries and his successors for all time to come a magnificent but most ambitious ideal for unfolding the culture and civilisation of Asia, making Calcutta a living centre of Asia's intellectual activities. The memorable words that he then uttered amply bear a repetition after 160 years, serving as they do to enable us to take stock of our achievements and to remind us of the unlimited field that yet remains to be covered before our founder's ideal can be worthily attained.

Defining the object of the society being to enquire into the history and antiquities, arts, science and literature of Asia, Sir William Jones proceeded as follows:

> You will investigate whatever is rare in the stupendous fabric of nature; will correct the geography of Asia by new observations and discoveries; will trace the annals and even traditions of those nations who, from time to time, have peopled or desolated it; and will bring to light their various forms of government, with their institutions, civil and religious; you will examine their improvements and methods in arithmetic and geometry—in trigonometry, mensuration, mechanics, optics, astronomy and general physics; their systems of morality, grammar, rhetoric and dialectic; their skill in surgery and medicine, and their advancement, whatever it may be, in anatomy and chemistry. To this you will add researches into their agriculture, manufacture and trade; and, whilst you enquire into their music, architecture, painting, and poetry, will not neglect those inferior arts, by which comforts and even elegances of social life are supplied or improved.

To give emphasis to these details, Sir William Jones added:

> If now it be asked, what are the intended objects of our enquiries within these spacious limits, we answer, Man and Nature: whatever is performed by the one, or produced by the other.

Himself a scholar deeply versed in western and eastern languages and schools of thought, the clarion call given by Sir William Jones was responded to by generations of scholars and administrators, some of whom held the highest offices both under the East India Company and the Crown. One has to turn the pages of the society's proceedings and journals during the last one century and a half, and one is struck by the manner in which knowledge spread in various branches of history and antiquity, language and philosophy, science and medicine. In fact, the pioneer works of stimulating original investigation in both letters and science, since the advent of British rule in India, stands to the credit of our society. It was at first conspicuously served by western scholars, some of whom, after their retirement from India, went back to their native land and carried on their activities in furtherance of the cause of learning. The encouragement given to the cause of Asiatic research, with special reference to Indian culture and civilisation, kindled the intellectual powers of many a brilliant Indian scholar of repute, thus coinciding with the movement of progressive expansion of western education in this country. The history of our society indeed records India's solid contributions to the progress of human civilisation. I cannot but here stress a characteristic feature of our activities. The men who have come to our society from generation to generation have belonged to various races and schools of thought, some of whom have had sharp differences in opinion and outlook amongst themselves, others following occupations widely divergent in character; but when they came into the rooms of the society they left behind them all extraneous controversies and differences and were actuated by one common ideal and that was how best to stimulate the intellectual activity of the country and to glorify the sacred traditions of truth and knowledge. Historically speaking, our society, which was unique of its kind at its inception, gradually witnessed the formation of other learned bodies and institutions devoted to specialised research in particular branches of knowledge, some of whom were the direct outcome of the 'mother' society's efforts. Calcutta and Bengal thus became the seat of the Indian Museum; the great scientific services organised by the Government of India, geological, botanical and zoological; a vast and progressive teaching and research university; the All-India Institute of Hygiene and Public Health; the Indian Association for the Cultivation of Science, a fine achievement of non-official efforts in the field of scientific education; the Indian Science Congress and the National Institute of Sciences; the Bose Institute; the Visva-Bharati, the international university embodying the idealism of Rabindranath Tagore and various other institutions. Similar intellectual activities also spread in other parts of India affecting the domains of both arts and sciences and Indian scholars have deservedly earned recognition throughout the civilised world.

Notwithstanding such a natural development of India's intellectual and cultural life, there still remains a paramount need of a society such as ours. In the first place, it continues to afford a meeting ground of scholarly men, old and young, wholly engaged in the pursuit of knowledge, following diverse branches of study in different organisations. It also brings them into contact with others who, while following administrative or business careers or belonging to some other learned professions, seek an opportunity not only to imbibe new ideas and knowledge but also to make their own contributions in some department or other. It is this latter class of non-specialists who have helped in no small measure to develop the love of Asiatic culture and civilisation through the agency of this society. In the second place, our society claims to its credit a rich and valuable library divided into four sections namely, General, Sanskritic, Islamic and Sino-Tibetan. Apart from its value as a reference and research library in various branches of Indological and scientific studies, it has a particularly rich collection of manuscripts ranging from the seventh to the nineteenth century. Our total strength of manuscripts in the Sanskritic languages is about 27,000 representing a variety of subjects such as literature from the Vedic time, philosophy, law, grammar, history, geography, astronomy, mathematics, medicine, art, architecture, music, theology and religion. At least 10,000 Sanskritic manuscripts still remain uncatalogued and undeciphered. Similarly, in the Islamic section we have more than 6,000 manuscripts ranging from the twelfth century to the nineteenth, covering an equal variety of subjects. Some of the manuscripts apparently formed part of the rich collections of Mughal emperors whose autograph they bear. More than 1,200 Islamic manuscripts still remain to be catalogued. Our collection of coins, from the early Hindu to those of Indo-Muslim rulers, numbers about 20,000; but this section has not developed on account of the policy adopted by the society, nearly forty years ago, to hand over its coins to the Indian Museum. Our collection of copper plates, numbering 40, ranges in date from the third century to the eighteenth and some of them constitute important landmarks of Indian history. During the last two years, we have carried on with vigour and earnestness our scheme of completing the catalogues of our manuscripts without which deeper investigation can hardly be undertaken. Many of our rare collections have been removed from Calcutta due to war emergency and our task of reorganisation will not be fully completed until the return of normal times. In any case, if the society is to do full justice to its large and valuable collections, it must be enabled to engage an adequate band of scholars and experts who will develop a well-coordinated plan of translating, editing and publishing special memoirs on the rich treasures that the society possesses. It is thus and thus alone and not by merely making the society a storehouse of antiquities that we can worthily contribute to the advancement of knowledge. Our publications, including our proceedings, memoirs and journals, suffered for some time for lack of proper publicity. The recent catalogue brought out by the society has promptly demonstrated the keenness of the demand for our publications from scholars far and near. We are thankful to government for the modest grant they have made for publishing our catalogues and manuscripts. The funds at the disposal of the society do not, however, permit it to engage a large number of scholars to develop our utilisation branch. If the task is to be completed within a reasonable period of time, our funds have to be generously supplemented both by the State and the public.

In the third place, the society, though remaining a learned one, must continue to be a well-equipped and functioning centre from where new information and knowledge may be disseminated to the public in various fields of intellectual activity, social and economic, literary and scientific. The society by its scheme of publications and public lectures must play an important part in bringing home to the people at large the fruits of investigations of scholars and savants. Without in any way allowing itself to become a machinery for propaganda, it may thus elevate the intellect of the people it serves, broaden their minds and sharpen their curiosity. The society readily organised special courses of discussion meetings, intended for civilians and members of the allied forces, where distinguished lecturers regularly speak in a non-technical manner on some aspect or other of Indian culture and civilisation, as part of the society's war services.

The future of the society depends on the zeal and devotion that its members and well-wishers may bring to bear on its affairs consistent with the great ideals of its founder. Limitless was the scope of activities propounded by him; it is for us to adjust them with due regard to our ever-changing conditions and environments. Today the war has placed human civilisation on its trial. Throughout the chequered history of mankind, there have been eras of remarkable progress and achievement often mixed with tragic clashes and conflicts reviving the barbaric impulses of the jungle man. The ancient history of the east records many an achievement of the Asiatic peoples in the domains of arts, science and religion. Indeed the greatest religious prophets of the world flooded humanity with light from the eastern horizon. But history also records that, for centuries, the east witnessed a decay of economic and scientific progress, and it laid greater stress on philosophy and religion than on literature, art and architecture. The west illumined itself and the rest of the world by great and startling discoveries of science and it felt glorified at the apparent mastery of man over nature. Science revealed to the human mind the great mysteries of nature and her infinite capacity to do good to suffering humanity. Science, however, was not permitted by man merely to serve or enlighten humanity, irrespective of race, creed and colour, but it was wedded to a policy of devastating greed and exploitation, both national and imperial, leading to distrust and conflict, and upsetting the peace and security of the world at large. The Second World War through which we are passing today, costing the lives and happiness of millions of combatants and non-combatants, will be a meaningless sacrifice unless the peace that follows it is based on fundamental ideals of equality, justice and liberty. A war to end war there may never be. But is a peace to end war beyond the contrivance of mortal thought? The safety of the world lies in the elimination of ideas of the ever-expanding spirit of material conquest and of domination and exploitation of one race or country over another. The world is large enough for all of us to stand by the maxim—*live and let live*—and to inaugurate the establishment of a confederation of free countries, each having the liberty to develop itself on the basis of its own culture and traditions and contributing its share to the spirit of man which recognises no barrier of race, religion or colour. Every country must learn the supreme value of giving all possible scope to its scholars and thinkers, men of letters and science, who will not allow their intellect and freedom of thought and opinion to be sacrificed at the altar of State politics.

The greatest antidote for tyranny is a powerful and fearless public opinion which scrutinises men and things from a detached point of view and speaks with knowledge and authority whenever the occasion demands it...India will have to pass through her period of post-war reconstruction and this society will, I hope, be enabled to play its appropriate role...let us march along the path of truth and knowledge and contribute to the best of our ability to the growth of that unity in diversity, that spirit of mutual respect, trust and understanding among individuals and nations which must form the foundation of a new world order dedicated to the cause of progress of human civilisation.

Speech delivered at the annual meeting of the Royal Asiatic Society of Bengal on 7 February 1944

With his mother Jogmaya Devi.

With Dr BR Ambedkar in Parliament.

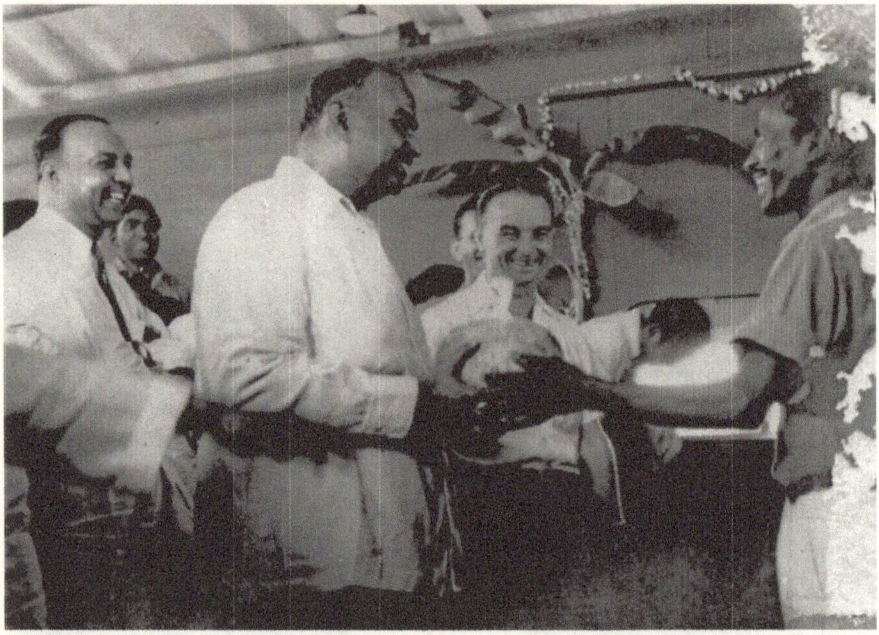

At the inauguration of a factory.

With the Mother during the Sri Aurobindo Memorial Convention, Puducherry.

With U Nu, first Prime Minister of Burma and Jawaharlal Nehru.

At his house.

DR SYAMA PRASAD MOOKERJEE: A PORTRAIT OF A SELFLESS PATRIOT

It is not very often that we come across a person who lives for fifty-two years and remains in politics only for fourteen years, but within that short period rises to great heights and makes history. Dr Syama Prasad Mookerjee was born on 6 July 1901 in Calcutta (now Kolkata) and breathed his last on 23 June 1953 in captivity at Srinagar under mysterious circumstances. His lifespan and manner of death bear an uncanny resemblance to his dearest disciple Pandit Deendayal Upadhyaya.

The second son of the great educationist, Sir Asutosh Mookerjee (1864-1924), who was known as *Banglar Bagh* ('tiger of Bengal'), Dr Syama Prasad Mookerjee, also began his life as an educationist and a lawyer. In fact, Sir Asutosh Mookerjee, who had multifarious talents as a lawyer, mathematician and educationist, had groomed his eldest son Rama Prasad for the legal profession and second son Syama Prasad for the field of education. After a brilliant career in the University of Calcutta and securing first position in his graduation and postgraduation, Syama Prasad studied Law to become a member of the 'Indian Bar' in the Calcutta High Court, and thereafter set sail for England to became a Barrister and enter the 'English Bar'. But Syama Prasad's principal intention of going to England was to study the working of the universities in Britain. After accomplishing what he had in mind, he returned to India to become a member of the syndicate of the University of Calcutta. At the age of twenty-three, he was the youngest member of this syndicate. At that time, the Dyarchy system had recently been introduced in India by the Montague–Chelmsford Reforms (1919) and Education was one of the 'Transferred Subjects', which simply means, one in which Indians had some say. In 1929, Syama Prasad entered the legislative council from the University Constituency as an Indian National Congress (INC) candidate. However, immediately following this, the Congress decided to boycott the Council. Syama Prasad disagreed with this and resigned his seat in the Council to come back as an independent candidate. At this juncture in his life, he was purely concerned with education and not with politics.

Syama Prasad gave such a good account of himself in running the affairs of the university that the great scientist, Acharya Prafulla Chandra Ray, once congratulated him as '*Baap ka beta*' (true son of his father). He became the vice chancellor of the University of Calcutta at an unbelievably young age of thirty-three and infused new life into the running of the university. He served two terms of two years each as vice chancellor from 1934 to 1938. As vice chancellor, Dr Mookerjee supported nationalist scholars who wished to undertake serious research in Indian history from an Indian viewpoint; he encouraged excavations, opened the first museum of Indian history, culture and archaeology in the university and also invited international universities to send their students to study Indian civilisation, culture and the Sanskrit language. He promoted the languages of India. In fact, in 1937, he invited Rabindranath Tagore to deliver the convocation address in Bengali—this was the first time ever that a convocation address was delivered in Bengali in the precincts of the University of Calcutta.

Syama Prasad had to face some personal tragedies. His elder sister, Kamala was widowed, remarried, again widowed and died early. His father, Sir Asutosh, a guiding light in his life, died prematurely at the age of sixty, in 1924. Then came the worst tragedy, when his beloved wife of only eleven years,

Sudha, died. Syama Prasad was left to take care of his four young children. He could remain in public life only because of the help he received from his sister-in-law, Smt Tara Devi, wife of his elder brother Justice Rama Prasad.

In 1935, the British Parliament passed the Government of India Act, which introduced more representation for Indians. Each province was to have an elected government run entirely by Indians, but under the executive governorship of a British governor and with a civil service manned by Indian and British officers of the Indian Civil Service. By this time, mainly because of the machinations of the British, considerable polarisation on religious lines had taken place in India and the Muslim League emerged as a powerful communal party. However, their hold on the Muslim masses was still, at best, tenuous. In Bengal, the Muslim League represented mostly the Muslim landowners and the Muslim middle class and clergy. The bulk of the Muslim peasants were supporters of the Krishak Praja Party led by Abul Kashem Fazlul Haq. Although supported almost entirely by the Muslim peasantry, Haq was not a particularly communal person, and the culture in his party developed accordingly. Thus, there were three comparable political parties in Bengal, namely, the Congress, Muslim League and Krishak Praja Party.

After the assembly elections were over, it was found that none of the parties had got a majority. In such circumstances, the logical thing would have been for the Congress to form a coalition with the Krishak Praja Party, which had the support of the Muslim masses and was relatively secular in character. However, for some inexplicable reason, the Congress Working Committee refused to give permission to the provincial unit to form this coalition. This was a mistake that cost Bengali Hindus very dearly in perpetuity. Had this coalition been formed, perhaps the whole of Bengal would have remained part of India. As a result of this short-sightedness of the Congress, the Muslim League and the Krishak Praja Party formed a coalition brokered by Nalini Ranjan Sarker, a Bengali Hindu industrialist.

After the formation of this coalition, the Muslim League gradually gobbled up the Krishak Praja Party and began to introduce draconian legislations in the province that favoured Muslims and worked against Hindus. At this stage, the Hindus were far ahead of Muslims in Bengal in terms of the educational and professional attainments. This ministry's attempt was to negate this advantage by totally stopping the entry of Hindus in government services without any regard for qualification or experience. Fazlul Haq himself was inducted into the Muslim League and was persuaded to move the infamous Lahore Resolution.

Conference of the Muslim League in 1940

Meanwhile the Hindus of Bengal, being persecuted in this manner, were looking for a leader who could look after their interests. As a result, the elders of the community, who could see clearly that the Bengali Hindus were an endangered lot under the Krishak Praja Party and the Muslim League ministry, turned to Dr Syama Prasad Mookerjee and persuaded him to leave the field of education and enter the rough terrain of politics. He thus came out of 'academic seclusion' and became politically active. Later, he once wrote, 'My tendencies lay in the sphere of educational administration and I did not feel attracted by the noisy and dusty career of a politician. I thought the best way to serve my country would be through the path of education.' Some have also observed that Dr Mookerjee was 'impelled to leave the university and enter the political arena due to the miserable plight of the Bengal Hindus who were being systematically humiliated and despoiled by the Muslim League with the connivance of the British'.

Dr Mookerjee's activism in politics also came at a difficult time. The Congress was powerful in Bengal but was, as always, hesitant to speak for the rights of the Hindus, often bowing down to the Muslim League's pressure tactics. The Communist Party of India was the other element, which supported the Muslim League but called the All-India Hindu Mahasabha or any other organisation that spoke up for the Hindus as 'communal and reactionary'. Interestingly, the Communist attitude has not changed even now, after nearly seven decades. Among those who were instrumental in bringing Dr Mookerjee into politics were NC Chatterjee (father of former Lok Sabha Speaker, Somnath Chatterjee), a well-known barrister at the Calcutta High Court, Ashutosh Lahiri, Justice Manmatha Nath Mookerjee and Swami Pranavananda (founder of the Bharat Sevashram Sangha and a great source of inspiration for Dr Mookerjee).

Vinayak Damodar 'Veer' Savarkar, the All-India Hindu Mahasabha leader came to Bengal in August-September 1939 and Dr Mookerjee came in close contact with him and joined the Hindu Mahasabha. His entry was welcomed by Mahatma Gandhi, who was greatly impressed by his thoroughly nationalistic outlook and told him that 'somebody was needed to lead the Hindus after Malaviya ji (Pandit Madan Mohan Malaviya)...' Dr Mookerjee is said to have replied, 'But you will call me communal.' Gandhi replied: 'Like Siva could drink poison after churning the sea, somebody must be there to drink the poison of Indian politics. It could be you.' In fact, Gandhi, without ever saying so in as many words, had a deep appreciation of Dr Mookerjee's abilities. It was at his insistence that Nehru had inducted him as a Minister for Industry and Supply in free India's first Cabinet in 1947. In his first year with the Mahasabha, Dr Mookerjee extensively toured Bengal calling upon the Hindus to dissolve their differences and unite. His energetic political leadership infused greater strength and cohesiveness in the Hindu Mahasabha in Bengal. As one of his biographers noted, 'For the first and the last time, the Hindus of Bengal found a spokesman who did not care at all for political expediency or personal interest.'

Within one year of Dr Mookerjee's entry into politics in 1940, Savarkar, in view of his own illness, appointed him as the working president of All-India Hindu Mahasabha. This enabled Dr Mookerjee to tour the length and breadth of the country taking his message to a wider cross-section and in the process, Dr Mookerjee became an all-India leader. He was noticed all over the country and his courage, determination for the cause, his organisational and oratorical skills, tireless capacity for reaching out to the people and his decisive leadership quickly propelled him to national fame and he became a rallying point for Hindus all over the country. It was in 1940 in Lahore that he addressed a 'rally of Rashtriya Swayamsevak Sangh' and observed: 'I see in this organisation the one silver lining in the cloudy sky of India.'

Dr Mookerjee, once having stepped foot in politics, spared no pains to fight the sinister designs of the Muslim League-led government of Bengal. The government was trying to take secondary education out of the purview of the university with a view to bringing it directly under the government and Muslimise it. As secondary education in Bengal was under the purview of the University of Calcutta and since taking it under control was difficult for the Muslim League, the League decided to weaken the institution by taking secondary education out of its academic jurisdiction and giving it over to a secondary education board, which would have a majority of League-nominated members. Dr Mookerjee could not accept this; in fact, this bill, when introduced in the Bengal Assembly, saw him come out in full force against it. He generated a debate in the House, organised movements outside and mobilised public opinion against this bill, which would, he argued, 'give educational administration' in Bengal an 'aggressively communal turn'. In opposing the Secondary Education Bill, Dr Mookerjee displayed his great deftness in using constitutional means to push forward the political objective. His expertise in this was so high that he managed to win over the other parties. Dr Mookerjee, as a Hindu Mahasabha leader, managed to persuade the Congress to support him in this opposition and stoutly resisted the bill in the legislative council. His successful resistance of the Secondary Education Bill 'purely through constitutional means, without once taking the fight to the streets, once again showed the quality of the man as a constitutional and parliamentary politician'.

The other modus operandi of the Muslim League was to foment riots, especially in East Bengal. There were serious anti-Hindu pogroms at this time in Dhaka, Noakhali and Narayanganj (all now in Bangladesh). Dr Mookerjee wanted to proceed to Dhaka to quell these riots in spite of great opposition by the British government. The plane for Dhaka on which he requested a seat, left without him. Not one to be daunted, Dr Mookerjee, at great risk, travelled in a small monoplane. He was the first Hindu non-official from outside to reach the city. On reaching Dhaka, he defied every attempt made against him from entering the city and went straight to the palace of the Nawab of Dhaka and persuaded the Nawab to cooperate with him in stopping the pogroms. He stayed back in Dhaka for the next few days at the house of the famous nationalist historian RC Majumdar, who was then vice chancellor of Dhaka University, and visited the strife-torn areas to inspire confidence among those affected. Such display of exemplary courage and fearlessness would often be seen in Dr Mookerjee's life. He wanted the rest of India to know what had transpired in Dhaka and also about the nefarious actions of the Muslim League, but since there was a gag order on the press, the only other way of highlighting the issue was to raise it in the Assembly. Again, by displaying great political sagacity, Dr Mookerjee wired Mahatma Gandhi asking for his support. In turn, Gandhi asked the then Congress president to direct the Congress legislators in Bengal to support Dr Mookerjee's move of raising the issue on the floor of the House. This is how the whole country came to know of the happenings in Dhaka.

In 1941, Dr Mookerjee managed to persuade Fazlul Haq to quit Muslim League and form a ministry with the Congress and Hindu Mahasabha. Fazlul Haq was to be the Chief Minister, the second man was to be Sarat Chandra Bose and Dr Syama Prasad Mookerjee was to be a member of the Cabinet. However, the British Governor of Bengal, Sir John Herbert (a scheming India-hater) got Bose arrested under Defence of India Rules and he was transferred to a jail in South India. Thereafter, there was no chance of his inclusion in the Cabinet and Dr Mookerjee became the principal Hindu face in the Cabinet. Because of his past association with Fazlul Haq, Dr Mookerjee ran the Cabinet very well, so much so that the Cabinet, formally called Progressive Democratic Coalition, came to be popularly called the 'Syama–Haq Cabinet'.

This coalition provided a secular administration in the state, and after four years of persecution, Hindus could expect to be treated at par with Muslims. Dr Mookerjee deftly handled the functioning of the finance ministry and other governance issues. In a letter to the Bengal governor, in July 1942, Dr Mookerjee wrote that 'for the first time in the history of British India, whatever democratic constitution has been handed over to us, in spite of its manifold defects, was sought to be worked in Bengal by Hindu and Muslim representatives who wielded considerable influence over their own community. The success of this experiment naturally would give a lie direct to the plea of communal disharmony standing in the way of India's political advancement'.

The Muslim League was completely sidelined and the British were at a loss to see their divide and rule policy fail for the first time. Dr Mookerjee 'was determined to demonstrate that in matters of state administration,

Hindu and Muslim representatives could work together in a spirit of common understanding'. He was of the firm opinion that even in a difficult state like Bengal, 'if leaders were in a position to assure their communities that their interests were being well looked after and once this public confidence was established, mischief-makers would naturally become powerless and eventually dissolve'. The story goes that a few Muslims leaders in Haq's party who had earlier opposed Dr Mookerjee were uncomfortable with this arrangement and approached Haq in protest. Haq is said to have replied, 'Listen you do not know Dr Mookerjee, I do. He is the son of Sir Asutosh. It doesn't matter that he belongs to the Hindu Mahasabha. You will not find a more liberal person or a better well-wisher of Muslims among Hindus. If you trust me, you must trust him too.' A widespread feeling of relief was felt among the people who wished to see the Muslim League ministry dissolve. Hindus of Bengal were especially relieved because the League ministry between 1937 and 1941 had discriminated against them and had 'retarded the real progress of Bengal as a whole'. However, this was not to last very long. Bengal Governor Herbert hated this ministry and, by using machinations, dismissed it in 1942. In the meantime, the Congress gave a call for Quit India Movement and all Congressmen were promptly put in jail.

Meanwhile, in Bengal, a Tsunami hit the town of Contai in East Midnapore district in October 1942 killing some 30,000 people in fifteen minutes. As a result, a huge number of people were orphaned. Also, at that time, the Japanese advanced in Southeast Asia and took over Burma, throwing out the British. As a result, Herbert launched a scorched earth policy. The bulk of foodstuff not needed for the military was deliberately destroyed. Similarly, the means of transportation that was being used for such foodstuff was also destroyed. The price of rice rose from Rs 2 per maund (about thirty-six kilos) to about Rs 100 per maund. There was a famine in which an estimated 15 lakh people perished. The colonial government also attempted to withhold relief to the affected area because of strong nationalist feelings and the revolutionary zeal displayed by the people. Dr Mookerjee, however, plunged into famine relief work and consolidated the different organisations set up for such relief and coordinated their work. In the absence of this act, the number of casualties would have been much more and India would have never known about this tragedy. Dr Mookerjee also resigned from the Cabinet when he realised that autonomy was a farce and that Indian ministers were obstructed at every step by the British civil servants and the governor. He was particularly incensed when repression was let loose on the people, and after trying to unsuccessfully talk to the viceroy and negotiate with the British government, so that they would step back, allow the formation of an 'Indian National Government' and declare that 'freedom is formally recognised', Dr Mookerjee, while resigning, said: 'The reign of repression that we have witnessed in India since August last [August 1942] has been directed not only against a so-called subversive movement but against every form of nationalist activities, calculated to mobilise the willpowers of Indians to throw off a foreign rule that they intensely dislike.'

At this point, the Second World War was raging and all Congress leaders were in jail, but Muslim League leaders were all outside and ruling in Bengal. The British government observed that Mahatma Gandhi's health was deteriorating and decided to release him for fear that his death in jail might precipitate further trouble. Then C Rajagopalachari met Gandhi and persuaded him to speak to Jinnah in order to reach a settlement on the partition of the country. Talks were held and proved to be abortive, but Gandhi and CR practically conceded Pakistan. Before talks began, Dr Mookerjee repeatedly advised Gandhi not to concede anything, but they did not listen to him and Jinnah had his way.

In 1945, the Second World War ended and the Congress leaders were released from jail and hailed as heroes. Election in the central legislative council was held, but before that, Dr Mookerjee tried to find a common ground with the Congress in order to fight the League. Sarat Chandra Bose was adamant and did not give any space to Dr Mookerjee. By this time, there was complete polarisation in the country on religious lines—Hindus in favour of Congress and Muslims in favour of Muslim League. The Muslim parties that had opposed the League, for example, Krishak Praja Party in Bengal and Unionist Party in Punjab, either folded up or merged with the League and Allah Baksh, an important Muslim leader of Sind who stood firmly to oppose the League, was assassinated. As a result of this polarisation, Dr Mookerjee was ignominiously defeated by a non-entity (candidate) of the Congress. Not only so, but he suffered a heart attack in the process of electioneering and was completely bedridden.

In 1946, the multi-party war Cabinet in Britain was replaced by the Labour Party, and Clement Attlee as the new Prime Minister sent a high-powered committee called the 'Cabinet Mission' to work out means of granting India independence. The Cabinet Mission made a plan for the grouping of provinces, by which India would have remained one. This was initially accepted by both the Congress and Muslim League. At this time, Jawaharlal Nehru replaced Maulana Abul Kalam Azad as the president of the Congress and immediately thereafter without consulting anyone, Nehru resiled from the acceptance of the grouping plan. Jinnah withdrew his acceptance as well and announced 'Direct Action Day' on 16 August 1946. On this day, began a bloodbath in Calcutta between Hindus and Muslims for four days in which an estimated 15,000 people died. Dr Mookerjee had now become a member of the provincial legislative council of Bengal. The government of Bengal was being run by the Muslim League under the leadership of Hussain Shaheed Suhrawardy who masterminded the entire carnage. In the provincial council, Dr Mookerjee lambasted Suhrawardy's role in perpetrating the riots. He also actively organised a resistance to this pogrom and worked to bring in normalcy in the city. Surprisingly, no All-India Congress leader visited Calcutta after this riot, for reasons best known to them.

Meanwhile, Lord Mountbatten had become viceroy of India. As the events unfolded later, the British under Mountbatten succeeding in inveigling upon Nehru to accept Partition. On 3 June 1947, the British Prime Minister made an announcement of granting independence to India and partitioning it. He also declared that the provinces of Bengal and Punjab would be partitioned as well.

After it became settled that India would be partitioned and it was proposed that the whole of Bengal would go to Pakistan, the reworking of the partition of Muslim-majority Bengal was forced by Dr Mookerjee by creating public opinion in favour of a homeland for Bengali Hindus and attaching the Hindu areas of Bengal to India. Dr Mookerjee began to build and mobilise public opinion in favour of the proposal. His cogent arguments and 'forceful advocacy of the scheme for the partition of Bengal' succeeded in winning over a large number of leaders in Bengal, including Congressmen to his side. In March 1947, Bengali Hindu members of the Central Assembly adopted a resolution with the support of Hindu Mahasabha's NC Chatterjee and Indian National Army's General AC Chatterjee. Following this, Dr Mookerjee convened a well-attended two-day conference of Hindu representatives from all parts of Bengal. Apart from Hindu Mahasabha members, a large number of other representatives convened from all over the province.

Leading intellectuals and scholars like RC Majumdar, Dr Suniti Kumar Chatterji, the veteran revolutionary Hemendra Prasad Ghosh, Lord SP Sinha, Dr Radha Kumud Mookerjee participated, among others. The conference unanimously passed a resolution that a 'separate province must be created comprising the Hindu majority areas in Bengal...' So widespread was the support for Dr Mookerjee's scheme of partitioning Bengal that an opinion poll held by the leading daily *Amrita Bazar Patrika* in April showed that 98.6 per cent voted 'yea', with only 0.6 per cent favouring a united Bengal. In April, Dr Mookerjee met Viceroy Mountbatten and pointed out why the partition of Bengal was necessary. It was thus Dr Mookerjee's forceful intervention and leadership that saved a portion of Bengal and the historic and strategically important city of Calcutta from going to the Muslim League-ruled Pakistan. This was, arguably, the greatest achievement of Dr Syama Prasad Mookerjee's life.

The Muslim League had opposed this partition because they wanted the whole of Bengal, particularly Calcutta, to remain in Pakistan. When they realised that they could not achieve this directly, they influenced some discredited Congress leaders of Bengal and tried to float the concept of Sovereign United Bengal independent of India or Pakistan. Dr Mookerjee fought and managed to kill the idea.

After India became independent on 15 August 1947, Dr Mookerjee was in Hindu Mahasabha, while the power was transferred by the British wholly to the Congress. Earlier in February 1946, Dr Mookerjee was elected unopposed to Bengal Legislative Assembly from the Calcutta University constituency, his old constituency. In July that year, so high was his popularity that he was nominated to the Constituent Assembly of India by the Bengal Congress to work for the framing of a new Constitution. His performance in the Constituent Assembly was captivating and displayed his old skill in the parliamentary set-up. An intervention he once made against efforts to obstruct the working of the Constituent Assembly was remarkable for its boldness. Dr Mookerjee sensed that some colonial officials may have been behind this, 'I would say Sir', he began, 'that we should say to the British people once for all: "We want to remain friendly with you. You started your career as traders. You came here as supplicants before the Great Mughal. You wanted to exploit the wealth of the country. Luck was in your favour. By forgery, fraud and force you succeeded in establishing—these are all matters of history—you governed this country but not with the willing cooperation of the people of this land. You introduced separate electorates; you introduced religion into Indian politics. That was not done by Indians. You did it only to perpetuate your rule in this country."'

Dr Mookerjee's mastery of parliamentary procedure and his skill in the debate made him instantly popular. 'His position as one of the topmost public figures' with a great 'record of service in the cause of the country's independence' was nationally recognised. He had also become the undisputed leader of Bengal by then. Even though he still led the Hindu Mahasabha, Mahatma Gandhi insisted that Dr Mookerjee be included in free India's first Cabinet. Gandhi argued that independence had come into place as a joint effort and because of the struggle of all 'nationalist forces' in the country and not only the Congress, and therefore, wanted a wide representation of leaders in the first Cabinet making it truly a national government. Dr Mookerjee was initially hesitant because he saw Congress's 'pitiable cowardice' in acceding to partition. But like Gandhi, Veer Savarkar too wanted him to join the Cabinet as that would give him an opportunity to work and serve independent India and strengthen the national government. Savarkar was not parochial; he saw independent India's first government as a national government that had to work to strengthen India's sovereignty and integrity. It was the Congress and its leaders who displayed parochialism and tried to obliterate Veer Savarkar's contribution to

India's freedom struggle. Dr Mookerjee joined the government and was made the Minister for Industry and Supply, though his natural inclination and area of expertise was in the field of education. Had he been given the portfolio of education, his field of specialisation since his youth, Dr Mookerjee could have perhaps given a new direction to India's national education policy and moulded young minds in the ideal of nationalism and national service. But the industrial and economic challenges facing the country were also immense and Dr Mookerjee rose to the challenge.

It must be mentioned here that Sardar Patel was very much in favour of Dr Mookerjee being included in the first Cabinet of free India. Sardar Patel greatly admired Dr Mookerjee's historic role in demanding the partition of Bengal and thus saving a part of it from Jinnah's Pakistan. He also admired Dr Mookerjee's refusal and opposition to the Muslim League's pipe dream of a 'sovereign, independent Bengal'. His leadership on both issues had saved India and Hindus. As one of Patel's biographer notes, 'Mookerjee, who represented the Hindu Mahasabha, had gained the Sardar's favour by demanding Bengal's partition in March 1947 and by refusing to join an abortive bid for a united and independent Bengal that Sarat Bose and Suhrawardy made in April and May [1947].'

Sardar Patel played a decisive role in inducting both Dr BR Ambedkar and Dr Mookerjee in the Cabinet. On the other hand, Dr Mookerjee was a great support to Patel and always worked to strengthen his hands in his great effort to create the Indian union. Especially in the case of Hyderabad, he constantly stood by Patel and demanded action, thus earning Nehru's wrath. While a minister, he had serious differences with other leaders of Hindu Mahasabha over the direction the party must take in independent India. He wanted the Mahasabha to evolve and grow with times developing a new perspective. Eventually, Dr Mookerjee's advice on these directions were not taken and he left the party in 1948. He was then a leader without a party and he continued in this way until 1950.

As Free India's First Industry Minister

It is inspiring to see the work Dr Mookerjee did as the Industry and Supply Minister in a short span of over two years. His 'experience as Finance Minister of undivided Bengal and his general grasp of things were a determining factor'. In fact, this gave him an 'opportunity to lay the foundations of India's industrial policy and prepare the ground for the industrial development of the country in the years to come. The loss to education and cultural life was thus a gain to the economy and industry.' One of Dr Mookerjee's early biographers notes: 'His record of work as Minister for Industry and Supply for two-and-a-half years he remained in office amply justified the faith and trust that had been put in him. He brought his solid intellectual grasp and realistic understanding of the problems of industrialisation in a predominantly agricultural country, whose industrial growth had been deliberately checked by the unsympathetic foreign government.' Dr Mookerjee's 'intellectual eminence, mental alertness and rock-like integrity' evoked spontaneous respect and fullest cooperation from all sections among the officers. 'Even his political opponents praised the way he handled the industrial problems and formulated industrial policies in the most formative years of independent India.' Dr Mookerjee had a clear perception of the industrial direction that India needed to take and was convinced that in a deindustrialised country like India, which had just achieved political independence, the 'primary task was to mobilise all resources, private and governmental, for a cooperative effort to make the country self-sufficient in essential goods, particularly those needed for the defence of the country'.

Dr Mookerjee's great contribution in setting the motion for India's industrial development has never been discussed and has never found place in history books. It would be interesting to see in some detail the work he did as free India's first Industry Minister and also try and understand some of his thoughts in this field. In those early years, Dr Mookerjee thought that the best method would be to give 'full scope to private enterprise under suitable government regulation and control, to play its part in India's industrialisation'. He wanted the State to utilise its meagre resources for developing that sector of the industry whose growth was essential for the defence of the country, but for which private capital was not [then] readily forthcoming. He, thus, wanted a rational coordination, in the light of the actual conditions in the country, between private and public enterprise for speedy but orderly industrialisation of the country. In formulating this policy, he was guided solely by a realistic assessment of the needs and circumstances of the country and not by abstract theories or dogmas, to which he had no attachment.

This was a time when failed economic theories were vigorously propagated by communist ideologues trained in the west and who were eager to develop a proletarian paradise in India. This was also a period when communists put up a resistance to India's industrial march by repeated obstructionism through violent strikes and bandhs. Dr Mookerjee always stood for cooperation between 'labour and capital in the interest of increasing production. The theory of class struggle as a means of progress never appealed to his rational mind'. Yet, he did not support cooperation of labour completely on the terms of the employers. 'He was all for profit-sharing between capital and labour so as to enable labour to develop a genuine interest in the industry. While his solicitude for the welfare of labour inspired confidence in the labour, his realistic and practical approach to the problem of capital reassured employers.'

'With an open mind', Dr Mookerjee 'judged every scheme and policy by the criteria of its practicability and usefulness to the people'. Apart from the basic objections to total nationalisation, he was convinced that India lacked the requisite resources, experience and trained personnel to nationalise all industries and still run them efficiently'. He emphasised on laying a strong industrial foundation, on developing a robust economic framework and on teaching skills to the youth. His speeches during this period point to his vision and ideas. Speaking to the Science and Technology Association of the Delhi Polytechnic, sometime in 1949, he observed that the 'economic safety of the vast masses of the people—their economic security and their standards of living—is the foundation on which all political institutions rest. Political freedom, therefore, has neither meaning nor stability unless its economic contents are realised'. He believed that a 'widespread technological revolution in industry and agriculture' was required to raise the standard of living of the general masses. Referring to the effort being made on the industrial front, Dr Mookerjee noted that spadework was being done for the 'establishment of a number of very vital industries and when these industries are actually established, they will form the solid groundwork on which the economic development of our country may proceed'. The Government of India's declaration of an industrial policy in 1948 saw the reflection of Dr Mookerjee's ideas. This declaration 'envisaged a mixed economy, with overall responsibility of ensuring planned development and regulation of industries in national development lying with the government'. Dr Mookerjee also laid great emphasis on developing and reenergising India's cottage and small-scale industries. During his tenure between 1948 and 1950, the All India Handicrafts Board, the All India Handloom Board and the Khadi and Village Industries Board were set up to 'supply the much-needed organisation and finance required by cottage and small-scale industries to survive and develop'. The textile research institutes were also conceived in his tenure. In July 1948, the Industrial Finance Corporation of India, 'a government-sponsored institution acting as an investment banker, collecting private savings on government guarantee of repayment and distributing them in form of advances and long-term loans to industrial borrowers', was formed.

As a Minister, Dr Mookerjee was credited with several pioneering schemes, such as Damodar Valley Corporation, fertiliser factory at Sindri, Chittaranjan Locomotive Works and Hindustan Aircraft of Bangalore—these were among the four most successful gigantic projects of free India. He also brought about great improvement in the cotton textile industry including handloom. In line with the plan to achieve self-sufficiency in some key sectors, under the initiative of Dr Mookerjee, in 1948, the locomotive factory at Chittaranjan in West Bengal was started and the first Indian locomotive from assembled parts 'named Deshbandhu, was produced in 1950'. Dr Mookerjee reconstituted the Hindustan Aircraft into a limited company and saw to it that it undertook the assembling of jet aircrafts for the Indian Air Force, manufactured the HT 2, a 'trainer aircraft for civilian and defence purposes' and also 'manufactured all-steel rail coaches for the Indian Railways and bus bodies for various state and private transport authorities'. Thus, the losses the company incurred in the first two years after the War were covered by profits in 1947-48 and 1948-49 under the able chairmanship of Dr Mookerjee. The company's sales in 1949-50 amounted to about Rs 2 crore. The then new model of third-class coaches of the Indian Railways manufactured by the Hindustan Aircraft was the result of Dr Mookerjee's personal interest in the matter.

The steel plant at Bhilai was initially conceived by Dr Mookerjee. His proactive approach to the project and detailed survey of whether it was feasible in the surroundings earmarked for it, demonstrated how thorough he was an administrator. 'His dream of establishing a new steel plant to improve the quantity and quality of steel production in India was fulfilled in 1955', when the agreement for setting up the Bhilai Steel Plant came up. It was during Dr Mookerjee's tenure that steps for the manufacturing of newsprint were initiated by setting up of the National Newsprint and Papers Mills limited in Central Provinces (now Madhya Pradesh). Similarly, the setting up of the fertiliser factory at Sindri, near Dhanbad in Bihar, finally took off at the behest of Dr Mookerjee, who was keen that India achieves self-sufficiency in the production of fertilisers. As always, his long-term vision on this front saw 'this vast and modern factory' go into production in October 1951.

Similarly, the multipurpose Damodar Valley Corporation (DVC) was another great achievement of Dr Mookerjee. His deft stewardship saw the central government and the government of Bihar and Bengal come together to cooperate for the establishment of this corporation for the development of the Damodar Valley that spanned both states. It is a tribute to Dr Mookerjee's farsighted vision that DVC was created and one of its chief functions was 'the promotion and operation of schemes for irrigation, water supply, generation and transmission of energy—hydroelectric and thermal', the implementation of schemes for flood control in the Damodar River, promotion of 'public health and of agriculture, industrial and economic well-being in the Damodar Valley and the adjoining areas'.

Along with these large-scale industrial schemes, Dr Mookerjee was also acutely sensitive to small industries and worked hard to alleviate their plight and strengthen their base. His intervention on behalf of about 200 small cottage factories manufacturing match by hand and situated mostly in Tamil Nadu, is a case in point. A Swedish combine produced matches in bulk in factories situated all over India and the cottage factories 'complained of their critical condition on account of the severe competition from the former and the loss of west India (now Pakistan) markets due to partition'. Dr Mookerjee addressed the grievances of the South Indian cottage match manufacturers by 'giving considerable relief in excise duty on handmade matches, making sufficient for import of the required raw materials and facilitating transport for the small-scale producers to move their goods to reach all destinations'. His ministry also directed the Madras government to bring these 'cottage industry workers under a cooperative organisation and finance them using its funds for facilitating supply of raw materials and distribution of finished products so as to eliminate 90 per cent of their troubles'.

In a similar manner, he addressed the problems and challenges faced by the woollen handloom industry 'not only for India's export trade but also for keeping the cottage workers perennially employed'. 75 per cent of this industry was concentrated in Uttar Pradesh, Punjab, Kashmir and Rajasthan. Dr Mookerjee identified the problems and solved them in a concerted manner. To tackle the problem of imparting technical guidance to workers in this sector, he proposed to start the Central Sheep and Wool Research Institute, which 'would train students in all phases of manufacture and instruct the village workers in improved appliances'. Dr Mookerjee promoted the idea of the Central Cottage Industries Emporium in Delhi 'to market and advertise the goods made in the provinces'. India's trade commissioners abroad were directed to organise exhibitions, sales and publicity drives to push Indian handloom products. For the improvement of the age-old Indian silk industry, Dr Mookerjee gave it a new impetus by establishing the Central Silk Board in 1948. He also worked towards putting the cotton handloom and textile industries in India on a sound footing.

As president of the Maha Bodhi Society of India, Dr Mookerjee took the lead in forging a link with the Buddhist nations of South and Southeast Asia, chiefly Burma (now Myanmar) and Ceylon (now Sri Lanka), Cambodia and Tibet (not yet annexed by the Chinese). In order to further cement these ties, Dr Mookerjee brought the relics of two chief disciples of Buddha, Mahamoggallana and Sariputra, from England and at the invitation of the leaders from the Southeast Asian region, Dr Mookerjee took a portion of the sacred relics to these countries and received a royal welcome. The legendary Cambodian monarch, Prince Norodom Sihanouk (1922-2012), invited him with the relics and more than half a million people turned up to listen to

Dr Mookerjee speak on the message of Buddha and of how India and the countries of Southeast Asia could work together to bring in a new Asian age. It was due to Dr Mookerjee's indefatigable efforts that a portion of these sacred relics was presented to the people of Burma from the Government of India, as a 'permanent loan'. The relics were installed at the legendary Kaba Aye Pagoda in Yangon. The Burmese Prime Minister, U Nu, wrote to him saying that his people shall forever remain grateful to Dr Mookerjee for this great sacred act of friendship. It was again due to the efforts of Dr Mookerjee that these relics were installed at a newly constructed vihara, adjacent to the ancient vihara in Sanchi near Bhopal.

Pakistan's Perfidy

In February 1950, the East Pakistan Government launched an anti-Hindu pogrom all over East Pakistan with the intention of de-Hinduising that country. Until then, the Hindus had a very large share of the cultural and intellectual space in East Pakistan and constituted the majority of professors, school teachers, lawyers, doctors and other professionals. As a result of this pogrom, there was a huge exodus of Hindus into India especially West Bengal, Tripura and Assam. According to Nehru, the solution to this problem laid in working out an agreement with Liaquat Ali Khan, the Prime Minister of Pakistan, and he proceeded to do the same. Dr Mookerjee argued that this was totally an irrational thing to do because it was the Liaquat Ali-led government itself that had started the pogrom and there was no point in making an agreement with it. However, Nehru did not listen to him, as a result of which Dr Mookerjee had no alternative but to resign from the Cabinet. Sardar Patel and a number of Dr Mookerjee's colleagues in the central Cabinet wanted him to continue. The other central minister from Bengal, KC Neogy, resigned along with him. The surging crowd that came to receive Dr Mookerjee at the Howrah Station in Kolkata, when he arrived from Delhi after the resignation, is said to have been phenomenal.

Meanwhile, the folly that Jawaharlal Nehru committed in Jammu and Kashmir, probably under the influence of Lord Mountbatten, is well known. When the Maharaja did not sign the Instrument of Accession in time but vacillated, Pakistan sent its soldiers in disguise as Pathan tribesmen to take over the state. All the approaches to Jammu and Kashmir at that time were from Pakistan—approach to Jammu from Sialkot and approach to Srinagar from Rawalpindi through Jhelum valley. The Maharaja signed the instrument as laid down on 26 October 1947. The Indian Army and Air Force thereafter acted with great courage and speed and entered Jammu and Kashmir from Pathankot, scaled the Pir Panjal Mountains, reached Srinagar and began to chase the marauders out of the valley. When the Indian Army was in hot pursuit, Nehru suddenly declared a unilateral ceasefire and announced that there would be a plebiscite in the state supervised by the United Nations. In the annals of warfare, perhaps, there were few examples of such supreme short-sightedness. The so-called Kashmir problem arose as a result of this and continues to this day. A part of the state covering the Mirpur and Muzaffarabad strip together with Gilgit and Skardu remained in the hands of Pakistan. A part of this subsequently was ceded by Pakistan to China.

Following this, Sheikh Mohammed Abdullah took oath as the Prime Minister (not Chief Minister) of the state of Jammu and Kashmir and Yuvraj Karan Singh as the Sadar-i-Riyasat (not Rajpramukh as was done in case of other Indian princely states). Abdullah started treating the state as almost independent. Not only that, he also adopted a totally stepmotherly attitude towards the people of Jammu and Ladakh as opposed to those of the Vale of Kashmir.

Formation of Jana Sangh

Dr Mookerjee, meanwhile, was a leader without a party. At this stage, he met Sri Guruji Golwalkar, Sarsanghchalak (organisation's head) of the Rashtriya Swayamsevak Sangh (RSS) who asked him to start a party for whom the RSS would give him some of its ablest workers. Among the people that were given were Pandit Deendayal Upadhyaya, Balraj Madhok, Atal Bihari Vajpayee, Kushabhau Thakre, Nanaji Deshmukh, Sundar Singh Bhandari, Jagdish Mathur and several others. Dr Mookerjee held a series of meetings with the leaders from all over the country, and after deliberating on several ideas and names, he finally founded Bharatiya Jan Sangh (BJS). Its formation was announced in a meeting held at Raghomal Arya Kanya Vidyalaya, Delhi on 21 October 1951 and was followed by a huge public meeting in Gandhi Grounds in front of Gurudwara Sis Ganj Sahib in Old Delhi.

In his presidential address before the mammoth gathering, Dr Mookerjee said, 'Our party must continue to function (even after the forthcoming general elections in 1951-52) carrying a message of hope and goodwill to all classes of people and try to draw out from them their best efforts in rebuilding a happier and more prosperous free India... One of the chief reasons for the manifestation of dictatorship in Congress rule is the absence of well-organised opposition parties that alone can act as a healthy check on the majority party... Bharatiya Jana Sangh emerges today as an all-India political party which will function as the principal party in opposition... We have thrown our party open to all citizens of India irrespective of caste, creed or community. While we recognise that in matters of customs, habit, religion and language, Bharat presents a unique diversity, the people must be united by a bond of fellowship and understanding inspired by a deep devotion and loyalty to the support of a common Motherland... While it will be dangerous to encourage growth of political minorities on the basis of caste and religion, it is obviously for the vast majority of Bharat's population to assure all classes of people who are truly loyal to their Motherland that they will be entitled to full protection under the law and to build equality in all matters of social, economic and political. Our party gives this assurance unreservedly... Our party believes that the future of Bharat lies in the proper appreciation and application of *Bharatiya sanskriti* and *maryada*.'

Referring to Pakistan, Dr Mookerjee called for 'a policy of strict reciprocity'. Talking about Kashmir, Dr Mookerjee said, 'Our party feels that the case should be withdrawn from the United Nations and there should be no further question of plebiscite. Kashmir is an inalienable part of India and should be treated as any other state'. Dr Mookerjee was also very critical of Nehru, who had, by now, repeatedly started using the word 'communal' against him. Dr Mookerjee said, 'Having repeatedly sacrificed Indian nationalism at the altar of Muslim communalism and even after Partition having surrendered to the whims and howls of the Pakistani government, it does not lie in the mouth of Pandit Nehru to accuse others of communalism. There is no communalism in India today, except the new policy of Muslim appeasement, which had been started by Pandit Nehru and his friends for the purpose of winning their vote at the forthcoming election. We have provincialism and other type of class or caste difference in the country today. Let us jointly try to remove these evils so as to lay a foundation of a truly democratic India.' Dr Mookerjee concluded his historic address with the following words, which still continue to inspire, 'We enter upon our task with full faith, hope and courage. Let our workers constantly remember that only through service and sacrifice will they be able to win the confidence of the masses. The great task of revitalising and reconstructing Bharat awaits us. The mother calls her children irrespective of class, caste or religion to come to her and serve her. However dark the present may be, Bharat has a great destiny to fulfil in the years to come. May our party, whose symbol in the forthcoming election is a humble earthen *pradeep* (lamp), try to carry this light of hope and unity, faith and courage to dispel darkness that surrounds the country. The journey has just begun. May providence endow us with strength and fortitude to remain ever on the right path, not cowed down by fears or tempted by favours and to help make Bharat great and strong especially so that she may become a fit and noble instrument in the preservation of wealth and prosperity.'

Referring to Nehru's threat of crushing Jana Sangh, Dr Mookerjee said, 'I say, I will crush this crushing mentality of yours.' In 1951-52, the first general elections took place in which the infant Jana Sangh got three seats—two from West Bengal and one from Rajasthan. Meanwhile, the Kashmir problem continued to worsen. Dr Mookerjee wrote to Nehru a number of times and there was a tripartite correspondence between him, Nehru and Sheikh Abdullah but with no results. The Praja Parishad, under the leadership of Pandit Prem Nath Dogra, began an agitation against Sheikh Abdullah and the neglect of Jammu. Dr Mookerjee held a meeting with Pandit Dogra and completely identified himself and his party with the agitation. He had emerged as a fiery and the most vociferous speaker in the entire opposition and succeeded in not only uniting the Opposition bloc, but also in being recognised as the unofficial leader of the Opposition.

First Session of Jana Sangh

The first annual session of Bharatiya Jana Sangh was held in Kanpur. This meeting saw the emergence of several young leaders of the party among whom the foremost was a young RSS *pracharak* called Deendayal Upadhyaya. Dr Mookerjee also recruited a *swayamsevak* called Atal Bihari Vajpayee as his general secretary, who later became the Prime Minister of India.

At this time, there was a system in vogue whereby Indian citizens had to take a permit from the Union Defence Ministry to enter the state of Jammu and Kashmir. On being requested by Pandit Premnath Dogra, Dr Mookerjee decided to travel to Jammu and to do so without a permit. He also wanted to personally survey the situation and the oppression unleashed on the protestors by Sheikh Abdullah's government. Accordingly, on 8 May 1953, he set out on a journey by passenger train from Delhi railway station accompanied by Vaid Guru Dutt, Atal Bihari Vajpayee, Tek Chand and Balraj Madhok along with a few members of the Press. He stopped at Ambala, Jalandhar and Pathankot where he attended a huge public meeting. Before arriving at Pathankot near the border of East Punjab and Jammu and Kashmir, the Deputy Commissioner of Gurdaspur district boarded the same train at Gurdaspur and said that he would probably have to arrest Dr Mookerjee if he tries to enter Jammu and Kashmir without a permit. However, by the time he reached the border at Madhopur, he, surprisingly, received a new order. Thereafter, he told Dr Mookerjee that he had been instructed to allow him and his companions to enter Jammu and Kashmir without a permit.

When Dr Mookerjee and his companions, Guru Datt Vaid and Tek Chand, reached the middle of the bridge over the Ravi River separating the two states, he was arrested by the police of Jammu and Kashmir on the grounds that he was about to act in a manner prejudicial to public safety and peace. It is important to note here that he was not arrested for entering Jammu and Kashmir without a permit because until this day such a permit could only be issued by the Union Defence Ministry, and a person could be arrested for entering Jammu and Kashmir without a permit only by Indian authorities and not by those of the state. Yet, significantly, the Deputy Commissioner of Gurdaspur district had clear instructions of not arresting him but to let him enter Jammu and Kashmir. In retrospect, this is very intriguing. It appears that he was cleverly pushed into Jammu and Kashmir without a permit, only to take him out of the jurisdiction of the Supreme Court of India. Had he been arrested at Gurdaspur, a petition of habeas corpus would have brought him out in no time.

Arrest in Kashmir

Apart from Dr Mookerjee, Guru Datt Vaid and Tek Chand were also with him. Immediately after the arrest, Dr Mookerjee was put in a closed jeep and whisked away to Batote. After spending the night there, he was taken to Srinagar the next morning where he was put in a small, secluded and bare cottage—a 'concrete hut'.

This cottage was converted into a sub-jail in which Dr Mookerjee had to spend time under great difficulty and in highly cramped and uncomfortable conditions. He had been medically advised to take long walks, but he was not permitted to do so here. As a result, he suffered excruciating pain in one leg. Surprisingly, Nehru and Dr KN Katju, his Home and State Minister visited Srinagar on 24 May 1953, but did not have the decency to look for Dr Mookerjee.

On the night of 19-20 June, Dr Mookerjee had pain in his chest and back along with a high temperature. The next day, the pain increased. On 22 June, quite early in the morning, his temperature fell and he broke into a sweat. At about 11:30 am, the jail superintendent reached his cottage with a taxi (not an ambulance) and they walked Dr Mookerjee from his bed to the taxi. Then he was moved, not to a nursing home, but to the gynaecological ward of a state hospital about ten miles away. Meanwhile, Barrister UM Trivedi had come to Srinagar to move a petition for his bail. On 22 June, he went to visit Dr Mookerjee and stayed with him until about 7:15 pm. He asked the attending physician about his actual medical state. The physician told Trivedi that there was no immediate cause for concern. But on 23 June, at about 3:45 am, Trivedi was woken up by the superintendent and told to rush to Dr Mookerjee's bedside. Pandit Premnath Dogra and the two fellow inmates were also asked to go. When they reached the hospital at 4 am, they were informed that Dr Mookerjee had breathed his last at 3:40 am.

This much is clear that Dr Mookerjee had been subjected to the worst possible neglect with startling incidents like being put in an isolated cottage that did not even have a telephone connection, not being allowed to walk and thereafter being made to walk from his cottage and brought to the gynaecological ward. Adding to this was Nehru's lack of decency in failing to search for him. Dr Mookerjee at that time was a highly respected parliamentarian and the de facto leader of the Opposition and a former Union Minister. Yet, he was not put in any VIP ward. One of his leading biographers, while working on his biography and having enquired from two prominent doctors, gathered that Dr Mookerjee must have suffered at least one or possibly two heart attacks while in the cottage and was possibly suffering from Deep Vein Thrombosis (DVT). Upon interviewing his elder daughter, (now late) Sabita Banerjee, one also came to know that immediately before his death, he had been injected with something that made his body burn and made him shout '*humko jal raha hai*' (I have burning sensation). This was told to her by Rajdulari Tiku, Dr Mookerjee's nurse, but was not corroborated.

The next day his dead body was flown to Calcutta, where a sea of humanity followed his cortège to the Keoratala Burning Ghat in south Kolkata, where incidentally in 1925 Deshbandhu CR Das's body was consigned to flames. The saddest and most regrettable event following his death was when Nehru refused Dr Mookerjee's mother's request for an enquiry into the death of her son.

Whenever a leading public figure dies or disappears under suspicious circumstances, there is always an enquiry, usually under the provisions of the Commissions of Enquiry Act 1952. As many as three such commissions had been constituted to conduct enquiry in relation to the disappearance of Netaji Subhas Chandra Bose—the Shah Nawaz Commission (1956), the GD Khosla Commission (1970) and the Manoj Mookerjee Commission (1999). Mahatma Gandhi's assassination was probed by the Kapur Commission, Indira Gandhi's by the Thakkar Commission, Rajiv Gandhi's by two commissions—JS Verma Commission and MC Jain Commission. All these assassinations (except Netaji's disappearance), it must be remembered, took place in public view, and therefore, there was no doubt left in anyone's mind as to how the person died. The enquiry was needed to find out the background and the conspiracy behind it. Dr Mookerjee's untimely and suspicious death, on the other hand, took place in secret, far away from family and friends in hostile territory, which was even beyond the jurisdiction of the Supreme Court of India. It is therefore natural that Dr Mookerjee's family, colleagues, admirers, party men and unrelated men who took an interest in public affairs would demand an enquiry into it.

The initiative was taken by Dr Mookerjee's mother Jogmaya Devi, who, in her reply to Nehru's condolence message, dated 30 June 1953, wrote thus on 4 July: 'I am not writing to you to seek any consolation. But what I do demand of you is justice. My son died in detention—a detention without trial. In your letter, you have tried to impress that Kashmir government had done all that should have been done. You base your impression on the assurances and information you have received. What is the value, I ask, of such information when it comes from persons who themselves should stand a trial? You say, you had visited Kashmir during my son's detention. You speak of the affection you had for him. But what prevented you, I wonder, from meeting him there personally and satisfying yourself about his health and arrangements?'

Nehru refused the enquiry! The reply, dated 5 July, is, to say the least, much less convincing to the mother in particular and all those who demanded inquiry in general: 'I can well understand a mother's sorrow and mental anguish at the death of a beloved son. No words of mine can soften the blow that you must have felt...I did not venture to write to you before without going into the matter of Dr Mookerjee's detention and death fairly carefully. I have since enquired further into it from a number of persons who had occasion to know some facts. I can only say to you that I arrived at the clear and honest conclusion that there is no mystery in this and that Dr Mookerjee was given every consideration.'

It was an acutely perfunctory reply to a solemn and rightful demand for an enquiry into the suspicious death of one of the foremost national leaders. 'I have since enquired further into it from a number of persons who had occasion to know some facts'. Ironically, the then Prime Minister of India, Pandit Nehru 'explained' the mysterious death of one of his foremost colleagues thus: 'I arrived at the clear and honest conclusion' and in my discretion 'I have decided to say no more! And after my clear and honest conclusion all arguments must stop.' Among those leaders who demanded the enquiry were Jayaprakash Narayan, Purshottam Das Tandon, Hari Vishnu Kamath, MR Jayakar, Master Tara Singh, Sucheta Kripalani, Pandit Hriday Nath Kunzru, SS More and others. Atulya Ghosh, the Congress president of West Bengal and Dr BC Roy also obliquely asked for an enquiry. But Nehru did not budge.

Thus, ended the life of one of the greatest sons of Mother India. But it did not go in vain. The party that Dr Mookerjee founded, the ideals for nation building that he set before the people and workers ultimately found their realisation in the form of commitment to protecting *bharatiya maryada* and to work towards realising a great and united India.

Sri Guruji Golwalkar, in his tribute to Dr Mookerjee, said, 'As a true fighter for his Motherland, Dr Mookerjee died in the forefront of the battle for integration of Kashmir, which is and which ought to be immediately declared an undivided and indivisible part of Bharat.'

Atal Bihari Vajpayee's tribute to Dr Mookerjee was a deeply moving one—he said, 'I had the privilege of working with Dr Mookerjee after he became the president of the Bharatiya Jana Sangh. I also accompanied him on his journey to Srinagar from where he was to never return. His last message to the people "I've entered Jammu and Kashmir defying the permit system", still rings in my ears. He was the first martyr to the cause of India's unity and integrity. His towering personality, debating skills, political sagacity and above all, his humanism will continue to inspire and guide generations to come.'

The ideas of Dr Mookerjee reverberated in his estimate by his contemporaries, as he inspired, and would do so in future as well, subsequent generations in public, political and intellectual life in India. Dr BR Ambedkar noted it, when he stated that he was shocked to hear about 'the sudden death of my old friend and erstwhile colleague Dr Syama Prasad Mookerjee. I am sure that the death has a void in public life which would hardly be filled.' Dr S Radhakrishnan, who knew Dr Mookerjee and his father Sir Asutosh Mookerjee as academic leaders wrote about Dr Mookerjee in glowing terms in 1959, as he developed 'great admiration and affection for him, for he was a man with wide knowledge and unshakeable purpose'. Further, he called him 'a staunch patriot' and 'an educationist, humanist and politician'. In the present generation, Narendra Modi, Prime Minister of India, remembered 'his rich contribution towards Indian history' as 'a great statesman, thinker and patriot'.

The life of Dr Mookerjee, as seen through the prism of ideas of many luminaries, will enthuse generations to come with his ideas and ideals for which he made the ultimate sacrifice.

References

1. Madhok, Balraj. *Portrait of a Martyr*, (1954), reprint New Delhi: Rupa & Co, 2001, 2009.
2. Mookerjee, Syama Prasad. *Leaves from a Diary*, New Delhi: Oxford University Press, 1993, 2000.
3. Banerjee, Anil Chandra. *A Phase in the Life of Dr Syama Prasad Mookerjee* 1937–1946, Kolkata: Asutosh Mookerjee Memorial Institute, 2000.
4. Chatterji, Prashanto Kumar. *Syama Prasad Mookerjee and Indian Politics*, New Delhi: Cambridge University Press, 2010.
5. Roy, Tathagata. *The Life and Times of Dr Syama Prasad Mookerjee*, New Delhi: Prabhat Prakashan, Delhi, 2012. (Also available in Hindi)

PERSONALITIES/INSTITUTIONS REFERRED TO BY SYAMA PRASAD MOOKERJEE

Adivar, Halide Edib (1884-1964): Woman novelist, advocate of women's rights, historian and educationist.

Agharkar, Gopal Ganesh (1856-1895): An ardent pleader for compulsory education for all and of co-education.

Andrews, Rev CF (1871-1940): A Christian missionary, educator and a friend of Mahatma Gandhi and Tagore during India's freedom struggle. Known by the honorific 'Deenabandhu'.

Azad, Maulana Abdul Kalam (1888-1958): First Education Minister, Government of India.

Bahadur, Rai Viharilal Mitra (d. 1933): A promoter of Hindu female education and donated the bequest of Rs 48,000 per annum to the University of Calcutta.

Banerjee, Rakhaldas (1886-1930): Pioneering archaeologist and epigraphist. He was the Manindra Chandra Nandy Professor of Ancient Indian History and Culture at the Banaras Hindu University from 1928 to 1930. The discoverer of Mohenjo Daro and Indus civilisation.

Banerjea, Captain Jitendra Nath: A Fellow of the University of Calcutta and a promoter of physical culture.

Bhadrabhau (433BC-357BC): Jain monk, known as spiritual teacher of Chandragupta Maurya.

Bhandarkar, Ramkrishna Gopal (1837-1925): A renowned Sanskrit scholar.

Bose, Acharya Girish Chandra: A pioneer of non-official educational institutions and founder of Bangabasi College.

Bose, Sir Jagdish (1858-1937): Indian scientist, seer and philosopher and founder of the Bose Research Institute, Calcutta.

Bose, Satyendranath (1894-1974): Indian physicist, best known for his path-breaking work in quantum mechanics and Bose–Einstein statistics. Bose was appointed Adharchandra Mookerjee Lecturer in science for the year 1935. The subject he chose was 'Recent Developments in Nuclear Physics'.

Brahmachari, Dr Indubhushan: He was long associated with the Calcutta University as a lecturer in pure mathematics in the Postgraduate Department.

Chakravarti, Prabhat Chandra: Teacher of Sanskrit in the Postgraduate Department in the University of Calcutta.

Chandavarkar, Narayan Ganesh (1855-1923): President of Royal Asiatic Society, Bombay and Vice Chancellor, University of Bombay. President of the 1900 session of the Congress.

Chiplunkar, Vishnu Krishna (1850-1882): Founder of modern Marathi prose.

Crohan, FX: He was associated with the Calcutta University as a Fellow for a period of 25 years.

Cunningham, Alexander: Major General in 1861 and excavator at Sārnāth and Sānchi, knighted in 1887.

Das, CR, known as **'Deshbandhu'** (1870-1925): President for the Congress session of Gaya in 1922.

Dev, Acharya Narendra (1889-1956): Legendary leader of the Congress Socialist Party, thinker, political philosopher, educationist and freedom fighter, was vice chancellor of Lucknow University.

Dipankara: An advocate and emissary of Indian civilisation beyond Indian shores.

Dutt, Gurusaday (1882-1941): Founder of the *Bratachari* movement (1932) for self-esteem and national awareness among people of undivided India irrespective of religion, caste, sex or age.

Edward VIII, born as **Albert Christian George Andrew Patrick David:** King of the United Kingdom and British dominions and Emperor of India from 20 January 1936 until his abdication on 11 December in the same year.

Ehrmann-Ewart, Dr Eugene: He came to India as a special delegate of the Austrian State Tourist Department, delivered lectures on Economics and Cultural Structure of Austria.

Fang-Kuei, Li (1902-1987): Also known as FK Li, was a well known Chinese linguist, sinologist and Professor of Chinese at the University of Washington.

Fisher, Ronald Aylmer: He was former Fellow of Mathematics at Gonville and Caius College, Cambridge, who delivered a course of lectures on the Theory of Statistical Estimation.

Gandhi, M K (1869-1948): Leader of India's freedom struggle, known as the 'Father of the Nation' for his contribution.

George V: King of the United Kingdom and British dominions and Emperor of India from 6 May 1910 until his death on 20 January 1936.

Ghose, Sir Bepin Behari: A barrister and later judge of Calcutta High Court, a member of the Calcutta University Senate for eight years (1927-1935).

Ghose, Rash Behary (1845-1921): Fellow from 1893 to 1895 of the University of Calcutta and member of its Syndicate from 1887 to 1899.

Ghosh, Dr PN: Professor of Applied Physics, University of Calcutta as Chairman and Principal.

Gupta, Chandra: Mauryan Emperor of Magadha empire (321-185 BC) with its capital Pataliputra, the grandson of Chandragupta Maurya.

Haque, Khan Bahadur Maulvi Azilul: Minister of Education and a member of the Senate of the University of Calcutta.

Hossian, Professor Syed: Lecturer in history of civilisation at the University of Southern California, and Reader in Calcutta University reader.

Indraji, Bhagwanlal (1839-1888): Indian archaelogist, epigraphist, member of Royal Asiatic Society. Made transcript of the Hathigumpha inscription and discovered the Mathura lion capital.

Jayaswal, Dr Kashi Prasad (1881-1937): Famous Indologist and well-known authority on Hindu law, author of the celebrated work 'Hindu Polity: A Constitutional History of India in Hindu Times' (1918). While practising at the Calcutta High Court came in contact with Sir Asutosh Mookerjee who encouraged him to undertake research in Indian polity.

Jeejeebhoy, Sir Jamsetjee (1783-1859): Member, Managing Committee of the Native Education Society in the first half of nineteenth century and on the Senate of the University of Bombay when it was established in February 1857.

Kempere, Dr AJ Barnet: Special University Reader on the development of Hindu–Japanese culture and art.

Kerr, Sir John: Acting Governor of Bengal and responsible for the Asutosh Building.

Lad, Ramakrishna Vithal, better known as **Bhau Dauji** (1822-1874): Supporter of Marathi drama.

Lévi, Dr Sylvain (1863-1935): French Indologist and Visiting Professor, Visva-Bharati, Santiniketan.

Madhavrao alias **Mahadeo Ballal Namjoshi** (1853-1896): An advocate of industrialisation and founder of Deccan Paper Mills, and industrial conference held in 1889, 1890, 1892 and 1893.

Mahalanobis, Prasanta Chandra (1893-1972): An Indian scientist and applied statistician, founder of the Statistical Laboratory in the Presidency College sometime in the 1920s.

Maharaj, Chhatrapati Shivaji (1627/1630-1680): The great Indian warrior who fought against the Mughal rule of Aurangzeb and founded Maratha Empire.

Maitra, Dr Jatindra Nath: Fellow of the University of Calcutta between 1922 and 1927.

Mandlik, Vishwanath Narayan (1833-1889): One of the pioneers in social, educational, religious and political reforms in Maharashtra. Became member of Bombay Legislative Council in 1874.

Mehta, Pherozshah (1845-1915): Founder of Swadeshi Bank, the Central Bank of India.

Moonje, Balakrishna Shivram (1872-1948): Nationalist leader, freedom fighter, political associate of Lokmanya Tilak, Sri Aurobindo, President of All India Hindu Mahasabha from 1927-1937, founder of Bhonsala Military School in Nasik.

Mookerjee, Dr Harendra Coomar: Private tutor of Dr Syama Prasad Mookerjee, Vice President of the Constituent Assembly (1946-49), and Governor of West Bengal from 1951 until his death in 1956.

Mookerjee, Dr Syamadas: Lecturer in Postgraduate Department of Calcutta University.

Mitra, Dr Heramba Chandra: The champion of purity in the students' world in Bengal. He was the Principal of City College, Calcutta (1907-37).

Mitra, Dr Mrigendralal: A surgeon and Fellow of the Calcutta University in 1927.

Mitra, Raja Rajendra (1822-1891): A pioneer ideologist.

Mulla, Sir Dinshaw: A judge of the Bombay High Court and law member of the Viceroy's Executive Council and the Tagore Professor of Calcutta University.

Mukerji, Sir Manmatha Nath: Judge of the Calcutta High Court in 1930s.

Mookerjee, Sir Asutosh: (1864-1924) Noted academician and Vice Chancellor of the University of Calcutta and father of Syama Prasad Mookerjee.

Nair, Sir Sankaran: President of the Indian National Congress in its Amraoti (Amravati) session in 1897, Advocate General of Madras, judge of the Madras High Court, member of the Viceroy's Executive Council and Chairman of Indian Reforms Committee.

Nandi, Dr Pramathanath: A medical practitioner of Calcutta and professor at Carmichael Medical College. Died in 1933.

Noguchi, Yone, also known as **Yonejiro Noguchi** (1875-1947): Japanese poet and litterateur and teacher of Arts and Literature of Japan at the University of Calcutta (1935-36).

Palit, Taraknath (1831-1914): Donor of seven lakh of rupees to the University of Calcutta on 15 June 1912 for Department of Physics and Chemistry, with a chair in each.

Paranjype, GR: Secretary, Royal Institute of Science, Bombay.

Parsvanatha: An eminent Tirthankara of the Jainas.

Pataliputra: A province that included within its boundaries Uruvilva and Nalanda, Uddandapur and Bikramasila, of Shilabhadra's discourse, of Gopala's piety and of Dharmmapala's charity.

Pratap, Maharana (1540-1597): King of Mewar who valiantly fought the Mughal rule.

Prinsep, James: An Assay Master (1820–30) of mints at Benares and Calcutta and Secretary of the Asiatic Society of Bengal, a British numismatist.

Radhakrishnan, S (1888-1975): The Spalding Chair of Eastern Religion and Ethics, University of Oxford; Vice Chancellor of Banaras Hindu University, 1939-1948; India's Ambassador to USSR, 1949-1952; first Vice President of India, 1952-1962 and later the President of India, 1962-1967.

Ranade, Mahadev Govind (1842-1901): An advocate of physical instruction and physical development in education.

Rajwade, Vishwanath Kashinath (1864-1926): A nationalist and Marathi author.

Roychand, Premchand (1831-1906): A merchant prince of Bombay who in July 1866 donated 2 lakh of rupees for founding university scholarships.

Saratchandra (1876-1938): Pre-eminent Bangla novelist of early twentieth century.

Sarkar, Sir Jadunath (1870-1958): Legendary historian of Sivaji, Aurangzeb and Mughal era.

Sarvadhikary, Sir Deva Prasad: Vice Chancellor of the University of Calcutta from 1914 to 1918.

Sarvadhikary, Jyotiprasad: Advocate of the Calcutta High Court and Professor of Hindu law in the University Law College.

Seal, Sir Brajendra Nath (1864-1938): In 1911, the first occupant of the Chair named King George V, Professor of Mental and Moral Science in the University of Calcutta from 1913 to 1920.

Sen, Kshitimohan (1880-1960): Scholar, polymath, Professor of Sanskrit, acting Upacharya of Visva-Bharati from 1953-1954, his work on the mystic saints of medieval India continues to be classic. Sen accompanied Tagore on his visit to China in 1924.

Sen, Rai Bahadur Narendra Nath: Controller of Examinations, the University of Calcutta.

Shirazi, Khan Bahadur Aga Mahomed Kazim: A native of Persia (Iran) and postgraduate lecturer in Persian at the University of Calcutta.

Shraddhananda, Swami (1856-1926): An educationist and a spiritual master and follower of Swami Dayananda Saraswati and his Arya Samaj.

Singh, Guru Gobind or **Guru Gobind Rai** (1666-1708): The tenth Guru of Sikhs, spiritual master, warrior, philosopher, poet, translator and founder of Khalsa Panth, the Sikh warrior community.

Sircar, Sir Nilratan: Vice Chancellor of the University of Calcutta from 1919 to 1921 and one of the founders and President of RG Kar Medical College.

Stamp, Dr L Dudley: Sir Ernest Cassel Reader in Economic Geography at the University of London, he invited delivered lectures in Calcutta University.

Suhrawardy, Sir Abdullah: Founder of the Pan-Islamic Society of London and Tagore Professor of Law in the University of Calcutta.

Suhrawardy, Hassan: Vice Chancellor of the University of Calcutta between 1930 and 1934.

Suri, Shershah (1486-1545): Emperor of north India (1540–45).

Tagore, Rathindranath (1888-1961): Rabindranath Tagore's son, one of the first five boys of the Brahmacharyashram at Santiniketan, studied agricultural science at the University of Illinois, spent around four decades serving Visva-Bharati, spearheading the rural reconstruction experiment at Sriniketan, held various positions at Visva-Bharati and when the university became a central university Rathindranath became its first Upacharya.

Tata, Jamshedji (1839-1904): A promoter of scientific and technical education.

Takacs, Zoltan De: Director of the Francis Hopp Museum of Eastern Asiatic Arts, Budapest, and Special Reader of the University for lectures on Pre-historic Motives in the Arts of Greater Asia and others on Eastern Asiatic Art Import in the Dark-Age Europe.

Telang, Kashinath Trimbak (1850-1893): Educationist.

Thackersey, Sir Vitthaldas Damodar (1873-1921): A promoter of Sanskrit *pathshala*s at Benares and Dwarka.

Thomas, Dr FW: Special Reader of the Calcutta University.

The All India Institute of Hygiene and Public Health: Established in Calcutta on 30 December 1932 with assistance from the Rockefeller Foundation.

The Indian Science Congress Association (ISCA): Initiated and established by two British chemists, Professors JL Simonsen and PS MacMahon.

The Royal Asiatic Society: Founded in 1823 by Henry Colebrooke.

Tulsidas (1532-1623): Renowned Bhakti poet and author of the *Ramacharitmanas*.

Turner, Dr CE: Chairman, Massachusetts Institute of Technology, Cambridge, and Special Reader of the University of Calcutta for course in Health Education.

Tyabji, Badruddin (1844-1906): Third President of the Indian National Congress and an eminent jurist.

Wacha, Sir Dinshaw Edulji (1844-1936): A prolific writer and educationist.

Walker, Sir Gilbert Thomas (1868-1958): A British mathematician and Director General of Observatories in the Indian Meteorological Service.

Woodroffe, Sir John (Arthur Avalon): A judge of the Calcutta High Court and Fellow of the University of Calcutta, known for his work on Tantra.

BIBLIOGRAPHY

Primary Works

Mookerjee, Syama Prasad and Chatterjee, Lalit Mohan. *Representative Indians*, The Popular Agency, Calcutta, 1936.

Mookerjee, Syama Prasad. *A Phase of Indian Struggle*, MV Bhowmick, Kushtia 1942.

Awake Hindusthan, New Delhi: Dr Syama Prasad Mookerjee Research Foundation, New Delhi, (rpt 2009).

Educational Speeches with Foreword by Dr Sarvepallli Radhakrishnan, A Mukherjee & Co. (private) Ltd, 1959.

Mookerjee, Syama Prasad. *Leaves from A Diary*, Oxford Univesity Press, hard cover 1992; pbk 2002.

Hereafter AMMI. Second edition edited by Dr Reena Bhaduri, 2015.

Secondary Works

Mookerjee, Uma Prasad (ed.) *Syama Prasad: Diary O Mritya Prasanga*, Kolkata, Mitra O Ghosh, II ed.

Panchasher Manvantar O Rashtriya Sangram (Bengali translation of 'Famine of 1943 and A Phase of Indian Struggle'), Mitra o Ghosh, Kolkata 2015. II ed.

Bhaduri, Reena (ed.). *Selected Speeches in Bengal Legislative Assembly 1937-1947*, Centenary Publications. 2001.

Bhaduri, Reena. *Kashmir Issue: Correspondence, Speeches and Reports 1947-1953*, Centenary Publication, 2001, AMMI pub.

Books on Dr Syama Prasad Mookerjee

Adak, Naba Kumar. *Syama Prasad Mookerjee: A Study of His Role in Bengal Politics*, 1929-1953, New Delhi, Kunal Books, 2013.

Adeney, Katherine and Saez, Lawrence. *Colonial Politics and Hindu Nationalism*, London: Routledge, 2005.

Anderson, Walter K and Damle, Shridhar D. *The Brotherhood of Saffron: The Rashtriya Swayamsevak Sangh and Hindu Revivalism*, New Delhi: Westview, 1987.

Chandra, Anil. *A Phase in the Life of Dr Syama Prasad Mookerjee*, 1937-1946, Calcutta: AMMI, 2000.

Basu, Rita. *Dr Syama Prasad Mookerjee and an Alternative Politics in Bengal*, Calcutta: Progressive Publishers, 2002.

Baxter, Craig. *The Jana Sangh: A Biography of an Indian Political Party*, Bombay: Oxford University Press, 1971.

Berglund, Henrik. *Hindu Nationalism and Democracy*, New Delhi: Shipra, 2004.

Bhatt, Chetan. *Hindu Nationalism: Origin, Ideologies and Modern Myths*, Oxford: Berg, 2001.

Brass, Paul R. *The Politics of India after Independence*, Cambridge: Cambridge University Press, 1993.

Burger, Angela Sutherland. *Opposition in a Dominant Party System: A Study of the Jana Sangh, the Praja Socialist Party and the Socialist Party in Uttar Pradesh, India*. Bombay: Oxford University Press, 1969.

Chatterjee, Jaya. *Bengal Divided: Hindu Communalism and Partition, 1932-1947*, (New Delhi: Foundation Books, 1995.

Chatterjee, Pranab Kumar. *Struggle and Strife in Urban Bengal, 1937-47*. Calcutta, Dasgupta & Co. 1991.

Chatterjee, Prasanta. *Dr Syama Prasad Mookerjee and Bengal Politics, 1938-1953: An Account of an Outstanding Political Leader*. New Delhi: Foundation Books, 2010.

Curran, JA. *Militant Hinduism in Indian Politics: A Study of the RSS*. New York: Institute of Pacific Relations 1951.

Gordon, Leonard. *Brothers Against The Raj: A Biography of Sarat and Subhas Chandra Bose*, New Delhi- Viking Penguin Books, 1990.

Graham, Bruce D. *Hindu Nationalism and Indian Politics: The Origins and Development of the Bharatiya Jana Sangh*, Cambridge: Cambridge University Press, 1990.

Gould, William. *Hindu Nationalism and the Language of Politics in Late Colonial India*, Cambridge: The University Press, 2005.

Hansen, Thomas Blom. *The Saffron Wave: Democracy and Hindu Nationalism in Modern India*. Princeton: Princeton University Press, 1999.

Jaffrelot, Christophe. *The Hindu Nationalist Movement and Indian Politics, 1925 to 1990s*, New Delhi: Penguin Books, 1999.

Jhangiani, Motilal A. *Jana Sangh and Swatantra: Profile of the Rightist Parties in India*, Bombay: Manaktalas, 1967.

Kanungo, Pralay. *RSS's Tryst with Politics: Politics: From Hedgewar to Sudarshan*, New Delhi: Manohar 2000.

Khandelwal, Devesh (ed.). *Pledge for an Integrated India: Dr Mookerjee in the Throes of Jammu & Kashmir 1951-1953*, New Delhi: Prabhat Prakashan, 2015.

Madhok, Balraj. *Portrait of a Martyr: Biography of Dr Syama Prasad Mookerjee*, Bombay: Jaico Publishing House, 1969.

Ray, Tathagata. *Life and Times of Dr Syama Parasad Mookerjee: A Complete Biography*, New Delhi: Prabhat Prkashan, 2012.

Veer, Peter Van Der. *Religious Nationalism: Hindus and Muslims in India*, Berkley: University of California Press, 1994.

Vijay, Tarun (ed.). *Thus Spoke Syama Prasad: selected quotes from the writings & speeches of Dr Syama Prasad Mookerjee*, New Delhi: Dr Syama Prasad Mookerjee Research Foundation.

In Bengali

Bhaduri, Reena. *Samudra Himadrir Mahasangame: Thakurbari—Asutosh Paribar Sangjog* Kolkata; Anjali Publishers, 2011.

Basu, Tarun. *Bharat Keshari Syama Prasad O Bharatvarsha*, Vol. I, Kolkata.

Chatterjee, Rudraprotap. *Kashmir Manche Syama Prasad*, Kolkata: 2000.

De, Amalendu. *Swadhin Bangabhumi Gathaner Parikalpana: Prayas O Parinati*, Calcutta Ratna Prakashani, 1975.

Majumdar, Biresh Chandra. *Syama Prasad: Bektittva O Krittiva*, Calcutta: General Printers and Publishers, 1969.

Ray, Kalidas. *Syama Prasad*, Calcutta AMMI Publication, 2001. Revised, supplemented and edited by Dr Reena Bhaduri &Sri Amitabha Chatteriee, AMMI, 2008.

Sanyal, Dr Arun. *Shiksha Brati Syama Prasad*, Kolkata: 1999.

Singha, Dinesh Chandra. *Syama Prasad: Banga Bibhag O Paschim Banga*. Calcutta: Grantha Rashmi, 2001.

Dr Syama Prasad Mookerjee Smarak Samiti. ed. *Satavarsher Aloy Syama Prasad*. Kolkata: Sristhi Prakashan, 2002.

Hindi

Prakashvir Shastri ed, Kashmir Ki Vedi Par, New Delhi: Dr Syama Prasad Mookerjee Research Foundation, New Delhi, 2011.

Tarun, Vijay. (ed.). *Agnipath*, New Delhi: Dr Syama Prasad Mookerjee Research Foundation, 2011.

Tarun, Vijay. (ed.). *Ameya Maitryee: Rabindranath Tagore & Syama Prasad*, New Delhi: Dr Syama Prasad Mookerjee Research Foundation, 2012.

Exhibition Online

'Dr Syama Prasad Mookerjee: a Selfless Patriot', a special exhibition curated by Dr Syama Prasad Mookerjee Research Foundation, New Delhi & Nehru Memorial Museum & Library, New Delhi, 2016, available at: http://www.spmrf.org/spmookerjee/special-exhibition-by-spmrf.pdf

INDEX